THESE FINAL DAYS

Part 1

THESE FINAL DAYS

Part 1

The Truth about the Rapture, the Four Horsemen, and the Prelude to the Great Tribulation

"Declaring the end from the beginning,
and from ancient times things that are not yet done…"
Isaiah 46:10

"When He, the Spirit of truth, has come,
He will guide you into all truth;
for He will not speak on His own authority,
but whatever He hears He will speak;
and He will tell you things to come."
John 16:13

Ryan Speakman

THESE FINAL DAYS, PART 1: The Truth about the Rapture, the Four Horsemen, and the Prelude to the Great Tribulation

© 2014 by Ryan Speakman

First Edition

Edited by Erin Speakman
Cover design by Rudolf Korv
Photos by Amber Kennedy

Scripture taken from the New King James Version®. Copyright © 1982 by Thomas Nelson, Inc. Used by permission. All rights reserved.

CreateSpace ISBN-13: 978-1500844813
CreateSpace ISBN-10: 1500844810

Library of Congress Control Number: 2014916626
CreateSpace Independent Publishing Platform
North Charleston, South Carolina

ALL RIGHTS RESERVED
No part of this publication may be reproduced, stored in a retrieval system, or transmitted in any form or by any means—electronic, mechanical, photocopying, recording, or otherwise—without prior written permission.

For information:
These Final Days Ministries • P.O. Box 1331 • Lake Havasu City, Arizona 86405

This book series is dedicated to my wife, Pamela, without whose continuing love, support, encouragement, prayer, and discernment my life's work would not be possible.

Acknowledgments

There are too many people who have supported me over the years as I've worked on this book series for me to thank everyone personally here, so many who have freely given their love and support, and who—most encouragingly for a writer—have shown genuine interest in this topic. But there are a few who I simply must mention by name.

First, I wish to thank my twin brother, Erin Speakman, and my brother in the faith, Brian McLaughlin, for their enthusiasm and encouragement as I've worked on this project. As a literature major in college, a professional editor, and a fellow writer himself, Erin's insights and advice along the way have been indispensable. Brian, one of the smartest guys I know, has read—and offered feedback on—every word that I've written; his friendship and shared enjoyment of in-depth discussion have been more valuable to me than he probably knows.

Next, I wish to thank my parents, Tom and Diane Speakman, who have, since the day I was born, instilled in me that I can do whatever I set out to accomplish—and I hope that this book series proves them right! No one has ever doted on their children more, and their love for my siblings and me is only surpassed by their love for God, His Son, and the Holy Spirit. As blessed as I was being born to wonderful parents, I was blessed again with wonderful in-laws, Ernie and Sharon Kaysen, who have likewise shown me years of love and encouragement; and who equally love the Father, Son, and Spirit.

And as if one man were not blessed enough to have such great parents and parents-in-law, I was blessed yet again with wonderful spiritual parents, Pastors Dan and Maureen Collins. It is thanks to their love and support for me and my family over the years—and the liberty and opportunities that they've given me to grow and mature in my gifts and calling—that I am fulfilling the assignment that God has given me. Pastor Dan is in the Glory Realm now, and I sense him cheering me on now more than ever. I also must thank my pastors' right-hand man and woman, Pastors Jimmy and Linda Bethoney. Their encouragement and belief in me over the years have kept my own enthusiasm high. I also must thank my church family in general—the extraordinary people of Living Word Family Church in Lake Havasu City, Arizona—my brothers and sisters in Christ who make this journey exceedingly enjoyable. You all help keep the spark bright in me, and I hope that I do the same for you.

Most of all, I could never thank my wife, Pamela, enough for all her years of love, support, encouragement, prayer and discernment—she is my greatest blessing, and all of my accomplishments in life are equally hers. And, last but most certainly not least, thank you to my daughter, Skylar, for her patience whenever Daddy is working. Writing means missed time with her, but what we might miss in quantity we make up for in quality! I hope that she's as proud of her Dad as I am of her...

Table of Contents

Introduction   xv

Section I
In Search of the Rapture   1

    Chapter 1
    What is the Rapture?   3

    Chapter 2
    Finding a Model for the Timing of the Rapture   9

    Chapter 3
    Building Confidence for Our Model   21

    Chapter 4
    The Second Coming   31

    Chapter 5
    The Pre-Tribulation Rapture   37
        Earlier Belief in a Pre-Tribulation Rapture?   39
        The "Loving Father" Argument   46
        We Are Not Appointed to Wrath   53

Jesus is Preparing Mansions for Us in Heaven	57
Rapture Depicted Prior to Great Tribulation in Book of Revelation	59
Church Not Mentioned During Depiction of Tribulation in Book of Revelation	64
Extensive Use of Old Testament Symbols and Language in Book of Revelation Indicative of Israel, not Christians	72
Bible Offers No Instructions on How to Live During Great Tribulation	81

Section II
The Book of Revelation: Prelude to the Prophecy   89

Chapter 6
The Book of Revelation	91
About the Author	94

Chapter 7
The Introduction	97
Revelation 1:1-1:3 ~ The Vision Begins	97
Revelation 1:4-1:8 ~ Salutations	101
Revelation 1:9-1:20 ~ The Seven Golden Lampstands	110

Chapter 8
The Letters to the Seven Churches	115
Revelation 2:1-2:7 ~ The First Letter: The Loveless Church	118
Revelation 2:8-2:11 ~ The Second Letter: The Persecuted Church	120
Revelation 2:12-2:17 ~ The Third Letter: The Compromising Church	123
Revelation 2:18-2:29 ~ The Fourth Letter: The Corrupt Church	125
Revelation 3:1-3:6 ~ The Fifth Letter: The Dead Church	127
Revelation 3:7-3:13 ~ The Sixth Letter:	

TABLE OF CONTENTS

The Faithful Church	130
Revelation 3:14-3:22 ~ The Seventh Letter:	
The Lukewarm Church	134

Chapter 9
John Prepared to Receive the Prophecy	139
Revelation 4:1 ~ John Summoned to Heaven	139
Revelation 4:2-4:11 ~ The Throne Room Described	141

Section III
The Book of Revelation: The Prelude to the Great Tribulation 153

Chapter 10
The Scroll with the Seven Seals: Prelude to the Great Tribulation	155
Revelation 5:1-5:14 ~ God's Decree of Judgment	158
Revelation 6:1-6:8 ~ The Four Horsemen	162
Daniel's "70-Weeks Prophecy"	163
The Gap in the 70-Weeks Prophecy	179
Back to the Four Horsemen	184
Revelation 6:9-6:11 ~ The Cries of the Martyrs	204
Revelation 6:12-6:17 ~ A Coming Nuclear Holocaust	207
Revelation 7:1-7:8 ~ We Are Not Appointed to Wrath	217
Revelation 7:9-7:17 ~ On the Other Hand...	229
Revelation 8:1-8:6 ~ It Begins	234

Conclusion	239
Does It Matter What We Believe?	240
Be Filled with the Holy Spirit!	248
How Can I Be Filled?	259

amazon.com

Thanks for reading! If you enjoy this book I'd be very grateful if you'd **post a short review on Amazon**. Your support really does make a difference, and I read all of the reviews personally: http://thesefinaldays.org/book1/review (redirects to Amazon)

While I'm asking for favors, might I also request:
- **Recommend this book to your friends**
- Like my Facebook page:
  http://facebook.com/thesefinaldays
- Subscribe to my YouTube channel:
  http://youtube.com/thesefinaldays

Finally, I invite you to **check out all of the books in this series**. You can find them on my Amazon author page:
http://amazon.com/author/ryanspeakman

Thanks for your support!

Introduction

"**G**od, please help me!" she shouted over the thundering noise of the helicopters overhead. A look of utter despair flashed across the woman's young face as one of them descended on her from behind. She fell to her knees in the wet mud, at the end of her strength. Water spray, kicked up by the blast of the helicopter's rotor blades, mixed with her long blonde hair as it whipped up into a tangled mess. She heard the sound of the soldiers' footsteps as they jumped onto the ground and darted toward her. A tall black boot, now covered in mud, splashed into the puddle in front of her. The rifle barrel hung in her face.

She knew she wouldn't die here under this dark sky, but her fate was undeniable. She was a Christian, one of the persecuted few who had come to accept Jesus following the Great Disappearance so many months earlier. Her mother and sister had tried for many years to lead her to the Lord, but she had foolishly thought there was time, time to live her life on her own terms. Then one day they were gone, along with millions of other believers. She'd heard about the Rapture in church growing up, and she, like many others, realized too late that it had all been true. Now she was facing quick death at the end of a guillotine blade.

She lifted her gaze to look into the face of her captor. Dark eyes peered down at her from behind an evil grin. A stylized tattoo of the number "666" showed prominently on his forehead. She glanced at the uniform, completely black from head to toe, the unmistakable insignia of the World Army on the chest. Another soldier grabbed her arm and abruptly pulled her to her feet. She would now be taken to the Holding Facility where she would await sentencing. There would be no trial, no hearing. She would refuse to receive the mark, and would be given the institutional punishment meted out to those who rebel against the Great Leader and his New World Order. She would be unceremoniously beheaded…

• • •

The smell of straw and dust permeated the air. I squirmed in my seat, and secretly wished that the film would get stuck in the projector and break, as happened so often when we watched films in school. I nervously glanced around the inside of the barn, hoping that my fear would be invisible to those who sat in the seats around me. After all, I was ten years old, and ten-year-olds aren't supposed to be scared. But this was heady stuff for a fifth-grader. I looked at my brother and sister, who were sitting near my parents and me. They looked like I felt, and I knew they were thinking the same thing I was—we'd better make absolutely sure we were saved, or we might get left behind, too, and have to suffer through the Great Tribulation like this poor girl on the rickety screen in front of us.

Such was my introduction to the ominous world of End Times prophecy. In the years that followed that barn meeting, my twin brother, Erin, and I became increasingly obsessed with the Book of Revelation and particularly with the vast supply of supporting literature. We latched onto every theory and storyline we encountered on the subject, and were able to quote Scripture—and posit popular interpretation—with the best of them. The locusts with "tails like scorpions," "breastplates of iron," and faces "like the

INTRODUCTION

faces of men" (Revelation 9:7-10) were military helicopters. Wormwood (Revelation 8:11) was some sort of mass chemical weapon. The ten horns on the fiery red, seven-headed dragon (Revelation 12:3) represented OPEC.

As the years went by, my devotion to the study of the topic began to wane a bit, but I never lost my fascination with End Times prophecy. My teen years saw little time spent actively pursuing the subject (though I thought about it every day), and by the time I was a young adult, my interest had taken a more secular turn. I was as intrigued as ever with the notions of world government, a global police force and military, and a one-world economy—indeed, the more I understood about the world and its history, the more it seemed unmistakably headed in this direction. A desire to study the topic began to surface in me again, but I felt that the Bible—at least as I'd heard it taught—had long ago offered up what it could, and I had long since grown weary of all the books, films, and sermons about the Last Days.

So, I decided to find out what the world had to teach me on the subject. In 1991, I moved from the Bay Area, where I'd grown up, to Arizona. My plan was to complete one year of junior college in the small central Arizona town of Prescott and then transfer to the political science program at the University of Arizona in Tucson. As a teenager in 1987, I'd traveled across the Soviet Union, and figured that the U.S.S.R. would play prominently in the End Times scenario—the Cold War was still going on, after all—so I would major in International Relations and minor in the Russian language. Just a month or so after arriving in Arizona—thanks to our two well-intentioned mothers who arranged a barbeque for just this purpose—I met my wife-to-be, Pamela. A month later, Pam—still just a friend at this point—accompanied me to Prescott to help me scout out a place to live during school. As we walked through downtown looking for a lunch spot, I happened to glance at a newspaper stand, and was taken aback by the world-altering headline: "Collapse of the Soviet Union." Nevertheless, I decided to stay on my planned course. A year later, I'd completed my first year of college, Pam and I had fallen in love and were married, and I transferred with a 4.0 GPA from Prescott to Tucson. I was very successful at the U of A, and in 1994 I was awarded a full scholarship to study in Kazakhstan—a desperate place at that time—where I conducted research on the former Soviet Republic's attempt to fit into the "new world order" that had emerged following the Cold War. My focus was always on globalism, and my goal was eventually to work for the U.S. Department of State, or perhaps even the Central Intelligence Agency.

In 1995, I graduated *summa cum laude* from the University of Arizona and was in the process of applying to the graduate program in International Relations at Georgetown University in Washington, D.C., when I felt that God, whom I'd learned to hear more than ever during my difficult months in Kazakhstan, was directing me to get on a different path. I heeded His voice and canceled my Georgetown application. I applied instead to Thunderbird, The American Graduate School of International Management, one of the top international business schools in the world. I was awarded a full scholarship, and spent the next year and a half studying international finance, economics, and law. Through my studies, I gained much insight into the structure and content of this world system and the direction that we're headed; I became more convinced than ever that Bible prophecy is true; and I developed an ever-deepening conviction that a right relationship with God—with the Holy Spirit at the center—is critical in these final days.

I've been a Christian my whole life (I first said the "prayer of salvation" when I was four years old), and over the years I've experienced the whole spectrum of Protestant Christianity, from mainline Southern Baptist to full Pentecostal/Charismatic. In my few short decades on this Earth, I've witnessed firsthand the steady maturing of the Body of Christ. As a group, we are gaining an increasing revelation of our Father—that He is not some cold, distant dictator looking for an excuse to squash us all like bugs. He's not a harsh taskmaster, and—for us, His children—He is not an angry, wrathful Dispenser of Divine Judgment. God loves us. He gave His only begotten Son to die on a cross so that we could be forever reconciled to Him,[1] and much more than this: so that we

---

[1] John 3:16

could have life, and have it more abundantly.² Indeed, God has wonderful blessings in store for all those who truly love Him. But—humans that we are—even this precious knowledge has its potential pitfalls. God only wants the very best for us, it's true; but this does not mean that we won't have to endure some trials and tribulations along the way. In fact, these contribute to our maturing process, our refinement as we become the pure and spotless Bride for whom Jesus is going to someday soon return.³ Jesus' brother, James, tells us as much in James 1:2-4:

> 2 My brethren, count it all joy when you fall into various trials,
> 3 knowing that the testing of your faith produces patience.
> 4 But let patience have its perfect work, that you may be perfect and complete, lacking nothing.

When we are not rooted and grounded in the tenets of our faith that cause real maturing—patience, longsuffering, the determination to overcome—then we risk a dangerously false perception of our God: that He would never permit His children to face any form of real hardship; that He would not allow our faith to be challenged to its extreme; that He would rather steal us away to Heaven than see us endure tribulation, especially of the variety foretold in the Book of Revelation…

After the credits rolled across the screen in that barn so many years ago, the preacher gave an altar call. Who wanted to escape the horrors we'd just witnessed on the movie screen? Who wanted to be raptured before the Antichrist showed up and started chopping peoples' heads off? All you had to do was say a little prayer, and you'd have your ticket out of here. Hands went up from one end of the barn to the other. Perhaps two dozen people were "saved" that night.

Of course, I don't diminish the miracle of salvation, and it is cause for rejoicing whenever a single person accepts Christ as Savior. But salvation should not be akin to escapism, at least not in the way that it seems to be for many in this generation. Certainly, at the core of

---

[2] John 10:10
[3] Revelation 19:7-8

our salvation is the promise of escape from the wages of sin; that is, eternal spiritual death. Salvation can also include deliverance from some of the pains of this life, including sickness, poverty, and sorrow. But God never promised us that we wouldn't go through some hard times, times of tribulation that emanate from the world around us. In His final message to His Disciples before going to the Cross, Jesus said something that is true—on some level and to varying degrees—for each of us who follows Him: "Then they will deliver you up to tribulation…and you will be hated by all nations for My name's sake" (Matthew 24:9; paraphrased). Many were saved at that barn meeting so many years ago, but under the questionable pretense that their salvation would ensure deliverance from this world before things get really bad. Is such an expectation truly justified?

And such is the basis for this book. In the past few decades, the notion that the Rapture—the sudden "catching up" of Christians to meet Jesus in the air at His return[4]—will take place prior to the seven-year period of tribulation that is coming upon the Earth (and that is described by the Prophet Daniel, the Apostle John, Jesus, and many others throughout the Bible) has become nothing less than the mainstream view among Evangelical Christians worldwide;[5] and it is becoming increasingly popular among other Christian groups as well. At the heart of this concept, known as the Pre-Tribulation Rapture, is the sentiment that God is a loving father and would therefore never allow His children to go through such a terrible time. Added to this reasoning is layer upon layer of other pieces of "evidence," Biblical or otherwise, that "prove" that the Church will be removed from this world before the horrors that comprise the Great Tribulation are unleashed upon it. But are we really promised this in the scriptures? If not, what is the basis for such widespread acceptance of the Pre-Tribulation Rapture view? What is the real truth about the Rapture and the End of the Age? And why does it matter?

---

[4] 1 Thessalonians 4:17
[5] Spirit and Power—A 10-Country Survey of Pentecostals (October 2006; Pew Research Center's Religion & Public Life Project); Global Survey of Evangelical Protestant Leaders (June 2011; Pew Research Center's Religion & Public Life Project)

INTRODUCTION

My approach to this topic is simple. After years of reading, hearing, and watching many differing views and interpretations on the last of the Last Days, I decided to do something extraordinary: read the Word myself. How many believers really do this? Among those who do study for themselves, many make the dangerous mistake of approaching the Word with a pre-determined idea or belief. In other words, they decide beforehand what the Bible says, or what they want it to say, and then dig through the scriptures in search of verses that support their view. Many others rely on their pastors—and other preachers, teachers, and writers whom they happen to like—to tell them about these things (to whatever degree); and, if they're content with what they hear, they accept it as gospel truth without ever testing it against God's Word. Still others, confused or overwhelmed by the topic, choose to ignore it altogether. None of these approaches is beneficial, and none produces what God desires for each His children: a clear, illuminated comprehension of the times that are coming. As Paul instructs us in 1 Thessalonians 5:19-21:

19 Do not quench the Spirit.
20 Do not despise prophecies.
21 Test all things; hold fast what is good.

And so, in our attempt to answer the question "When will the Rapture occur?", we will approach the Bible with a completely open mind and will examine the entire Word, not just the bits of Scripture that seem to give us the answer that we want. None of us would desire to go through the Great Tribulation, but if God's Word tells us that we or some future generation of believers must, it's imperative that we understand and prepare—to do otherwise could be to our own peril. As we enter into the complex realm of End Times prophecy, we will use the Word of God as our primary guide. When a point or concept requires clarification, we will turn to Scripture first to seek our answer. In all matters, God's Word should be—must be—our final authority.

The first half of this book will present a careful examination of the Rapture, particularly regarding its timing relative to the Great Tribulation. This task will take us to many places in our Bibles, some familiar, some less familiar. Our in-depth analysis of the Rapture will, in fact, form the foundation for this entire book series, *These Final Days*. Then, once sufficient light has been shed on that topic, we'll begin to explore what the future really holds for God's people and for this world by delving into what is arguably the most complex—and, many might say, the most formidable—book of the Bible, its final text, the Book of Revelation.

I will offer a couple of comments on the Word of God, and then we'll begin our journey. First, I believe that the Bible is supremely simple for those who are willing to invest the time and effort to study it. Jesus said, "Ask, and it will be given to you; seek, and you will find; knock, and it will be opened to you. For everyone who asks receives, and he who seeks finds, and to him who knocks it will be opened." (Matthew 7:7-8). The answers we seek are freely available to us. They are also important. If this were not so, God would not have had men put it all down on paper. The prophets Isaiah, Ezekiel, and Daniel, the apostles Matthew, Mark, Luke, John, and Paul, and many other contributors to the Bible all knew the Last Days to be an exceedingly important topic and they wrote much on this subject. Jesus, knowing that He was about to be arrested and crucified, surely chose His final words to His Disciples carefully. According to three of the four gospels—Matthew, Mark, and Luke—Jesus' last sermon was on the End Times. Only the Apostle John seemed to marginalize this topic in his Gospel—he's the only one of the four Gospel writers who did not recount Jesus' words about the Last Days. And yet it is John who later coined the term "Antichrist," and it was to him that God gave the monumental task of recording the message that is the Book of Revelation, the last book of the Bible, God's final written word to mankind.

A very wise father once instructed his son, "And in all your getting, get understanding." (Proverbs 4:7). While sometimes it seems that there are as many differing views on the Rapture (and on the Last Days in general) as there are Christian preachers, teachers and writers, I believe that the answers must be plain, and with the benefit of the Holy Spirit they can be found. So, let's begin...

Section I

In Search of the Rapture

Chapter 1

What is the Rapture?

Merriam-Webster's Collegiate Dictionary defines "rapture" as "a mystical experience in which the spirit is exalted to a knowledge of divine things."[6] This barely offers us a hint of the meaning of this word in popular Christianity. Surprisingly, the word "rapture" does not appear once in the Bible, at least not in any English-language version. But the concept is definitely there.

The word "rapture" is derived from the Latin word *rapiemur*, found in the fourth-century Latin Vulgate,[7] an early translation of the scriptures that eventually became the official Latin Bible of the Roman Catholic Church and from which many early English translations were made. This, in turn, had been translated by Saint Jerome (who penned most of the Vulgate[8]) from the Greek

---

[6] *Merriam-Webster's Collegiate Dictionary* (2008; Merriam-Webster, Inc.)
[7] *Biblia Sacra Vulgata (Vulgate): Holy Bible in Latin*, Institute for NT Textual Resea (2007; German Bible Society)
[8] *The Grammar of the Vulgate: Introduction to the Study of the Latinity of the Vulgate Bible*, W.E. Plater & H.J. White (1997; Oxford University Press Reprints)

harpazō, which means "to snatch or catch away."[9] Paul tells us in 1 Thessalonians 4:13-17 (emphasis mine):

> 13 But I do not want you to be ignorant, brethren, concerning those who have fallen asleep, lest you sorrow as others who have no hope.
> 14 For if we believe that Jesus died and rose again, even so God will bring with Him those who sleep in Jesus.
> 15 For this we say to you by the word of the Lord, that we who are alive and remain until the coming of the Lord will by no means precede those who are asleep.
> 16 For the Lord Himself will descend from heaven with a shout, with the voice of an archangel, and with the trumpet of God. And the dead in Christ will rise first.
> 17 Then we who are alive and remain shall be *caught up* together with them in the clouds to meet the Lord in the air. And thus we shall always be with the Lord.

This, by many accounts, is the quintessential Rapture passage. By other accounts, it is the only Rapture passage. In fact, this is only one of many passages in the Bible that deal with this event—the "catching up" of the Saints at Christ's return—as we'll see. In the meantime, let's carefully examine Paul's words here. There's a lot going on in these five verses, and it's critical that we incorporate our "open mind" strategy at this early juncture. Much of what we believe about the Rapture, as taught to us by mainstream Christianity, may be challenged as we study Paul's description of the Rapture event.

In verse 13, Paul admonishes us to receive the knowledge that he is about to bestow concerning the dead in Christ (verse 16), whom he describes here as "those who have fallen asleep." Paul is simply referring to all believers whose physical bodies have died and are buried (or otherwise dispatched) prior to Christ's return. This is a very large group of individuals whose generations date back to Jesus' time, and even earlier—after all, won't Noah, Abraham, David, Daniel, Ezekiel and many other Old Testament faithful be

---

[9] *Vine's Complete Expository Dictionary of Old and New Testament Words*, W. E. Vine (1996; Thomas Nelson)

counted among those worthy to take their place in the Kingdom that is to come? Won't they likewise be included in the mass resurrection that—according to Paul's words above—will immediately precede the Rapture?

In any event, Paul advises the Thessalonians not to "sorrow (for this group) as others who have no hope." They, like the rest of us, no doubt felt grief when a loved one died, and Paul is offering them some comfort. But there is more to it than this. The Thessalonians—like every generation of Christians since—believed that theirs was the last generation, the one that would experience Christ's return. Apparently, they were concerned about the status of those who had passed away in the meantime. But notice that Paul does not console them with promises of Heaven for the spirits of their deceased loved ones, but rather with assurance of the eventual resurrection of their physical bodies. Paul, and perhaps his audience, seemed to understand something that recent generations of believers often miss: that man was not created to live in Heaven, but to live in a perfected, redeemed physical state here on Earth.

In verse 14, Paul goes on to say, "For if we believe that Jesus died and rose again, even so God will bring with Him those who sleep in Jesus." Let's consider this reference to Jesus' death and resurrection. We all know that it was not Jesus' spirit that died and rose again, but His physical body. Recall that the first clue that Jesus had risen from the dead was that His tomb was found to be empty (John 20:1-10). There was no body there. Later, when Jesus appeared to His Disciples, they became frightened and thought that He'd returned as a ghost. But He assured them that He was not a spirit, but was of "flesh and bones" (Luke 24:39). He directed Thomas, who'd always had a bit of a problem believing, to stick his finger into the holes in His hands and his hand into the sword wound in His side to see that it really was Jesus in physical form. Jesus even asked for some food, and then enjoyed a meal of fish and honeycomb (Luke 24:42-43). Nevertheless, in His resurrected physical body, Jesus was able to appear and disappear as if He were a spirit. But remember that even *before* His death and resurrection Jesus had been able to perform feats that seemed to defy physical laws, such as walking on water. More extraordinary yet, Peter, who was not God in the flesh but merely a man like the rest of us, responded to Jesus' invitation and joined Him on the surface of the waves, at least for a moment (Matthew 14:22-33). These facts should cause us to question just how vast is the chasm between the physical and spiritual realms: perhaps they are more intertwined than we imagine, simply two aspects of a single realm. After all, when Jesus finally went to His Father, it was not merely His spirit that ascended. His redeemed *physical* body "was parted from them and carried up into heaven" (Luke 24:51).

Is such a miraculous state of being reserved for the Son of God only? Apparently not. In fact, this event was not unprecedented. Paul tells us in Hebrews 11:5 that Enoch, named in the bloodline of Noah, was "taken away (by God) so that he did not see death" (see also Genesis 5:24). Similarly, we read in 2 Kings 2:1-11 that the Prophet Elijah, when his time on Earth was complete, was "taken up by a whirlwind into heaven." It was not only Elijah's spirit that was taken, but his physical body as well. Enoch's and Elijah's bodies were presumably translated to a state of perfection during these events, since corruptible flesh cannot exist in Heaven. Paul writes concerning these things in 1 Corinthians 15:50: "Now this I say, brethren, that flesh and blood cannot inherit the kingdom of God; nor does corruption inherit incorruption." However, perfected flesh—human bodies in a redeemed state—can go, and have gone, to Heaven. And humans—those who are in God—are destined likewise to receive glorified, perfected physical bodies on a massive scale at Christ's return.

In verses 15 and 16 of our passage, Paul writes, "For this we say to you by the word of the Lord, that we who are alive and remain until the coming of the Lord will by no means precede those who are asleep. For the Lord Himself will descend from heaven with a shout, with the voice of an archangel, and with the trumpet of God. And the dead in Christ will rise first." Notice that last sentence. In verse 14, we read that when Christ returns "God will bring with Him those who sleep in Jesus." If deceased Christians are coming with Him, how can they simultaneously rise to meet Him? The answer is simple: Their spirits will return with Jesus from Heaven, and their redeemed bodies will rise to be rejoined with their spirits in the air.

Those believers who are still alive at that time will also be transformed when we are "caught up together with them in the clouds to meet the Lord in the air" (verse 17). In 1 Corinthians 15:51-54, Paul explains this transformation in detail:

> 51 Behold, I tell you a mystery: We shall not all sleep, but we shall all be changed—
> 52 in a moment, in the twinkling of an eye, at the last trumpet. For the trumpet will sound, and the dead will be raised incorruptible, and we shall be changed.
> 53 For this corruptible must put on incorruption, and this mortal must put on immortality.
> 54 So when this corruptible has put on incorruption, and this mortal has put on immortality, then shall be brought to pass the saying that is written: "Death is swallowed up in victory."

Notice the mentions of a trumpet sounding and the dead being raised, and compare these to our Rapture passage above (1 Thessalonians 4:16). Clearly, Paul is talking about the same event in both passages; so we confirm at this early juncture that 1 Thessalonians 4:13-17 is not, in fact, the only scripture that deals with the Rapture. In any event, when the Resurrection and Rapture occur, all believers, deceased and living, will be given new physical bodies just like Enoch, Elijah, and Jesus (and perhaps others).

So, the popular image of millions of Christians suddenly ascending into the clouds to meet Jesus is entirely accurate. But the question of timing remains. Here, Paul has given us a wonderfully detailed account of the event that we call the Rapture, but he's given us no clue whatsoever as to when it occurs in relation to the Great Tribulation. If 1 Thessalonians 4:13-17 were indeed our only scriptural glimpse of the Rapture, we would be at an utter loss to determine whether Christians will have to endure the cataclysmic events foretold by the Apostle John in the Book of Revelation. Surely, God has known from the beginning that as the last of the Last Days draw near, Christians would be wondering about this and would be striving for correct understanding.

Would He have concealed the truth from us?

Chapter 2

Finding a Model for the Timing of the Rapture

Jesus is coming back for His Church, this we know. But when will He come? So often I've heard fellow Christians—teachers, preachers, evangelists, and just plain believers—make the statement, "Jesus could come back at any moment." Is this really accurate? Or are certain events slated to transpire first?

In the preceding chapter, we gained some understanding of what the Rapture is, but we weren't given any clues about when it will occur—before, during, or after the Great Tribulation. If we are removed from this planet before the Tribulation, we have much to rejoice about. After all, the details offered in the Bible about this coming period of human history paint a horrifying picture of anguish and terror "such as has not been since the beginning of the world until this time, no, nor ever shall be" (Matthew 24:21). But if we are going to be around for part, or all, of this time, we must be ready. We must prepare ourselves and others.

There is a popular sentiment among Christians today that we can't really know the answer to the question of when the Rapture will happen, so what's the point of trying? We read book after book, hear sermon after sermon on the subject, and all seem to be little more than individual opinions with a bit of Scripture woven in. If the answer clearly presents itself in the Bible, certainly there would not be such a wide spectrum of theories on the topic; there would be no theories at all, only facts, factually given. Great men and women of God posit the theory that the Rapture occurs before the seven-year Great Tribulation. Others, equally devoted to the Lord and His people, insist that it occurs at the halfway point. Still others argue that it occurs at the Tribulation's end. And perhaps not surprisingly, these three scenarios are not the only ones offered—there are a multitude of peripheral theories, ranging from the notion that there is no such thing as the Rapture to the idea that there actually will be not one, but perhaps several Rapture events.

With a presumed lack of any clear answer about the timing of the Rapture, why should we bother to consider this issue yet further? For one thing, it is one of our duties as believers to gain knowledge. Paul tells us in 2 Timothy 2:15, "Be diligent and study to present yourselves approved to God, workers who do not need to be ashamed, rightly dividing the word of truth." And God tells us through the Prophet Hosea, "My people perish for lack of knowledge" (Hosea 4:6a)—a statement that takes on special poignancy when applied to the timing of the Rapture, as we shall see. But where could we possibly find an answer if a definitive one has not already been found?

I stated in the introduction to this book that the Word of God must be our final authority on all things. All of our knowledge and understanding must begin there and end there. As we study the issue at hand, we must dig deep into the scriptures. However, if we take a "shotgun approach," we may end up with a smorgasbord of verses and passages that offer no coherent answer. I am highly critical of any approach that constructs a model outside the Word and then tries to find supporting scriptural evidence. But if we don't begin with a model of our own, we'll have no basis from which to explore our question.

Fortunately, we are not at a loss. All we need is one passage in Scripture that gives us a chronology of End Times events that includes the elements that we're attempting to relate: the Great

Tribulation and the Rapture. As it happens, there is not one, but many of these in God's Word. This assertion may surprise you. After all, most of today's popular teachers on the subject claim quite the contrary: that the Bible offers no timeline that would allow us to relate the timing of the Rapture to the Great Tribulation. Such is the basis of the widespread, and dangerous, notion that we can't know the truth. But if what I'm suggesting is accurate—if there really are chronologies in the Bible that relate the timing of the Rapture to the Tribulation—why would so many teachers proclaim otherwise? The answer is simple in many cases: these passages do not fit their predetermined models, so they ignore them, claim that they are talking about something else, or find some other way to dismiss them.

Not only does the Word give us several chronologies of Last Days events, but, amazingly, one of the most detailed is given by Jesus Himself. Jesus had just delivered His famous denunciation of the religious leaders of the day.[10] This showdown had been a long time—one might say centuries—in coming, and this would be the confrontation that would ultimately drive the corrupt Pharisees to conspire to have Jesus crucified. Jesus had little time left before He was to be delivered into the hands of Pontius Pilate, and the sermon that followed was to be His last. One would expect that Jesus would choose His parting words carefully, that the content of His final message would be of extreme import. As it happened, He chose to tell His Disciples—and, by extension, us—about the Last Days. He wasn't vague. He didn't bury his description of things to come in poetic symbolism. He explained things in terms that His audience would clearly understand, and He presented future events in the order in which they are to occur. We find Jesus' great End Times dissertation in Matthew chapter 24, which begins with a prophecy about what was to become of the Jewish Temple that was standing in Jesus' day (Matthew 24:1-3):

> 1 Then Jesus went out and departed from the temple, and His disciples came up to show Him the buildings of the temple.

---

[10] Matthew chapter 23

2   And Jesus said to them, "Do you not see all these things? Assuredly, I say to you, not one stone shall be left here upon another, that shall not be thrown down."
3   Now as He sat on the Mount of Olives, the disciples came to Him privately, saying, "Tell us, when will these things be? And what will be the sign of Your coming, and of the end of the age?"

In response to His Disciples' question, Jesus goes on to explain the events and conditions that will lead up to the last of the Last Days (Matthew 24:4-14):

4   And Jesus answered and said to them: "Take heed that no one deceives you.
5   "For many will come in My name, saying, 'I am the Christ,' and will deceive many.
6   "And you will hear of wars and rumors of wars. See that you are not troubled; for all these things must come to pass, but the end is not yet.
7   "For nation will rise against nation, and kingdom against kingdom. And there will be famines, pestilences, and earthquakes in various places.
8   "All these are the beginning of sorrows.
9   "Then they will deliver you up to tribulation and kill you, and you will be hated by all nations for My name's sake.
10 "And then many will be offended, will betray one another, and will hate one another.
11 "Then many false prophets will rise up and deceive many.
12 "And because lawlessness will abound, the love of many will grow cold.
13 "But he who endures to the end shall be saved.
14 "And this gospel of the kingdom will be preached in all the world as a witness to all the nations, and then the end will come.

Finally, Jesus describes those final years of human history that we refer to as the Great Tribulation (Matthew 24:15-31):

15 "Therefore when you see the 'abomination of desolation,' spoken of by Daniel the prophet, standing in the holy place" (whoever reads, let him understand),
16 "then let those who are in Judea flee to the mountains.
17 "Let him who is on the housetop not go down to take anything out of his house.
18 "And let him who is in the field not go back to get his clothes.
19 "But woe to those who are pregnant and to those who are nursing babies in those days!
20 "And pray that your flight may not be in winter or on the Sabbath.
21 "For then there will be great tribulation, such as has not been since the beginning of the world until this time, no, nor ever shall be.
22 "And unless those days were shortened, no flesh would be saved; but for the elect's sake those days will be shortened.
23 "Then if anyone says to you, 'Look, here is the Christ!' or 'There!' do not believe it.
24 "For false christs and false prophets will rise and show great signs and wonders to deceive, if possible, even the elect.
25 "See, I have told you beforehand.
26 "Therefore if they say to you, 'Look, He is in the desert!' do not go out; or 'Look, He is in the inner rooms!' do not believe it.
27 "For as the lightning comes from the east and flashes to the west, so also will the coming of the Son of Man be.
28 "For wherever the carcass is, there the eagles will be gathered together.
29 "Immediately after the tribulation of those days the sun will be darkened, and the moon will not give its light; the stars will fall from heaven, and the powers of the heavens will be shaken.
30 "Then the sign of the Son of Man will appear in heaven, and then all the tribes of the earth will mourn, and they will see the Son of Man coming on the clouds of heaven with power and great glory.
31 "And He will send His angels with a great sound of a trumpet, and they will gather together His elect from the four winds, from one end of heaven to the other.

Jesus' teaching in Matthew chapter 24 arguably comprises the most authoritative narrative on the End Times, and yet it is inexplicably omitted from many scholarly works on the Rapture or on the Last Days in general. Or, if it is not omitted, it is sorely misrepresented. However, Jesus herein undeniably describes the Rapture, and He clearly places this event at the end of the Great Tribulation. Let's examine this carefully:

Our first task is to determine whether this passage is describing events in *chronological order*. If not, we need not go any further: if the events are not listed in the order in which they occur, Jesus' words will not help us to determine the timing of the Rapture relative to the Great Tribulation. How can we be sure that Jesus is, in fact, describing events in their actual order? Our primary evidence for this is the use of the word "then." Merriam-Webster's Collegiate Dictionary defines the word "then" as "next in order of time; following next after in order of position, narration, or enumeration."[11] Few of us would debate the purpose of the word "then" in a narrative—its purpose is to construct a chronology—and this word appears no less than ten times in Jesus' discourse on things to come.

Our second task is to determine whether Jesus is, in fact, referring to the End Times as described in the Book of Revelation, or if He is merely describing events that would occur in His listeners' near future. This is a pertinent question since the first part of the Disciples' inquiry, "Tell us, when will these things be?" (verse 3), is in response to the comment that Jesus had just made about the future of the Temple in Jerusalem (verses 1-2):

1 Then Jesus went out and departed from the temple, and His disciples came up to show Him the buildings of the temple.
2 And Jesus said to them, "Do you not see all these things? Assuredly, I say to you, not one stone shall be left here upon another, that shall not be thrown down."

---

[11] *Merriam-Webster's Collegiate Dictionary* (2008; Merriam-Webster, Inc.)

Jesus' prediction of the destruction of the Temple was realized at the hands of the Roman general Titus in A.D. 70, just a few decades after Jesus' death and resurrection. But it was His Disciples' follow-up question to which Jesus responds in verses 4 through 31 (and beyond, but we'll save the rest of the passage for later): "And what will be the sign of Your coming, and the end of the age?" (verse 3). This question sets the stage for everything that Jesus says from here. As we examine this passage more closely, we'll clearly see that Jesus is, in fact, describing the events that are leading up to His "Second Coming" and the end of this age.

Next, let's confirm our delineation of Matthew chapter 24 above; that is, let's confirm that verses 4 through 14 depict the events that will lead up to the Great Tribulation, and that verse 15 begins Jesus' description of the Tribulation itself. In verse 6, Jesus predicts "wars and rumors of wars," but assures us that "the end is not yet." He then describes other conditions, all as evidence that the end of the age is approaching. Finally, in verse 14, he says that His gospel "will be preached in all the world," and "*then* the end will come." The "end" that Jesus is referring to is none other than the period that we call the Great Tribulation, which He begins to describe in the very next verse, verse 15. Here, Jesus makes reference to something called the "abomination of desolation" as described by the Prophet Daniel—this is a description of the self-deification of the Antichrist, an event that occurs *during* the Great Tribulation (see Daniel 9:27; we'll take a close look at this later). A few verses later, in verse 21, Jesus says: "For then there will be *great tribulation*, such as has not been since the beginning of the world until this time, no, nor ever shall be" (emphasis mine). This, in fact, is the only verse outside of the Book of Revelation where the term "great tribulation" appears (so we see that it is Jesus Himself who coins this term). We plainly see, then, that verses 15 through 24 are describing the period that we know as the Great Tribulation.

Now that we've confirmed where the Great Tribulation occurs in Jesus' chronology, our final task is to identify the Rapture. By doing so, and then by examining where this event is depicted in relation to the Tribulation, we will be able to conclusively determine whether the Rapture is going to take place before, during, or after the Great Tribulation period. Remember, many scholars would argue that the verses that we are about to examine do not describe the Rapture event. With this in mind, remember, too, that most agree that 1 Thessalonians 4:13-18 *does* describe the Rapture. Let's look at verses 30-31 in our Matthew passage:

> 30 "Then the sign of the Son of Man will appear in heaven, and then all the tribes of the earth will mourn, and they will see the Son of Man coming on the clouds of heaven with power and great glory.
> 31 "And He will send His angels with a great sound of a trumpet, and they will gather together His elect from the four winds, from one end of heaven to the other."

Pretty exciting stuff! But is this describing the Rapture? Let's compare Jesus' words here to the core verses in our quintessential Rapture passage in 1 Thessalonians (1 Thessalonians 4:16-17):

> 16 For the Lord Himself will descend from heaven with a shout, with the voice of an archangel, and with the trumpet of God. And the dead in Christ will rise first.
> 17 Then we who are alive and remain shall be caught up together with them in the clouds to meet the Lord in the air. And thus we shall always be with the Lord.

Do we see any correlation between these two accounts? We do. And the points that these passages have in common are substantial:

1. Both accounts begin with Jesus appearing in the heavens.
2. Both describe highly conspicuous events (widely visible, loud).
3. Both depict an accompaniment of angels.
4. Both include mention of a trumpet in conjunction with the angels.
5. Both conclude with believers being gathered to join Jesus in the air.

These two passages seem to be describing one and the same event, the Rapture of the Church. Some scholars, however, argue that the "gathering of the elect" described in Matthew 24:31 refers not to the Rapture but to the calling together of God's heavenly armies—

including, perhaps, believers raptured seven years earlier, prior to the Great Tribulation—for the Battle of Armageddon. This claim is, in fact, crucial to the veracity of the Pre-Tribulation Rapture model. After all, if Matthew 24:31 is describing the Rapture, it means that not only did Jesus Himself talk about the Rapture (and He did several times, as we'll see), but He described it as occurring not before, but *after* the Great Tribulation. Let's explore this carefully:

First, we'll confirm who the "elect" are. By "His elect" Jesus is obviously referring to His Church. In His Matthew chapter 24 discourse on the Last Days, He uses the word "elect" twice before mentioning their gathering together—first, in verse 22, to comfort us in the fact that "for the elect's sake" the days of great tribulation will be shortened; and second, in verse 24, to warn us that, if possible, false christs and false prophets (in particular, the Antichrist, as we'll see) will deceive "even the elect" during that time. Some teachers argue that "the elect" refers to the nation of Israel, not Christians. This term is, in fact, used in the Old Testament to describe Israel, specifically by the Prophet Isaiah.[12] But it is used in at least five post-Gospels books of the New Testament to describe Christians. For example, Paul, writing to the Christians in Colosse, writes, "Therefore, *as the elect of God*, holy and beloved, put on tender mercies, kindness, humility, meekness, longsuffering; bearing with one another, and forgiving one another, if anyone has a complaint against another; even as Christ forgave you, so you also must do" (Colossians 3:12-13; emphasis mine). So, when Jesus uses the term "elect," He is referring simply to the people of God, whether pre-Christ Israel or post-Christ believers.

The next question is, when the elect are mentioned as being gathered together in verse 31, from where are they gathered? From Heaven, or from Earth? If from Heaven, then this verse must not be describing the Rapture, and its correlation to 1 Thessalonians 4 is just a coincidence. The wording of verse 31 might seem to suggest this at first glance: "…and they will gather together His elect from the four winds, *from one end of heaven to the other*" (emphasis

---

[12] Isaiah 45:4; 65:9; 65:22

mine). Fortunately, we have a couple of other resources to help us resolve this—namely, the books of Mark and Luke. Most of us are aware that the Gospels of Matthew, Mark, Luke, and John all record the same history—that is, the life, death, and resurrection of Jesus Christ. The first three of these—Matthew, Mark, and Luke—are referred to as the "Synoptic Gospels" because these narratives cover much of the same material. Varying details are offered, but there is significant overlap among these books, even to the point of nearly identical wording in some places. And, as it turns out, each of these three includes, with just enough variance to help increase our understanding, Jesus' discourse on the Last Days. By comparing Matthew's record of Jesus' words about the gathering of the elect to Mark's and Luke's, we can easily resolve the question of the elect's location at the end of the Great Tribulation; that is, whether at Jesus' Second Coming we will be gathered from Heaven or from the Earth. Let's start with Luke's account (Luke 21:25-28; emphasis mine):

> 25 "And there will be signs in the sun, in the moon, and in the stars; and on the earth distress of nations, with perplexity, the sea and the waves roaring;
> 26 "men's hearts failing them from fear and the expectation of those things which are coming on the earth, for the powers of the heavens will be shaken.
> 27 "Then they will see the Son of Man coming in a cloud with power and great glory.
> 28 "*Now when these things begin to happen, look up and lift up your heads, because your redemption draws near.*"

These four verses directly parallel Matthew 24:29-31, so the "gathering of the elect" correlation here would be the last sentence, verse 28. Here, Jesus instructs us to "look up" because our "redemption draws near." Surely, if we are going to be returning from Heaven with Jesus at this time—if, as the Pre-Tribulation Rapture model posits, we have already been raptured up to Heaven some seven years prior to this moment—there is no need for us to look up at anything, nor to hope for a redemption that has long since come. Is it possible, then, that Matthew's wording, "from the four winds, from one end of heaven to the other," is just a poetic way of saying "from around the entire world"? Let's look at how Mark quotes Jesus' teaching (Mark 13:24-27; emphasis mine):

> 24 "But in those days, after that tribulation, the sun will be darkened, and the moon will not give its light;
> 25 "the stars of heaven will fall, and the powers in the heavens will be shaken.
> 26 "Then they will see the Son of Man coming in the clouds with great power and glory.
> 27 "And then He will send His angels, and gather together His elect *from the four winds, from the farthest part of earth to the farthest part of heaven.*"

Here, Mark specifically mentions Earth. Taken together, then, the three Synoptic Gospels make it clear: the Resurrection/Rapture event is going to take place at Christ's return, *at the end of the seven-year Great Tribulation.*

And so, Jesus' great End Times dissertation makes it abundantly plain when the Rapture will occur in relation to the Great Tribulation. Matthew 24:15-24 describes the period that we call the Great Tribulation. Verse 29, a few verses later, begins with the phrase, "Immediately after the tribulation of those days..." And this is then followed in verses 29 through 31 by a depiction of the Second Coming and Resurrection/Rapture event. It seems undeniable: Jesus is not going to return to rescue His Church from this world until *after* the terrible times that comprise the Great Tribulation have concluded, a fact that we will confirm more and more as our study progresses.

I recently asked a pastor friend of mine whether he was "Pre-Trib," "Mid-Trib," or "Post-Trib," the popular terminology used to describe a person's belief about the timing of the Rapture. He replied, "I'm Pan-Trib—Whatever happens, it will all pan out in the end!" He was not the first to tell this joke, and he certainly is not alone in his sentiment. Most Christians have been so inundated with disparate teachings on this topic that they've thrown their arms in the air and surrendered all hope of ever knowing the truth about how the last of the Last Days will play out. But God did not intend to hide the answer from us. The chronology we've just examined, given by Jesus Himself, substantiates this. And while Jesus' dissertation in Matthew 24 alone should be sufficient to convince us about the timing of the Rapture, this, as it turns out, is only the beginning of the light that the Word sheds on this subject…

Chapter 3

Building Confidence for Our Model

Jesus' chronology of the End Times should be a startling revelation to many. After all, if Jesus Himself very plainly places the Rapture "immediately after" the Great Tribulation, why is there so much debate about this issue? It seems surprising—given what we've commonly been taught—that such a timeline exists at all in the Word. It's even more amazing that the one provided by Jesus in Matthew 24 is not unique. There are several others—some simple, some complex. We won't fully dissect all of these in this chapter. However, a quick glance at a few of them will help to strengthen our Post-Tribulation Rapture model. But before we proceed with our study, it will be encouraging for us to examine evidence that, in fact, God *does* intend for His people to know about these things.

We're certainly pushing the envelope of contemporary mainstream Christian thought by suggesting that the timing of the Rapture can be known. There are oft-quoted scriptures that seem quite to the contrary, the most formidable taken directly from Jesus' great End Times dissertation, introduced in the prior chapter. After presenting us with His Last Days chronology, Jesus tells us in Matthew 24:36-44:

> 36 "But of that day and hour no one knows, not even the angels of heaven, but My Father only.
> 37 "But as the days of Noah were, so also will the coming of the Son of Man be.
> 38 "For as in the days before the flood, they were eating and drinking, marrying and giving in marriage, until the day that Noah entered the ark,
> 39 "and did not know until the flood came and took them all away, so also will the coming of the Son of Man be.
> 40 "Then two men will be in the field: one will be taken and the other left.
> 41 "Two women will be grinding at the mill: one will be taken and the other left.
> 42 "Watch therefore, for you do not know what hour your Lord is coming.
> 43 "But know this, that if the master of the house had known what hour the thief would come, he would have watched and not allowed his house to be broken into.
> 44 "Therefore you also be ready, for the Son of Man is coming at an hour you do not expect."

Just a few verses prior to this passage, Jesus had described the Rapture event, in verses 29 through 31 (as we discussed in the last chapter). Notice verses 40 and 41 here: these clearly comprise a reference to the Rapture. And yet, at first glance, the surrounding verses seem to be implying that the timing of this event cannot be known. Jesus says in verse 36 that no one knows the "day and hour" but God Himself. And in verse 44, He states that He is "coming at an hour you do not expect." How can we reconcile this against the fact that Jesus had just given us a timeline that tells us exactly when the Rapture will happen? First, notice that Jesus is referring here to *absolute* time, as opposed to *relative* time. He explains that we cannot know the exact "day and hour" of the Rapture, but He does not say that we can't make some inferences about its timing based on corresponding events. Quite the contrary: Just prior to the above verses, we read in Matthew 24:32-35:

32 "Now learn this parable from the fig tree: When its branch has already become tender and puts forth leaves, you know that summer is near.
33 "So you also, when you see all these things, know that it is near—at the doors!
34 "Assuredly, I say to you, this generation will by no means pass away till all these things take place.
35 "Heaven and earth will pass away, but My words will by no means pass away.

In verse 32, Jesus gives us a mini-parable about a fig tree. When the fig tree manifests certain conditions (tender branches and budding leaves), the observer knows by these signs that summer is near. He explains in verse 33 that, likewise, when the conditions appear and the events occur that He has just described in verses 15 through 24 (His depiction of the Great Tribulation), we will know that "it (the Second Coming/Resurrection/Rapture event) is near." In verse 34, Jesus tells us that "this generation" will witness the Rapture. Later Biblical writings suggest that the first Christians mistook "this generation" to mean the generation Jesus was speaking to; that is, them. What He actually was referring to, however, was the generation that experiences all of the conditions and events that He had just described. Those within that future generation who have prepared themselves by receiving the knowledge Jesus is offering *will not be surprised* when the Rapture occurs, because He has clearly told us the signs to watch for. Paul affirms this in the conclusion to his own famous discourse on the Rapture event. In 1 Thessalonians 5:1-8, he tells us (emphasis mine):

1 But concerning the times and the seasons, brethren, you have no need that I should write to you.
2 For you yourselves know perfectly that the day of the Lord so comes as a thief in the night.
3 For when they say, "Peace and safety!" then sudden destruction comes upon them, as labor pains upon a pregnant woman. And they shall not escape.
4 *But you, brethren, are not in darkness, so that this Day should overtake you as a thief.*
5 You are all sons of light and sons of the day. We are not of the night nor of darkness.

6   Therefore let us not sleep, as other do, but let us watch and be sober.
7   For those who sleep, sleep at night, and those who get drunk are drunk at night.
8   But let us who are of the day be sober, putting on the breastplate of faith and love, and as a helmet the hope of the salvation.

Paul tells us here in very plain language that when Jesus returns to gather His Church, it will indeed be a great surprise to many—but not to all. Those who are not "in darkness" (that is, in ignorance) but in "light" (having gained the knowledge about these things, and having had this knowledge illuminated by the Holy Spirit) will not be caught unawares. We'll know that the Rapture is upon us because we'll have witnessed the things that the Bible tells us will occur beforehand. But we must know what the Word says in order to know what to watch for. Jesus implied this as well in the passage that we read a few moments ago. In verses 45 through 47 of Matthew 24, he compared His return to the "days of Noah" and said that the recipients of God's judgment did not know what was coming "until the flood came and took them all away." They didn't know what to expect because they had not received the knowledge of this event from God. They didn't recognize the signs of an impending deluge, such as an old man—one who happened to be in close relationship with God—and his sons building a giant boat in the middle of the desert. Noah, on the other hand, had heard the Word of the Lord and had received it, and thus wisely prepared for what was coming. Most were completely surprised when the flood came; the man of God was not.

Now that we've gained some confidence that we *can* know the timing of the Rapture—not the absolute time (a specific day or hour), but the relative time (that is, relative to corresponding events and seasons, such as those that comprise the Great Tribulation)—let's proceed with strengthening our model. Again, Jesus seems to tell us in Matthew 24 that the Great Tribulation will occur at some point in the future, and that this period will conclude with the Second Coming and Resurrection/Rapture event. As we're about to see, Jesus' account does not stand alone. Paul, who gave us our primary (according to many scholars)

Rapture passage in his first letter to the church at Thessalonica,[13] had more to say about the End Times in his second letter to the Thessalonians. In 2 Thessalonians 2:1-12, Paul writes (emphasis mine):

1. Now, brethren, *concerning the coming of our Lord Jesus Christ and our gathering together to Him,* we ask you,
2. not to be soon shaken in mind or troubled, either by spirit or by word or by letter, as if from us, as though the day of Christ had come.
3. Let no one deceive you by any means; for *that Day will not come unless the falling away comes first, and the man of sin is revealed,* the son of perdition,
4. who opposes and exalts himself above all that is called God or that is worshiped, so that he sits as God in the temple of God, showing himself that he is God.
5. Do you not remember that when I was still with you I told you these things?
6. And now you know what is restraining, that he may be revealed in his own time.
7. For the mystery of lawlessness is already at work; only He who now restrains will do so until He is taken out of the way.
8. And then the lawless one will be revealed, whom the Lord will consume with the breath of His mouth and destroy with the brightness of His coming.
9. The coming of the lawless one is according to the working of Satan, with all power, signs, and lying wonders,
10. and with all unrighteous deception among those who perish, because they did not receive the love of the truth, that they might be saved.
11. And for this reason God will send them strong delusion, that they should believe the lie,
12. that they all may be condemned who did not believe the truth but had pleasure in unrighteousness.

In this passage, Paul admonishes us to not be deceived about the timing of the Rapture ("the coming of our Lord Jesus Christ and

---

[13] 1 Thessalonians 4:13-17; see Chapter 1 "What is the Rapture?"

our gathering together to Him"; verse 1). He explains that the Rapture *will not happen* until two specific events have occurred beforehand:

First, Paul tells us in verse 4, a "falling away" will take place. This is often referred to as the Great Falling Away or the Great Apostasy, and is touched on briefly in Paul's first letter to his protégé, Timothy: "Now the Spirit expressly says that in latter times some will depart from the faith, giving heed to deceiving spirits and doctrines of demons…" (1 Timothy 4:1). Note that Paul specifically says that the group he is writing about "depart from the faith" during the "latter times." In other words, a number of Last Days Christians, for some reason that is not specified here, surrender their Christianity and perhaps even forfeit their salvation. (This is a critical point that we'll study in detail later.)

Second, Paul tells us that "the man of sin is revealed" (verse 3). Paul also refers to this individual as "the son of perdition" and "the lawless one." The fact that Paul does not use the term "Antichrist" here should not discourage us from acknowledging that this is, in fact, who he is talking about. The term "Antichrist" only appears in the first and second epistles of John (1 John and 2 John), and is not used in any other book of the Bible, including the Book of Revelation. We are told in detail that this individual "opposes and exalts himself" above God; that he will come "with all power, signs, and lying wonders" and "according to the working of Satan"; that many will "be condemned" because of his "unrighteous deception"; and that, ultimately, he will be "consumed" and "destroyed" by the Lord. Paul is obviously talking about the Antichrist, and in verse 4 he gives us a description of the "abomination of desolation" mentioned by Jesus in Matthew 24:15: "…so that he sits as God in the temple of God, showing himself that he is God." As we'll see, the Book of Daniel places this event—the Abomination of Desolation, the Antichrist's self-deification—at the Tribulation's halfway point; that is, precisely three-and-a-half years into the seven-year Great Tribulation.

So, according to Paul's account, the Rapture will not occur until *after* the Great Falling Away and the rise to power of the Antichrist. We won't yet discuss the timing of the Great Falling Away in the context of the Great Tribulation, but there is no debating that the consolidation of the Antichrist's power will occur *during* the Tribulation; this event practically defines this period. And so, when we consider Paul's account of End Times events in conjunction with the one that Jesus provides in Matthew chapter 24,[14] a Pre-Tribulation Rapture becomes increasingly implausible.

In addition to the substantial chronologies offered by Jesus in Matthew chapter 24 and by Paul in 2 Thessalonians chapter 2, there are several other such passages that are short by comparison and without as much detail. As such, they don't necessarily stand well on their own, but they do complement our primary passages quite nicely. For example, six years after his second letter to the Thessalonians, Paul wrote his first (as far as we know) letter to the church at Corinth. In this letter, Paul tells us (1 Corinthians 15:20-25):

> 20 But now Christ is risen from the dead, and has become the firstfruits of those who have fallen asleep.
> 21 For since by man came death, by Man also came the resurrection of the dead.
> 22 For as in Adam all die, even so in Christ all shall be made alive.
> 23 But each one in his own order: Christ the firstfruits, afterward those who are Christ's at His coming.
> 24 Then comes the end, when He delivers the kingdom to God the Father, when He puts an end to all rule and all authority and power.
> 25 For He must reign till He has put all enemies under His feet.

Here, Paul gives us a description of the Rapture similar to his earlier explanation in 1 Thessalonians chapter 4. In verses 20 through 22, he tells us that just as Christ was resurrected in physical form from the dead, many others who are in Christ will likewise be raised at some point in the future, when Christ returns. In verse 24, Paul tells us that this event is followed by "the end," when all worldly power and authority is destroyed or subjugated. This

---

[14] See Chapter 2 "Finding a Model for the Timing of the Rapture"

unquestionably is a reference to what the Book of Revelation calls the fall of Babylon and the cataclysmic war that we refer to as the "Battle of Armageddon," which mark the end of all earthly rule. This coincides with the establishment of Christ's government on Earth—the ushering in of His Millennial Reign—which Paul describes in verses 24 and 25: "when He delivers the kingdom to God the Father... For He must reign till He has put all enemies under His feet." All of this we'll study in detail later, but the point here is that Paul does not indicate that the Rapture occurs and then is followed by seven years of Tribulation. On the contrary—he seems to imply that the Resurrection/Rapture happens in conjunction with events that, according to the Book of Revelation and elsewhere in Scripture, take place *at the end of the Great Tribulation.*

Let's look at one more passage, from the Book of Daniel. The Old Testament, you might be surprised to learn, is rich in prophecy about the Last Days. In fact, the Old Testament contains about five times as much prophecy about Jesus' Second Coming (and the conditions and events that surround it) as it does about His First Coming. Daniel, an Old Testament prophet who lived some six hundred years before Christ, provides one of the most comprehensive bodies of information about the End Times to be found anywhere in the Bible. Daniel's, however, is not the easiest text to decipher. The Apostle John gets much credit for offering a bewildering account of the Last Days in his Book of Revelation; but the Book of Daniel is every bit as challenging, perhaps even more so. Nonetheless, it is important—critical—that we integrate Daniel's writings as we proceed in our study, and doing so will do much to enrich our understanding of the Rapture, the Great Tribulation, and other aspects of the last of the Last Days. Let's begin with a brief chronology from Daniel that will help to reinforce our Post-Tribulation Rapture model. Daniel 12:1-3 reads as follows:

> 1 "At that time Michael shall stand up, the great prince who stands watch over the sons of your people; and there shall be a time of trouble, such as never was since there was a nation, even to that time. And at that time your people shall be delivered, every one who is found written in the book.

> 2 "And many of those who sleep in the dust of the earth shall awake, some to everlasting life, some to shame and everlasting contempt.
> 3 "Those who are wise shall shine like the brightness of the firmament, and those who turn many to righteousness like the stars forever and ever."

Daniel (who is recording a prophecy delivered to him by the Archangel Gabriel) is referring in verse 1 to the Archangel Michael, whom we'll see mentioned later in the Book of Revelation. Daniel tells us that, sometime in the future, "there shall be a time of trouble, such as never was since there was a nation, even to that time" (verse 1). Notice the similarity between this and Jesus' description of the Great Tribulation in Matthew 24:21: "For then there will be great tribulation, such as has not been since the beginning of the world until this time, no, nor ever shall be." Daniel is clearly describing this same period.

Daniel then writes, "And at that time your people shall be delivered, every one who is found written in the book" (verse 1). This would seem to be a depiction of the Rapture. In fact, recall that Luke relates the concept of deliverance to the Rapture in His account of Jesus' sermon on the End Times (Luke 21:27-28):

> 27 "Then they will see the Son of Man coming in a cloud with power and great glory.
> 28 "Now when these things begin to happen, look up and lift your heads, because your redemption draws near."

Here, the Rapture is referred to as our "redemption," which is essentially synonymous with the concept of deliverance, as mentioned by Daniel. Daniel then writes, "And many of those who sleep in the dust of the earth shall awake." If there was any doubt that Daniel is talking about the Resurrection/Rapture event, there shouldn't be now. This mention of "those who sleep" suddenly waking can be directly related, of course, to Paul's Rapture passage in 1 Thessalonians, where he tells us not to sorrow for "those who have fallen asleep" because "the dead in Christ will rise first" (1 Thessalonians 4:13-17). It is clear: Daniel's prophecy is describing the Resurrection and Rapture, and he seems to place these events *at the end of the Great Tribulation.*

The fact that the Rapture is described in the Old Testament is amazing in light of most contemporary teachings on the subject. Again, many teachers claim that the Rapture is barely dealt with at all in the Bible. We've already seen substantial evidence to the contrary. And here, six hundred years before Christ, Daniel has given us a chronology that appears to completely support our assumption about the timing of the Rapture. In both the Old and New Testaments, we find strong evidence in favor of our *Post-*Tribulation Rapture model.

We've now studied several chronologies of the End Times that seem to place the Rapture at or around the conclusion of the Great Tribulation, including one very detailed account by Jesus Himself. But, remarkably, the most comprehensive chronology is yet to come. The majority of End Times teachers assert that the Rapture is not mentioned in the Book of Revelation, and that this neglect contributes greatly to the difficulty in determining when it occurs. It's very exciting to realize that this is, in fact, not the case at all. On the contrary, the Rapture is dealt with quite extensively in John's account of the Last Days. The key is to understand how Revelation is written, and to accept some things about the book that many scholars seem to resist. The exploration of this remarkable prophecy will comprise much of the rest of our study. But before we dive in, there are two more topics that we should examine: first, the event that we call the "Second Coming," and second, the main arguments in support of the Pre-Tribulation Rapture model…

Chapter 4

The Second Coming

Like the word "Rapture," the term "Second Coming" does not actually appear anywhere in the Bible. It, too, is simply a term invented by the Church to conveniently describe a concept—in this case, the return of our Lord Jesus Christ.

In Acts 1:9-11, we read about Jesus' ascension to Heaven following His resurrection, and a corresponding promise (bracketed comments mine):

> 9 Now when He [Jesus] had spoken these things, while they [the Disciples] watched, He was taken up, and a cloud received Him out of their sight.
> 10 And while they looked steadfastly toward heaven as He went up, behold, two men stood by them in white apparel,
> 11 who also said, "Men of Galilee, why do you stand gazing up into heaven? This same Jesus, who was taken up from you into heaven, will so come in like manner as you saw Him go into heaven."

Here, Luke (or whoever wrote the Book of Acts; we're not certain) gives us a description of Jesus' ascension into Heaven (or, more precisely, into our planet's atmosphere, where physical beings are somehow translated from this Universe to the spiritual realm of Heaven; but that's another topic). The key verse here is verse 11, where the angel tells us that Jesus will return exactly as He departed. This means He will *not* be born as a human again, not even to a "virgin" mother. He won't walk out of the desert. He won't suddenly appear in the streets of Jerusalem. He won't climb the ladders of politics or religion. And He won't come down in a UFO. Just as He ascended into the clouds, He will return in the clouds. In Mark's Gospel account of Jesus' End Times dissertation, we read (Mark 13:26): "Then they will see the Son of Man coming in the clouds with great power and glory." Paul similarly describes Christ's return in his famous Rapture passage: "For the Lord Himself will *descend from heaven* with a shout…" (1 Thessalonians 4:16). There are similar such descriptions of the Second Coming throughout the Bible. To internalize this reality, even for believers, is to help to avoid deception, as Jesus tells us in Matthew 24:23-27:

23 "Then if anyone says to you, 'Look, here is the Christ!' or 'There!' do not believe it.
24 "For false christs and false prophets will rise and show great signs and wonders to deceive, if possible, even the elect.
25 "See, I have told you beforehand.
26 "Therefore if they say to you, 'Look, He is in the desert!' do not go out; or 'Look, He is in the inner rooms!' do not believe it.
27 "For as the lightning comes from the east and flashes to the west, so also will the coming of the Son of Man be.

The Second Coming is a pivotal event in the Last Days, and in Christianity in general. Indeed, the return of Jesus Christ to Earth is arguably the most important event in all of human history. Approximately six thousand years ago, the first creatures to have the spirit of God breathed into them—that is, to become His children—were Adam and Eve. These two had the opportunity to walk in perfect communion with God all the days of their lives, and to pass this heritage on to their children and their children's children. But, as we all know, they messed up in a big way and fell into sin instead. Jesus' first incarnation—that is, His First Coming, as Messiah, some 2,000 years ago—was intended to reverse Adam and Eve's mistake, or at least to begin this process. We as believers no longer have to pay for our sins by suffering for even a single moment in Hell, because Jesus became the ultimate sacrifice for all those who would follow Him. But the Garden of Eden—that perfect state of the world, where no sin existed and man served only God—did not return when Jesus was crucified, nor when He was resurrected, nor when He ascended to the Father. There was to be a long history of the development of God's New Covenant Church first, and there are still several things that must be fulfilled before we finally step into that state of "perfection" that will begin the redemption of all of nature—the restoration of Eden, if you will. This latter period will commence with Jesus' *Second* Coming to this world, which will happen when we, His Church—the Bride of Christ—have made ourselves fully ready for His return.

As key as the Second Coming event is, it, too, is often seriously misunderstood by teachers of the Last Days. One common misconception about the Second Coming is that this is distinct from the Rapture: that these are two separate events that take place at different times. This is a confusing and overly complicated interpretation that requires much juggling of the Word of God. One popular contemporary teacher of the Last Days suggests that there is only one Second Coming, but that it occurs in two installments.[15] He, like most teachers who promote the Pre-Tribulation Rapture doctrine, suggests that the first time Jesus comes (that is, the "first installment" of His Second Coming), it will be in secret, a covert operation to snatch Christians off the face of the Earth, much to the confusion and anguish of those who remain. Many of us have seen the bumper sticker that reads, "WARNING: in case of Rapture, this car will be unmanned." There is great concern about patients in the middle of open-heart surgery suddenly being without the benefit of a surgeon; about traffic piling up for days all over the world when millions of drivers suddenly and inexplicably vanish from their vehicles; about airplanes suddenly losing their pilots and falling out of the sky. Indeed, many popular fictional works on the End Times, whether in book form or on the big screen, include such dramatic imagery.

---

[15] *Revelation Unveiled*, Tim LaHaye (1999; Zondervan)

It's true that the world will be very upset when the Rapture occurs, but not because a bunch of Christians have mysteriously disappeared. In Matthew 24:30 Jesus tells us, "Then the sign of the Son of Man will appear in heaven, and then all the tribes of the earth will mourn, and they will see the Son of Man coming on the clouds of heaven with power and great glory." No cloak-and-dagger stuff here. No trench coat and dark glasses. Jesus is going to show up in full, brilliant glory, and no one on Earth will misinterpret what they're witnessing. Every nation will mourn because they'll suddenly realize—too late—that Jesus, the true Lord of all creation, is real. And they'll know that He's not showing up to debate issues of religion or morality or free choice. Jesus Christ is returning as King, Priest, and absolute ruler over this whole world. And every person on Earth will know it.

Even our quintessential Rapture passage demonstrates that Jesus will not return in secret to gather His church. 1 Thessalonians 4:16 tells us, "For the Lord Himself will descend from heaven with a shout, with the voice of an archangel, and with the trumpet of God. And the dead in Christ will rise first…" A shout. The voice of an Archangel (this is the highest order of angels, the most powerful and authoritative of the heavenly host, likely not known for having a quiet disposition). And the trumpet of God. Paul's depiction of the Second Coming certainly doesn't make it sound like a quiet little affair.

It seems plain: the picture of a "secret Second Coming" is simply not scriptural. Again, the reason that this idea has become so popular as to be considered absolute truth by the majority of modern Christians (at least mainstream Evangelical Christians) is that it fits the Pre-Tribulation Rapture model and is therefore promoted in most popular teachings on the subject. But there is no covert first Second Coming of Jesus to gather His Church that is followed seven years later by a very public *second* Second Coming. As should now be clear, there is one monumental event at the conclusion of the seven-year Great Tribulation that is comprised of the Second Coming of Christ, the Resurrection, and the Rapture. Let's review our main scriptural evidences for this, noting in each passage the reference to the Second Coming and the corresponding reference to the Resurrection/Rapture (bracketed comments and emphasis mine in all passages):

- "For *the Lord Himself will descend from heaven* [Second Coming] with a shout, with the voice of an archangel, and with the trumpet of God. And *the dead in Christ will rise first* [Resurrection]. *Then we who are alive and remain shall be caught up* [Rapture] *together with them in the clouds to meet the Lord in the air. And thus we shall always be with the Lord.*" (1 Thessalonians 4:16-17)

- "Then the sign of the Son of Man will appear in heaven, and then all the tribes of the earth will mourn, and they will see *the Son of Man coming* [Second Coming] on the clouds of heaven with power and great glory. And He will send His angels with a great sound of a trumpet, and they will *gather together His elect* [Resurrection/Rapture] from the four winds, from one end of heaven to the other." (Matthew 24:30-31)

- "For as in the days before the flood, they were eating and drinking, marrying and giving in marriage, until the day that Noah entered the ark, and did not know until the flood came and took them all away, so also will *the coming of the Son of Man* [Second Coming] be. Then *two men will be in the field: one will be taken and the other left. Two women will be grinding at the mill: one will be taken and the other left* [Rapture]. Watch therefore, for you do not know what hour your Lord is coming." (Matthew 24:38-42)

- "For as in Adam all die, even so in Christ *all shall be made alive* [Resurrection]. But each one in his own order: Christ the firstfruits, afterward those who are *Christ's at His coming* [Second Coming]." (1 Corinthians 15:26-27)

- "Now, brethren, concerning *the coming of our Lord Jesus Christ* [Second Coming] and *our gathering together to Him* [Rapture], we ask you, not to be soon shaken in mind or troubled, either by spirit or by word or by letter, as if from us, as though the day of Christ had come." (2 Thessalonians 2:1-2)

These scriptures all deal with Christ's return, and each one describes it in conjunction with the Resurrection and/or Rapture. The Second Coming, Resurrection, and Rapture are all aspects of a single, extraordinary event.

Our in-depth analysis of the Book of Revelation will substantiate this. But we have one more matter to deal with before we get started.

Chapter 5

The Pre-Tribulation Rapture

I was recently having a casual conversation with a friend from church about the subject of this book. This friend is older than me, a devout and committed believer, and well-versed in many matters of the Word, including End Times prophecy. He's read all of the mainstream literature, seen the movies, and heard the teachings. He, like so many of us, assumes that if the majority of popular teachers promote a Pre-Tribulation Rapture view, then it must be based in fact—or is at least the best interpretation. After a brief exchange, he teased me a bit with the remark, "If you want to hang around for the Tribulation, go ahead, but I'm leaving in the Rapture!" Similar comments that I often hear include, "I can't wait for the Rapture to come so we can all go home," and, "The Rapture could happen tomorrow."

All such sentiments are meant to comfort, but are they founded in truth? In previous chapters, we examined evidence, from the Word of God, that the Rapture will not occur until all of the events that comprise the seven-year Great Tribulation have concluded; that is, a *Post*-Tribulation Rapture is what the Bible actually teaches. But if this is the case, then we must ask: what is the Pre-Tribulation

Rapture view based upon? What evidence—scriptural or otherwise—is presented by proponents of this doctrine as "proof" that God will rescue His people from this Earth prior to the Tribulation plagues, the Antichrist, the War of Armageddon, and the other frightening elements that comprise the Tribulation period?

I've already mentioned that the popularization of the Pre-Tribulation Rapture is a relatively recent phenomenon. In fact, there is no compelling evidence that this doctrine existed at all prior to the nineteenth century. The historical record strongly suggests that for the first 1,800 years of Christianity, believers universally interpreted the teachings of the prophet Daniel, the apostles Paul and John, Jesus, and others to indicate a Post-Tribulation Rapture. We might argue that, in and of itself, this is not absolute proof that the Pre-Tribulation Rapture model is incorrect. But it should catch our attention that, apparently, the unanimous belief among Christians for some eighteen centuries following Jesus' First Coming—from the time that Jesus walked among us in the flesh and taught from His very own mouth—was that He would return to gather His saints not prior to, but at the conclusion of, the seven-year Great Tribulation. This view apparently remained unquestioned all the way up to the year 1827. In that year, an Irish Protestant clergyman named John Nelson Darby published a paper proposing a "secret Second Coming" for Christians.[16] Darby's new doctrine posited that before the Second Coming of Christ—which the Bible plainly tells us will occur at the end of the Tribulation, as we've seen—there would be another, "secret" return whereby Jesus would rescue His followers from the Earth before the trials of the Great Tribulation begin. Darby spent the rest of his days traveling around Europe, Canada, and the United States working to spread his views. He managed to gain some followers, but it has only been in recent decades—only in our time, with this generation—that the Pre-Tribulation Rapture has become the mainstream belief among Evangelical Christians.[17]

---

[16] *The Origin of the pre-Tribulation Rapture Teaching*, John L. Bray (1992; John L. Bray Ministry, Inc.)
[17] Spirit and Power—A 10-Country Survey of Pentecostals (October 2006; Pew Research Center's Religion & Public Life Project); Global Survey of

Earlier Belief in a Pre-Tribulation Rapture?

Proponents of the Pre-Tribulation Rapture realize that the late arrival of this doctrine poses a bit of a challenge. If the Pre-Tribulation Rapture model is correct, why was it absent from the Body of Christ for nearly the first two millennia of Christianity? One prominent teacher of this view, Grant Jeffrey, set about in the 1980s to identify earlier examples of a belief in a Pre-Tribulation Rapture. In 1995, he claimed to have found just that in an eighth-century Latin translation of a seventh-century Syriac text composed by a writer who has come to be known as Pseudo-Ephraem.[18] No one is quite sure who Pseudo-Ephraem was, since he did not write under his own name but rather attributed his work to a prominent fourth-century theologian known as Saint Ephrem the Syrian.[19] Adding to the confusion is the fact that the eighth-century Latin translation[20] barely resembles Pseudo-Ephraem's seventh-century Syriac text.[21] Rather, they appear to be two different works entirely.

But whatever the case—whoever Pseudo-Ephraem was and however poor may be the Latin translation of his work—if the Latin text discovered by Grant Jeffrey indeed presents a Pre-Tribulation Rapture view, then this would place this doctrine at least as far back as the eighth century. Such a dubious writing from such an obscure writer would not be a major triumph for the Pre-Tribulation Rapture model, but it would at least demonstrate that this doctrine was not an entirely new invention by John Darby. However, does the Latin translation of Pseudo-Ephraem even truly posit a Pre-

---

Evangelical Protestant Leaders (June 2011; Pew Research Center's Religion & Public Life Project)
[18] *Triumphant Return: The Coming Kingdom of God*, Grant R. Jeffrey (2001; WaterBrook Press)
[19] *Symbols of the Cross in the Writings of the Early Syriac Fathers*, C A Karim (2004; Gorgias Press LLC)
[20] *Briefe, Abhandlungen Und Predigten Aus Den Zwei Letzten Jahrhunderten Des Kirchlichen Alterthums Und Dem Anfang Des Mittelalters*, Carl Paul Caspari (2012; Ulan Press)
[21] *Des heiligen Ephraem des Syrers Sermones, III. Syr. 138. (Corpus Scriptorum Christianorum Orientalium)*, Deborah Beck (1972; Peeters)

Tribulation Rapture, as Jeffrey claims? The "evidence" that Jeffrey points to is found in Section 2 of the text:

For all the saints and elect of God are gathered, prior to the tribulation that is to come, and are taken to the Lord lest they see the confusion that is to overwhelm the world because of our sins.[22]

At first glance, this sentence indeed seems to suggest a Pre-Tribulation Rapture view. Compare the verbiage here to Jesus' words in Matthew 24:31:[23]

> 31 "And He will send His angels with a great sound of a trumpet, and they will gather together His elect from the four winds, from one end of heaven to the other."

As we discussed in Chapter 2 of this book, here Jesus is describing the Rapture event, and our Latin text uses very similar language: the writer, inarguably, is likewise describing the Rapture. And since he says that this event will take place "prior to the tribulation that is to come," our Latin writer must mean to indicate belief in a Pre-Tribulation Rapture, right? Well, it depends on what he means by "the tribulation that is to come." In modern Christian vernacular, the term "the tribulation" has come to refer most commonly to the seven-year Great Tribulation. But is this what the writer of our Latin text means to indicate? Let's take a look at the same sentence in a slightly broader context (we'll include the sentences before and after it):

See to it that this sentence be not fulfilled among you of the prophet who declares: "Woe to those who desire to see the day of the Lord!" For all the saints and elect of God are gathered, prior to the tribulation that is to come, and are taken to the Lord lest they see the confusion that is to overwhelm the world because of our sins. And so, brothers most dear to me, it is the eleventh hour, and the end of the world comes to the harvest, and angels, armed and

---

[22] *Briefe, Abhandlungen Und Predigten Aus Den Zwei Letzten Jahrhunderten Des Kirchlichen Alterthums Und Dem Anfang Des Mittelalters*, Carl Paul Caspari (2012; Ulan Press)

[23] Discussed in Chapter 2 "Finding a Model for the Timing of the Rapture"

THE PRE-TRIBULATION RAPTURE

prepared, hold sickles in their hands, awaiting the empire of the Lord.[24]

Here, we find two clues about what the writer most likely actually means by "the tribulation that is to come." In the first sentence, he quotes a declaration by the Prophet Amos, "Woe to those who desire to see the day of the Lord!"[25] Generally speaking, the term "the Day of the Lord" always refers in Scripture to Jesus' Millennial Reign—the thousand-year period that follows the seven-year Great Tribulation, during which Jesus will rule and reign over the whole world from Jerusalem[26]—and, in particular, the moment that begins this period: Jesus' Second Coming, when He defeats the Antichrist and the armies of this world at the so-called Battle of Armageddon.[27] We see this plainly in the first occurrence of this term in the Bible (Isaiah 2:12, 17; emphasis mine):

> 12 For the *day of the Lord* of hosts shall come upon everything proud and lofty, upon everything lifted up—And it shall be brought low...
>
> 17 The loftiness of man shall be bowed down, and the haughtiness of men shall be brought low; the Lord alone will be exalted in that day.

Later, in Zechariah 14:1-4a, we read (emphasis mine):

> 1 Behold, the *day of the Lord* is coming, and your spoil will be divided in your midst.
> 2 For I will gather all the nations to battle against Jerusalem; the city shall be taken, the houses rifled, and the women ravished. Half of the city shall go into captivity, but the remnant of the people shall not be cut off from the city.
> 3 Then the Lord will go forth and fight against those nations, as He fights in the day of battle.

---

[24] *Briefe, Abhandlungen Und Predigten Aus Den Zwei Letzten Jahrhunderten Des Kirchlichen Alterthums Und Dem Anfang Des Mittelalters*, Carl Paul Caspari (2012; Ulan Press)
[25] Amos 5:18
[26] Revelation 20:1-6
[27] Revelation 19:11-21

> 4 And in that day His feet will stand on the Mount of Olives, which faces Jerusalem on the east...

Here, in defining "the Day of the Lord," the Prophet Zechariah describes God gathering "all the nations to battle against Jerusalem" (verse 2)—a reference to the so-called Battle of Armageddon—and the physical return of Jesus to Earth (to the Mount of Olives, from where He ascended to Heaven and to where He will return[28]) to fight against those nations (verses 3-4), events that the Bible teaches (and virtually all teachers of the Word agree) will take place at the very end of the seven-year Great Tribulation. Jesus' triumphant victory at this battle ushers in His thousand-year rule over the Earth...which lines up nicely with the third sentence of the passage from our Latin text above, wherein our writer mentions "the empire of the Lord," a clear reference to the Millennial Reign.

We see, then, that by the phrase "the tribulation that is to come," the Latin translator of Pseudo-Ephraem's work does not appear to mean the seven-year Great Tribulation but rather the "tribulation" that the world—all those who are led by the Antichrist—will be thrust into upon Christ's return at the Great Tribulation's very end. Later in the same sentence, our writer describes this as "the confusion that is to overwhelm the world." Let's compare this verbiage to a later passage in his text (Section 10), wherein our writer uses the very same word, "confusion" (emphasis and bracketed comment mine):

And when the three and a half years have been completed [the last half of the Great Tribulation[29]], the time of the Antichrist...on the day which the enemy of the son of perdition does not know, will come the sign of the Son of Man, and coming forward the Lord shall appear with great power and much majesty... Then Christ shall come and the enemy shall be thrown into *confusion*, and the Lord shall destroy him by the spirit of his mouth. And he shall be

---

[28] Acts 1:9-12
[29] Matthew 24:15-22

bound and shall be plunged into the abyss of everlasting fire alive with his father Satan...[30]

Here, it is clear that our writer uses the word "confusion" not to refer to some sudden and mysterious disappearance of millions of Christians at the onset of the seven-year Great Tribulation, but rather to describe the Battle of Armageddon and Jesus' defeat of the Antichrist at the *end* of this period. And so, with all due respect to Grant Jeffrey, it appears that his "discovery" was a misinterpretation. The eighth-century Latin translator of Pseudo-Ephraem's seventh-century work was not an early proponent of the Pre-Tribulation Rapture at all. On the contrary, this writer, whoever he was, believed that Jesus would come to rescue His elect only at the very end of the Great Tribulation.

Another oft-touted early proponent of the Pre-Tribulation Rapture is Hermas, who is believed by many scholars to have penned a text called *The Shepherd of Hermas*. Hermas was a brother of Pius, Bishop of Rome, during the second century, and his book was considered by many in the early Church as canonical; that is, as legitimate as any of the books of the New Testament. And so, *The Shepherd of Hermas* is a much earlier work than the writings of Pseudo-Ephraem and seems to be much more credible as an example of early Christian doctrine. If, as many Pre-Tribulation Rapture proponents claim, Hermas indeed was an advocate of the Pre-Tribulation Rapture doctrine, this would certainly benefit their claim that this was not the sole invention of John Darby. Let's take a look at the passage in question (from *The Shepherd of Hermas*, Vision Fourth, Chapter II) and judge for ourselves:

You have escaped from great tribulation on account of your faith, and because you did not doubt in the presence of such a beast. Go, therefore, and tell the elect of the Lord His mighty deeds, and say to them that this beast is a type of the great tribulation that is coming. If then you prepare yourselves, and repent with all your heart, and turn to the Lord, it will be possible for you to escape it, if

---

[30] *Briefe, Abhandlungen Und Predigten Aus Den Zwei Letzten Jahrhunderten Des Kirchlichen Alterthums Und Dem Anfang Des Mittelalters*, Carl Paul Caspari (2012; Ulan Press)

your heart be pure and spotless, and you spend the rest of the days of your life in serving the Lord blamelessly.[31]

Like the Pseudo-Ephraem text, Hermas' words seem on initial examination to indicate belief in a Pre-Tribulation Rapture. In his vision, a sort of spiritual being—which he describes as "a virgin...adorned as if she were proceeding from the bridal chamber,"[32] apparently a symbol of the Church—instructs Hermas, following an encounter with a certain "beast," to "tell the elect of the Lord" that if "you prepare yourselves, and repent with all your heart, and turn to the Lord, it will be possible for you to escape...the great tribulation that is coming" (paraphrased). Here again, at first glance, this early Christian writer seems to be telling us that, assuming that we are in proper relationship with Christ, it will be possible for us to entirely miss the seven-year Great Tribulation at the end of this age. The assumption, of course, is that he means that we'll be raptured to Heaven before this period begins.

But is this really what Hermas means to tell us? In this case, it seems that the writer is, in fact, referring to the whole period that we call the Great Tribulation, not just its conclusion, as we determined that Pseudo-Ephraem meant in his text. But, we might ask, what does Hermas mean by "escape"? Does he mean that Christians will be entirely absent from the Earth during the Tribulation period? Here again, we need to look at the whole context. As we noted, the "virgin" communicates this message to Hermas following an encounter he'd just had with some sort of "beast," which, the text above tells us, "is a type of the great tribulation that is coming." We might surmise, then, that Hermas' encounter with the beast is indicative of Christians' "encounter" with the Great Tribulation. In other words, examining the details of the beast incident may shed some light on Hermas' perceptions about Christians during the Tribulation period. Let's have a look:

---

[31] *The Pastor of Hermas*, Hermas of Rome (2014; CreateSpace Independent Publishing Platform)
[32] *The Shepherd of Hermas*, Vision Fourth, Chapter II

Twenty days after the former vision I saw another vision, brethren—a representation of the tribulation that is to come... And while I was glorifying (God) and giving Him thanks, a voice, as it were, answered me, "Doubt not, Hermas;" and I began to think with myself, and to say, "What reason have I to doubt—I who have been established by the Lord, and who have seen such glorious sights?" I advanced a little, brethren, and, lo! I see dust rising even to the heavens. I began to say to myself, "Are cattle approaching and raising the dust?" It was about a furlong's distance from me. And, lo! I see the dust rising more and more, so that I imagined that it was something sent from God. But the sun now shone out a little, and, lo! I see a mighty beast like a whale, and out of its mouth fiery locusts proceeded. But the size of that beast was about a hundred feet, and it had a head like an urn. I began to weep, and to call on the Lord to rescue me from it. Then I remembered the word which I had heard, "Doubt not, O Hermas." Clothed, therefore, my brethren, with faith in the Lord and remembering the great things which He had taught me, I boldly faced the beast. Now that beast came on with such noise and force, that it could itself have destroyed a city. I came near it, and the monstrous beast stretched itself out on the ground, and showed nothing but its tongue, and did not stir at all until I had passed by it.[33]

In this vision, Hermas encounters a beast that is symbolic of the Great Tribulation: "a representation of the tribulation that is to come." It's a frightful sight—something that Hermas clearly does not want to face—and he calls upon the Lord "to rescue (him) from it." But then he remembers what God told him before the beast even appeared, the simple instructions that God gave him to prepare him for what was coming: "Doubt not, O Hermas." In other words, there would be no rescue, no miraculous escape from the beast. But Hermas was not to fear it. Instead, Hermas tells us, "Clothed, therefore, my brethren, with faith in the Lord and remembering the great things which He had taught me, I boldly faced the beast." And what Hermas discovers is that, in spite of the terrifying visage that the beast presents, he was able to pass by the entire length of it—or, to correlate with what the beast symbolizes, to pass through the entire Great Tribulation period—without being

---

[33] *The Shepherd of Hermas*, Vision Fourth, Chapter I

harmed. This, as we'll see more and more as our study progresses, is precisely the message that God wants to convey to His elect—to us—today.

And so, in spite of the claims of Grant Jeffrey and other proponents of the Pre-Tribulation Rapture, it seems that even Pseudo-Ephraem and Hermas believed what every other Christian did before 1827, when John Nelson Darby had his "special revelation": they believed in a *Post*-Tribulation Rapture.

Despite its utter absence from the Body of Christ throughout the first nearly two millennia of Christian history, today the Pre-Tribulation Rapture view dominates mainstream Evangelical Christian thought. Again, we must ask: what "proofs" do proponents of the Pre-Tribulation Rapture model offer in favor of this relatively recent doctrine? Let's take a look at the most popular arguments.[34]

The "Loving Father" Argument

Perhaps the most emotionally-charged Pre-Tribulation Rapture argument proclaims that God is a loving Father who would never "require" His children to suffer through a time so horrible as the Great Tribulation. But we've already read in Jesus' great End Times dissertation in the Book of Matthew that "they [the world] will deliver you up to tribulation and kill you, and you will be hated by all nations for My name's sake" (Matthew 24:9; bracketed comment mine). Jesus was speaking to His Disciples when He said this, and we know that He is addressing His Church because he says that this persecution will be "for My name's sake." In other words, those who come *in His name*—that is, Christians—will be hated, will suffer tribulation, and in some cases will even be killed.

The fact is, Christians have suffered because of their faith from the very beginning, since the time of Christ. The Bible records the first Christian martyr (besides Jesus Himself) as Stephen, a leader of the church in Jerusalem, who was stoned to death by an angry mob for

---

[34] *Revelation Unveiled*, Tim LaHaye (1999; Zondervan)

his proclamation of Jesus Christ.[35] Paul, Peter, and many others were imprisoned and beaten for their faith. John himself was a prisoner on the island of Patmos when he penned the Book of Revelation. We've all heard about, read about, or watched on the big screen innocent Christians thrown to the lions or murdered by gladiators to the amusement of Roman audiences. Not all suffered such a dramatic demise, but most early Christians were severely persecuted by their contemporaries. Such persecution is quite common even in this present day. Chinese Christians must conduct church in secret or risk arrest, torture, and even death at the hands of government agents. In North Korea, tens of thousands of Christians have been thrown into prison camps because of their faith. And throughout the Middle East, Christians are being murdered in record numbers by radical Islamists who seek to purge Christianity from the region. It is clear: Christians are not exempt from real tribulation. And yet, many believers in the United States (and other Christianity-tolerant places) seem to presume otherwise. For many, "suffering for Jesus' sake" means that we have to be nice when someone cuts in front of us in line at the grocery store. But do we really believe that this is all the Word means when it says that we will experience trials and tribulations in this life?

As it turns out, there are scriptures that seem to imply this, verses in the Bible that at first glance seem to suggest that we, as Christians, are indeed exempt from any real testing of our faith; most especially, that time that we call the Great Tribulation. For example, in Luke's account of Jesus' teaching on the Last Days, we read (Luke 21:34-36; emphasis mine):

> 34 "But take heed to yourselves, lest your hearts be weighed down with carousing, drunkenness, and cares of this life, and that Day come on you unexpectedly.
> 35 "For it will come as a snare on all those who dwell on the face of the whole earth.
> 36 "Watch therefore, *and pray always that you may be counted worthy to escape all these things that will come to pass*, and to stand before the Son of Man."

---

[35] Acts 7:54-60

Just prior to these verses, Jesus had presented the events and conditions that will comprise the Great Tribulation, and here He seems to say that it is possible to "escape" all of the things that He had just described. In the Book of Revelation, John quotes an even stronger statement along these lines, made by Jesus in a general message to the Body of Christ—and in particular the Last Days Church—that comprises Revelation chapters 2 and 3, and that we refer to as the Seven Letters to the Seven Churches (Revelation 3:10):

> 10 "Because you have kept My commandment to persevere, I also will keep you from the hour of trial which shall come upon the whole world, to test those who dwell on the earth."

In both of these passages, Jesus seems to be saying that true believers will escape the last of the Last Days; that—to apply this to the Pre-Tribulation Rapture doctrine—the Church will be removed from this world before the terrible time that we call the Great Tribulation begins. The latter verse in particular (Revelation 3:10) is one of the principal ones touted by Pre-Tribulation Rapture proponents as evidence that their model is correct. But does the idea of "keeping us from" a moment of trial in the world indicate that we will not be present on Earth—that, instead, we'll be safely tucked away in Heaven—when it occurs? This sounds logical, and yet it doesn't mesh with a sentiment that Jesus expresses in a prayer to His Father in John 17:15 (emphasis and bracketed comment mine):

> 15 "I do not pray that You should take them [Jesus' followers] out of the world, but that You should *keep them from* the evil one."

Here, Jesus uses the exact same phrase that He uses in Revelation 3:10—"keep them [or you] from"—but, clearly, the idea is not that we are removed from the situation. On the contrary, in this verse Jesus specifically prays that God *not* "take [us] out of the world." So, how do we properly view the term "keep you from" in Revelation 3:10? As it turns out, this, like many other verses in our modern versions of the Bible (including the King James Version), is simply a victim of weak translation. The Greek word for "to persevere" (the term used in our verse to describe the believers whom Jesus says He will "keep") is *hupomone,* which conveys the meaning of having unswerving purpose and loyalty to faith and piety in the midst of even the greatest trials and sufferings.[36] And the Greek word for "keep" here is *tereo,* which means "to guard; to watch over"; this word carries the idea of protecting someone while they are in danger, not keeping them out of danger altogether.[37] So, a better translation of Revelation 3:10 might be, "Because you have kept My commandment to remain faithful through great trials, I also will guard and protect you *through* the hour of trial which shall come upon the whole world, to test those who dwell on the earth."

All of that said, Jesus may not even have been referring to the entire seven-year Great Tribulation when He said "all these things that will come to pass" (Luke 21:36) and "the hour of trial which shall come upon the whole world" (Revelation 3:10). In the latter verse, let's consider Jesus' use of the word "hour." By this, did He mean a protracted length of time—the whole seven-year Great Tribulation—or just a brief period, just a small part of the Tribulation, comprised perhaps of a few days or even literally one hour? The only other place in this same section of Revelation— Jesus' message to the Last Days Body of Christ, the so-called Seven Letters to the Seven Churches—where He uses the word "hour" is in Revelation 3:3. Here, He says:

> 3   "Remember therefore how you have received and heard; hold fast and repent. Therefore if you will not watch, I will come upon you as a thief, and you will not know what hour I will come upon you."

Recall from Chapter 3 of this book that the concept of Jesus coming "as a thief" refers to the Second Coming and corresponding Resurrection/Rapture event at the end of the Great Tribulation. Could this be what Jesus means by "the hour of trial" a few verses later in Revelation 3:10? His return to Earth will certainly

---

[36] *Enhanced Strong's Lexicon,* James Strong (1996; Woodside Bible Fellowship)
[37] *Ibid.*

be a moment of extreme trial for the world; that is, for all those who have rejected Him and followed after the Antichrist. Pseudo-Ephraem (discussed in the previous section) certainly had it right when he referred to Jesus' return at the end of the Great Tribulation as "the confusion that is to overwhelm the world."[38]

A closer look at our Luke passage supports this interpretation—that what Jesus is saying that His faithful will escape is not the seven-year period that we call the Great Tribulation, but rather the moment of divine wrath that He will deliver upon this world system at its conclusion. In this passage, Jesus instructs us to "pray that we may be counted worthy to escape all these things that will come to pass" (verse 36). What "things" is Jesus referring to? Does He mean all of the events of the Tribulation period, or only those that comprise His return at its very end? Two clues are found in this passage. First, in verses 34 and 35, Jesus mentions "that Day," which "will come as a snare on all those who dwell on the face of the whole earth." In the previous section,[39] we discovered that the phrase "that Day" in the context of End Times prophecy refers to the moment of Christ's return at the end of the Great Tribulation, or, more broadly, to "the Day of the Lord," His Millennial Reign that begins with His Second Coming (again, at the Tribulation's end).[40] Our second clue is the last part of verse 36, which mentions "(standing) before the Son of Man" (paraphrased), another clear reference to Jesus' Second Coming at the conclusion of the Great Tribulation. But our greatest clue about what Jesus means by the "things that will come to pass" that we should hope to "escape" is found just a few verses prior this passage, in Luke 21:25-27:

> 25 "And there will be signs in the sun, in the moon, and in the stars; and on the earth distress of nations, with perplexity, the sea and the waves roaring;

---

[38] *Briefe, Abhandlungen Und Predigten Aus Den Zwei Letzten Jahrhunderten Des Kirchlichen Alterthums Und Dem Anfang Des Mittelalters*, Carl Paul Caspari (2012; Ulan Press)
[39] Chapter 5 "The Pre-Tribulation Rapture"; section "Earlier Belief in a Pre-Tribulation Rapture?"
[40] Matthew 24:36; Isaiah 2:17; Zechariah 14:1-4

26 "men's hearts failing them from fear and the expectation of those things which are coming on the earth, for the powers of the heavens will be shaken.
27 "Then they will see the Son of Man coming in a cloud with power and great glory."

From this passage, it becomes abundantly clear what Jesus is saying that we may escape: not the seven-year Great Tribulation, but rather the world-shaking events—distress and perplexity (or, as Pseudo-Ephraem called it, confusion), tumultuous seas, unbelievers dying from sheer terror—that comprise Jesus' Second Coming, His return to Earth at the Tribulation's very end.

And so, we see that the idea that God loves us too much to ever let us go through times of trial and tribulation—and that He therefore means to rescue us from this world before the greatest of all tribulations begins—is simply not Biblical. Happily, though, God *does* love us too much to let us go through these times without Him. It should be increasingly clear from our study that we are destined to go through the seven-year Great Tribulation, right up to the return of our King at its very end, but God will protect us, provide for us and otherwise cover us during this time. God does not deliver His people *out* of tribulation, but He keeps us through it, and Biblical precedent proves this.

Most of us know the story of Hananiah, Mishael, and Azariah, otherwise known as Shadrach, Meshach and Abed-Nego. These were friends of the prophet Daniel who refused to worship a golden idol set up by King Nebuchadnezzar of Babylon (where they were living in captivity along with many other Jews nearly five hundred years before Christ). For their lack of obedience, they were sentenced by the king to burn in a fiery furnace, which was heated to seven times the normal temperature used for executions. The furnace was so hot that the men who threw the three faithful into the furnace were burned to death. But not even the clothes or hair of Shadrach, Meshach, and Abed-Nego were singed. Even more amazing, as they walked about unscathed in the furnace, Nebuchadnezzar spotted a fourth man, who he described as "like the Son of God" (Daniel 3:19-25). God did not spare Shadrach, Meshach, and Abed-Nego from the furnace—they had to go through the fire—but He did send His Son (six centuries be[fore] He came into the world as Jesus) to protect them throug[h]

Another example that is even more pertinent [to] whether God's people will go through the Gre[at] story of the Jews in Egypt during God's "negotia[tion with] Pharaoh. In this story, we actually see several stro[ng] John's depiction of the Tribulation in the Book of [...] had admonished Pharaoh, via Moses and Aaron, to [let His] people go, that they may hold a feast to [Him] in the [wilderness] (Exodus 5:1). God's ultimate intent, of course, was for [the] Israelites to be delivered from bondage after more than 400 years of slavery. But Pharaoh could see no reason to comply with God's "request," and so began a tug-of-war between Pharaoh's will and God's. No less than ten plagues were sent upon Egypt by the hand of God because of Pharaoh's stubbornness—terrible tribulations, including water turning into blood, livestock becoming diseased, boils and hail, locusts and darkness. The final plague—the one that finally caused Pharaoh to relent—was the most horrifying of all: the death of every firstborn, whether of man or of beast, in Egypt. These were some scary times in the land of Egypt. But did God remove His people before He sent these afflictions? No, He did not. The Israelites went through this time—they experienced every one of the Ten Plagues—right alongside their Egyptian neighbors. And yet—miraculously—the Israelites were not affected like the Egyptians were: God shielded His people from His plagues. The Book of Exodus provides several specific examples: in chapter 8, verse 22 (which depicts the pestilence of flies that comprised the fourth plague) we read, "And in that day I will set apart the land of Goshen, in which My people dwell, that no swarms of files shall be there, in order that you may know that I am the Lord in the midst of the land" (Exodus 8:22). Exodus 9:4 concerns the fifth plague, the affliction of livestock, and states, "And the Lord will make a difference between the livestock of Israel and the livestock of Egypt. So nothing shall die of all that belongs to the children of Israel." Regarding the seventh plague, great and destructive hail, we read, "Only in the land of Goshen, where the children of Israel were, there was no hail" (Exodus 9:26). And the ninth plague, pervasive darkness, likewise did not fall upon the Jews: "They [the Egyptians] did not see one another; nor did anyone rise from his place for three days. But all the children of Israel had light in their dwellings" (Exodus 10:23). One of the most profound examples in the Bible of God's distinction between those of this world and those who are of Him came with the tenth and final plague: per God's instructions, the people of Israel marked their doorways with the blood of a lamb "without blemish" (a type and shadow—an antetype—of Christ), and were thus passed over by "the destroyer" who came to kill the firstborn of every Egyptian household (Exodus 12:1-30). Many Egyptians perished that night but not a single Israelite was harmed. Again, the Egyptian plagues comprised a time of terrible tribulation. And God's people were present—they remained in the land of Egypt—to the very end. The Red Sea crossing—which was the ultimate deliverance from what was at that time the "world system," and which we might therefore call a type and shadow of the Resurrection/Rapture—came, but not until God's wrath against Egypt was complete.

So, while God does not spare His children from trials and tribulations—even those sent by His very own hand—we see that He *does* provide us miraculous provision and protection through them. As believers, we should not have an escapist mentality but rather a deep, abiding faith in our Father, whatever the outward circumstances. Through tests and trials our faith is matured and our obedience affirmed. God is indeed a loving Father, but One who guides His children through, not spares them from, bad times. This notion likely comports well with most Christians' personal experiences in this life: we go through trials—some quite severe—but God gives us supernatural grace and strength to endure them, and He provides us miraculous victory at the end. The generation of Christians who will one day go through the Great Tribulation will have the greatest of all testimonies of this wonderful truth.

We Are Not Appointed to Wrath

In 1 Thessalonians 5:9-10, Paul tells us:

> 9 For God did not appoint us to wrath, but to obtain salvation through our Lord Jesus Christ,
> 10 who died for us, that whether we wake or sleep, we should live together with Him.

We can see how easily this verse might be interpreted to suggest that God does not intend to leave His people on Earth when His fury—one aspect of the Great Tribulation, to be sure—is unleashed upon it. Equally compelling, in the first chapter of this same book, Paul writes (1 Thessalonians 1:10):

> 10 and to wait for His Son from heaven, whom He raised from the dead, even Jesus who delivers us from the wrath to come.

In both of the above passages, Paul says that God will spare us from His coming wrath. We read similar verses throughout Scripture that indicate quite clearly that God's wrath is reserved not for His children but for His enemies alone. But does this mean that God will remove us from Earth before He initiates the Tribulation? Do these passages support the Pre-Tribulation Rapture view?

As we saw in the previous section, there is a difference between being present for God's wrath and being the target of it. But to fully address this argument—the idea that because we are not appointed to God's wrath we must therefore be absent from Earth during the Great Tribulation—let's consider the distinction between the concepts of "wrath" and "tribulation." Merriam-Webster's Collegiate Dictionary defines the word "tribulation" as "distress or suffering resulting from oppression or persecution; a trying experience." The word "wrath," conversely, is defined as "strong vengeful anger or indignation; retributory punishment for an offense or a crime; divine chastisement."[41] Tribulation, according to this definition, emanates from one's surroundings, from outward circumstances, or from other people. Wrath, on the other hand, means, in a Biblical context, direct punishment from God. Tribulation and wrath are not the same thing. Therefore, it is possible to be subject to one without being subject to the other. It is possible for us to experience tribulation without experiencing wrath.

---

[41] *Merriam-Webster's Collegiate Dictionary* (2008; Merriam-Webster, Inc.)

It might also be useful to distinguish between God's *partial* (or limited) wrath and His *total* (complete) wrath. The Great Tribulation, as we'll see, will begin when God strikes the Earth with severe judgment in the form of what we might term the Tribulation plagues. In the years that follow, things will grow progressively worse as God unleashes more and more punishment upon this world system. Finally, seven years after the Tribulation's start, God's anger will reach its climax—His *total* wrath will come—with the return of Jesus Christ to Earth to confront the Antichrist and his armies, whom He "will consume with the breath of His mouth and destroy with the brightness of His coming."[42] And, as we've determined, God's people—both Christians and Jews—will be on Earth to witness every moment of this process, right up to the instant that God's wrath reaches its apex.

Historically, this is always the case: God's people are always present as God's wrath against His enemies builds, and are then delivered at the precise moment that the fullness of His judgment comes. Let's consider some examples of this. The first recorded instance of God unleashing His full wrath is found in the first book of the Bible. We read in Genesis 6:5-8:

> 5   Then the Lord saw that the wickedness of man was great in the earth, and that every intent of the thoughts of his heart was only evil continually.
> 6   And the Lord was sorry that He had made man on the earth, and He was grieved in His heart.
> 7   So the Lord said, "I will destroy man whom I have created from the face of the earth, both man and beast, creeping thing and birds of the air, for I am sorry that I have made them."
> 8   But Noah found grace in the eyes of the Lord.

We read on through chapters 6 and 7 that God instructed Noah to build an ark (a very large boat) for himself, his family, and representatives of every species of land animal. God's judgment was decreed: He was going to destroy all of the inhabitants of the Earth who were not in the ark with a great flood. Over the course of many

---

[42] 2 Thessalonians 2:8

months—or, more likely, years—Noah and his sons worked while the rainclouds gathered.[43] Finally, God loosed the Flood upon the Earth, and Noah and his family were lifted up in the ark upon the rising waters—their deliverance coincided with the precise moment that God released the fullness of His wrath. We see another example of this pattern just a few chapters later. In Genesis chapter 19, we read of the depravity of Sodom and Gomorrah, and God's judgment against these cities: they and their inhabitants were to be destroyed. In this case, a man named Lot—the nephew of Abraham and the only righteous resident of Sodom—was to be spared, along with his wife and two daughters. The drama played out: two angels came to warn Lot; the wicked men of the city threatened to molest them; the angels struck the men with blindness; and Lot and his family fled. Again, the moment of deliverance coincided precisely with God's complete wrath—as Lot and his family entered the nearby city of Zoar (which was not slated for destruction), God rained fire and brimstone down upon Sodom and Gomorrah and the surrounding cities of the plain, and they were wiped from the face of the Earth. Finally, let's consider again God's deliverance of the Israelites in the Exodus story.[44] As we saw in the previous section, it was only when all ten plagues, God's gathering judgment against Pharaoh, had taken place—only when His ultimate wrath had been unleashed in the form of the tenth and final plague—that God's people were supernaturally led across the Red Sea and delivered from their bondage in Egypt.

All of these examples—the stories of Noah, Sodom and Gomorrah, and the Israelites' deliverance from Egypt—establish precisely the same precedent: God's people are "rescued" only at the moment that God's full judgment is unleashed upon the unrighteous. To fully substantiate this, let's consider the context of our passages in question, the scriptures that tell us that we will be spared from God's wrath. In 1 Thessalonians 5:9-10, Paul tells us that we will "obtain salvation through our Lord Jesus Christ…[that] we should live together with Him"; and in 1 Thessalonians 1:10, he instructs us to "wait for [God's] Son from heaven." In both cases, Paul relates our exemption from God's wrath to a very specific moment

---

[43] Genesis 7:4
[44] Exodus chapters 1 through 15

in time: Jesus' Second Coming, which, as we know, takes place at the *end* of the Great Tribulation.

We are not appointed to God's wrath—this is true—but this does not mean that we do not witness the times of tribulation that lead up to it. On the contrary, God's destruction always comes on the very heels of the righteous at the moment of their escape. We should not be surprised, then, that one day God's people will be rescued from this world system, in the form of the Resurrection and Rapture, only at the moment that Jesus returns to Earth to deliver God's ultimate judgment upon it, at the conclusion of the seven-year Great Tribulation.

Jesus Is Preparing Mansions for Us in Heaven

In John 14:2-3, Jesus makes an intriguing statement about His Second Coming and the Resurrection/Rapture:

> 2   In My Father's house are many mansions; if it were not so, I would have told you. I go to prepare a place for you.
> 3   And if I go and prepare a place for you, I will come again and receive you to Myself; that where I am, there you may be also.

Jesus' words here seem to strongly suggest a Pre-Tribulation Rapture: He says that there are "many mansions" in "[His] Father's house"; that He is going to "prepare a place for [us]" (verse 2); and that He will "come again and receive [us] to [Himself]" (verse 3) so that we may be with Him forever. This seems to fit perfectly with the *Pre*-Tribulation Rapture model: Jesus will return to this world to gather His elect, whom He will then take to Heaven to safely reside in beautiful dwellings while the Great Tribulation commences on Earth. However, is this really what Jesus is saying here?

In order to properly understand what Jesus is telling us in this passage, let's take a close look at the unusual statement at the beginning, "In My Father's house are many mansions" (verse 2). The easiest assumption to make about the term "My Father's house"—and the one that supports a Pre-Tribulation Rapture position—is that it means Heaven. However, in all of Scripture, we find only one other instance where Jesus used this term, and it was not to refer to God's heavenly abode (John 2:13-16):

> 13 Now the Passover of the Jews was at hand, and Jesus went up to Jerusalem.
> 14 And He found in the temple those who sold oxen and sheep and doves, and the money changers doing business.
> 15 When He had made a whip of cords, He drove them all out of the temple, with the sheep and the oxen, and poured out the changers' money and overturned the tables.
> 16 And He said to those who sold doves, "Take these things away! Do not make My Father's house a house of merchandise!"

Here, Jesus is angry with various merchants who are exploiting the Temple in Jerusalem; that is, they are seeking profit from those who are coming to worship there. And the words that Jesus uses to refer to the Temple is "My Father's house" (verse 16). Clearly, this term, for Jesus, does not simply mean "Heaven." The Temple in Jerusalem might best be understood as an extension of God's Kingdom, and, as such, we might best interpret the term "My Father's house" to mean not Heaven in particular, but rather the Kingdom of God in general.

Now let's take a look at the term "many mansions" (verse 2 of our passage). The word "mansions" here is derived from the Greek word *monē*, which occurs in only one other place in Scripture (John 14:23; emphasis mine):

> 23 Jesus answered and said to him, "If anyone loves Me, he will keep My word; and My Father will love him, and We will come to him and make Our *home* with him."

Here, the Greek *monē* is translated as "home"—not something so elaborate as mansions in Heaven, but rather, simply, the humble believer's heart. So, we see that the translators may have been somewhat overzealous in their rendering of this word in our passage in question. In reality, the Greek *monē* simply means a place to reside, or room to live.

Taking these points—the true meanings of the terms "My Father's house" and "many mansions"—into consideration, John 14:2-3 might more reasonably be rendered, "In My Father's Kingdom, there is plenty of room; if it were not so, I would have told you. I go to prepare a place for you. And if I go and prepare a place for you, I will come again and receive you to Myself; that where I am, there you may be also." This more precise translation is completely compatible with our *Post*-Tribulation Rapture view, and it also fits nicely with our understanding of the broader storyline of the Last Days: that Jesus' Second Coming—His return at the end of the seven-year Great Tribulation—will usher in the consummation of His Father's Kingdom in this world, the Millennial Reign, Jesus' thousand-year rule on Earth. So, to be where Jesus is, as our passage promises, means that we will be on Earth, not in Heaven. In fact, this is precisely what Scripture tells us: our destiny is to rule and reign with Christ *on Earth*.

Jesus is indeed preparing a place for us in His Father's house…but He means *here*, in this world—destined to be fully an extension of God's Kingdom—at His return.

Rapture Depicted Prior to Great Tribulation in Book of Revelation

In chapters 2 and 3 of the Book of Revelation, John records Jesus' message to seven churches contemporary to John's time and in his region of the world. As mentioned, this message—referred to as the Seven Letters to the Seven Churches—actually constitutes a general message to the Church as a whole, from John's time until Jesus' return. Following the letters is a depiction, in Revelation chapters 4 and 5, of Heaven as it prepares for the events that will comprise the last of the Last Days. This is followed by a very detailed account of the Great Tribulation that spans fourteen chapters. So, John's prophecy of Last Days events essentially begins in chapter 4, and this chapter begins as follows (Revelation 4:1-3):

> 1   After these things I looked, and behold, a door standing open in heaven. And the first voice which I heard was like a

> trumpet speaking with me, saying, "Come up here, and I will show you things which must take place after this."
> 2 Immediately I was in the Spirit; and behold, a throne set in heaven, and One sat on the throne.
> 3 And He who sat there was like a jasper and a sardius stone in appearance; and there was a rainbow around the throne, in appearance like an emerald.

In verse 3, we see some highly symbolic speech depicting God. Jasper (probably better translated as "diamond") most likely symbolizes God's holiness and purity; sardius, a deep red stone, His wrath; and the rainbow His mercy. The verses that follow this introduction describe a scene of complete and continuous worship of God by various entities that reside in Heaven. Here, in verse 1, God calls John up to Heaven with a voice "like a trumpet" (recall the mention of a trumpet in our primary Rapture passage, 1 Thessalonians 4:16-17), where he is to be shown all of the events that comprise the Last Days. The Pre-Tribulation Rapture argument here is this: John is symbolic of the Church; his catching up to Heaven is symbolic of the Rapture; and since this event occurs before John is shown the vision of the Great Tribulation, this must indicate that the Rapture will take place *before*, not during or after, the Tribulation.

Although its conclusion is erroneous (as we'll discuss in a moment), there are two positive things about this argument. First, it allows that the Rapture is, in fact, described in the Book of Revelation. Considering the extreme importance of this event—the Rapture is our "blessed hope" (Titus 2:13); it is the extension of Christ's resurrection to all of His followers; and it is a matter that, as God is no doubt well aware, has been in the forefront of His people's minds since Old Testament times—it seems unthinkable that the Rapture would be omitted from the most comprehensive account of the End Times in the Bible.

The second thing that I like about this argument is that it presumes that the Book of Revelation is written in some sort of chronological order. This is a notion that most scholars reject. As we've discussed, many approach the Book of Revelation (and many believers approach the Bible in general) with predetermined ideas and desires. When they encounter a verse or passage that contradicts their view, there is a strong temptation to ignore it, take it out of context, or twist it to fit their belief system. Of course, one way to effectively neutralize a text like the Book of Revelation when it doesn't say what is desired is to decide that it is "out of order"; that is, we presume that the events depicted must not be recorded in a logical, decipherable fashion. To believe this about the Book of Revelation is a mistake that leads to error upon error. Because the Book of Revelation describes such a complex time in history, it is not laid out in a precisely linear fashion, but it *is* nevertheless in "perfect" chronological order.

The layout of the Book of Revelation might be compared to an account of World War II. In describing the war, one would reasonably start at the beginning with the annexation of Austria by Hitler, and would conclude with the dropping of the atomic bomb on Hiroshima and the surrender of the Japanese. But in the course of chronicling the war, one would likely jump around a bit, from the European theater, to the Pacific theater, to the North African Campaign, and perhaps to an examination of the war effort in the United States. Various events in otherwise unconnected places might be discussed, political and economic implications might be addressed, and different personalities would be examined. The resulting chronicle might fill volumes, and if not approached carefully might seem to be a mishmash of unrelated events that are presented in no particular order, even though this is not actually the case. The Book of Revelation is likewise a compendium of complex events describing a very complex period, and, as such, could seem at first glance to represent no clear sequential order. However, the prophecy portion of Revelation is, in fact, divided into distinct parts that are presented in the precise order in which they occur. First, the events that lead up to the Great Tribulation are presented. Next, the Tribulation's start and the plagues that comprise its first few years are described. This is followed by a depiction of the Third Temple and the rise of the Antichrist; then the collapse of the world system (and the culmination of this process, the War of Armageddon); and, finally, the consummation of the Kingdom of God here on Earth. If Revelation were in fact pieced together in a hodgepodge way, with events dropped into the text at random, it would be confusing to the point of being essentially useless to us as a revelation of things to come. Is this what we would expect from God? 1 Corinthians 14:33 tells us, "For God is not the author of confusion but of peace…"

The acknowledgements that the Book of Revelation depicts the Rapture and that it is, in fact, in chronological order are points in favor of our current Pre-Tribulation Rapture argument. That said, there is a fundamental problem with this argument's core assumption; that is, that John's location during the prophecy is indicative of the location of the Church during the Last Days. For starters, this interpretation would effectively place the Rapture immediately prior to the start of the seven-year Great Tribulation—just as Pre-Tribulation Rapture proponents would like—if this was, in fact, where Revelation's timeline of End Times events begins. But it is not. As we'll see, the chronology that is revealed to John immediately after his arrival in God's throne room begins not at the start of the Tribulation but rather many years—centuries, in fact—prior to it. If John being summoned to Heaven were indeed indicative of the timing of the Rapture relative to other End Times events, this would mean that the Rapture will have taken place hundreds of years *before* the Great Tribulation, an assumption that certainly does not agree with the Pre-Tribulation Rapture view nor with any other model that I am aware of.

And this argument only faces more challenges from here. Following the conclusion of the Tribulation, all believers—as we'll see—will be not in Heaven but rather on Earth, to rule and reign with Christ during His Millennial Reign. If John's location during the prophecy were indeed a reflection of the Church's location during the Last Days, would we not then expect to see John return to Earth for the part of the vision that depicts the Millennium? It seems that we would. But there is no such return of John to Earth at that point in the prophecy; that is, at the Tribulation's conclusion. John does, however, return to Earth for a brief moment *during* the Tribulation (Revelation 13:1; emphasis mine):

1 Then I *stood on the sand of the sea.* And I saw a beast rising up out of the sea, having seven heads and ten horns, and on his horns ten crowns, and on his heads a blasphemous name.

This verse depicts the appearance and rise to power of the Antichrist, and this event is followed by some of the details of his terrible reign. If John's location is indeed an indicator of the location of the Church during the Last Days, then Revelation 13:1 would place the Body of Christ back on Earth at a very awkward time—sometime in the middle of the Great Tribulation. This does not fit any of the usual analyses of the End Times, and is especially contradictory to the Pre-Tribulation Rapture model.

A few chapters later, further along in our chronology of the Last Days but still somewhere in the middle of the Great Tribulation, we read (Revelation 17:1-3; emphasis mine):

1   Then one of the seven angels who had the seven bowls came and talked with me, saying to me, "Come, I will show you the judgment of the great harlot who sits on many waters,
2   "with whom the kings of the earth committed fornication, and the inhabitants of the earth were made drunk with the wine of her fornication."
3   *So he carried me away in the Spirit into the wilderness.* And I saw a woman sitting on a scarlet beast which was full of names of blasphemy, having seven heads and ten horns.

Notice in verse 3 that John is "carried...into the wilderness." As we'll see, the angel is preparing to show John the fall of Babylon, a symbolic representation of the world system (or, more accurately, the nation that heads the world system). This event occurs just prior to the War of Armageddon and, in fact, helps to spark that cataclysmic clash. Again, if John's location during the prophecy is symbolic of the Church's location, this is a very awkward time for John to be returning to Earth.

Finally, we see in Revelation chapter 21 a depiction of the Bride of Christ and the New Jerusalem (Revelation 21:9-11; emphasis mine):

9   Then one of the seven angels who had the seven bowls filled with the seven last plagues came to me and talked

with me, saying, "Come, I will show you the bride, the Lamb's wife."

10 *And he carried me away in the Spirit to a great and high mountain, and showed me the great city, the holy Jerusalem,* descending out of heaven from God,

11 having the glory of God. Her light was like a most precious stone, like a jasper stone, clear as crystal.

This is an account of what is arguably the most monumental occasion in the history of the world—one that, incidentally, will take place about a thousand years after the end of the Great Tribulation. The evil that exists in men's hearts—and that will, surprisingly, continue to exist throughout the Millennial Reign—will have finally been crushed after so many millennia of rebellion, and God's children will manifest upon a new, redeemed Earth in the form of a New Jerusalem. The point here is that the Church is assumed to be *inside* the New Holy City (or, more accurately, will *comprise* it), but John is displaced from this scene, being shown it from a distance. If John's location were truly symbolic of the location of the Church, John would not be merely an observer of this event but would be in the very heart of it.

John's various perspectives during his vision simply do not line up logically with any reasonable assumptions about the location of the Church during the Last Days. The calling up of John to Heaven in Revelation 4:1, therefore, cannot reasonably be interpreted as symbolic of the Rapture of the Church.

Church Not Mentioned During Depiction of Tribulation in Book of Revelation

There are two variations of this argument, one very simple and one rather sophisticated. Let's start with the simple.

The word "church" appears approximately seven times in the Book of Revelation, depending on the translation. These all occur in chapters 2 and 3, which, as mentioned earlier, constitute seven letters to seven churches (or, more precisely, a message to the Body of Christ as a whole). Since the word "church" does not appear again throughout the remainder of the Book of Revelation, most of which comprises John's record of the prophecy of the End Times, one might assume that the Church is absent during this period. In other words, the Church is not mentioned during John's account of the Great Tribulation because we are not there—we have been raptured and are in Heaven.

However, while it is true that the word "church" does not appear in the prophecy portion of the Book of Revelation, let's remember that neither do the terms "Rapture," "Second Coming," "Great Tribulation," or "Antichrist"; and all of these topics are all dealt with quite extensively in John's depiction of the Last Days. But the real weakness of this argument is its assumption that the Church can only be referred to with the word "church." Especially in Revelation, arguably the most richly symbolic book of the Bible, we should expect otherwise. Jesus, for example, is referred to in Revelation not only by His name, but also as "the faithful witness," "the firstborn from the dead" (a reference to the Resurrection/Rapture), "the ruler over the kings of the earth," "the Alpha and the Omega," "the Beginning and the End," "He who is and who was and who is to come," "the Almighty," "One like the Son of Man," and "the First and the Last." And that's just in chapter 1. Jesus is referenced many other ways throughout the rest of Revelation, and this is true of His Church as well. For example, the word "saints" appears no less than thirteen times in Revelation chapters 5 through 20, which constitute most of the prophecy portion of the book, including John's account of the Great Tribulation. The word "saints" was used throughout the Old Testament to describe God's pre-Christ faithful—faithful Jews—and in the New Testament books preceding the Book of Revelation this term is used no less than 49 times, and always to describe the Church. I'll offer but a single example, from the Apostle Paul's first letter to the Corinthians (1 Corinthians 1:2a; emphasis mine):

> 2   To the church of God which is at Corinth, to those who are sanctified in Christ Jesus, called to be *saints*, with all who in every place call on the name of Jesus Christ our Lord...

Even where the word "church" is used in Revelation, it is never to refer to the Church—as in the whole Body of Christ—but only to seven specific churches located in a small region of what is today western Turkey. John simply chooses to use the very common alternative term "saints" to refer to the Body of Christ as a whole throughout the rest of the Book of Revelation. As it turns out, the Church is referred to in many other ways as well, some fairly clear, some highly symbolic; as our study progresses, we will identify and decipher each of these.

The second variation of this argument is more sophisticated than the first, and thus requires a bit more analysis. In Chapter 5 of this book,[45] we discussed the origins of the Pre-Tribulation Rapture model and the fact that this doctrine appears to have been non-existent in the Body of Christ prior to John Nelson Darby's publication of his "special revelation" in 1827. If this is the case, we may well ask: how did Darby come up with the idea of a Pre-Tribulation Rapture? Some critics of his view have claimed that Darby was influenced by the "visions" of a young Scottish parishioner named Margaret MacDonald, who, during a religious revival in 1830, conveyed revelations—purportedly divinely inspired—about the Second Coming, the Antichrist, and other the End Times matters. However, notice that the revival at which MacDonald conveyed her visions did not take place until some three years *after* Darby first published his ideas. Also, Darby and his colleagues in actuality considered the "revival" where MacDonald conveyed her vision as demonic in origin.[46] Finally, a careful look at MacDonald's words seems to reveal a *Post*-Tribulation Rapture perspective:

"I saw the people of God in an awfully dangerous situation, surrounded by nets and entanglements, about to be tried, and many about to be deceived and fall. Now will THE WICKED be revealed, with all power and signs and lying wonders, so that if it were possible the very elect will be deceived—This is the fiery trial which is to try us. It will be for the purging and purifying of the real members of the body of Jesus; but Oh it will be a fiery trial. Every soul will he shaken to the very centre... The trial of the Church is

---

[45] Chapter 5 "The Pre-Tribulation Rapture"
[46] *For Zion's Sake: Christian Zionism and the Role of John Nelson Darby (Studies in Evangelical History and Thought)*, Paul Richard Wilkinson (2008; Wipf & Stock Pub)

from Antichrist. It is by being filled with the Spirit that we shall be kept... This is what we are at present made to pray much for, that speedily we may all be made ready to meet our Lord in the air - and it will be."[47]

And so, in fairness to Darby, it was not the visions of a teenage girl that inspired his formulation of a Pre-Tribulation Rapture view, as some have claimed. Instead, this doctrine reportedly was spawned from Darby's awareness of the distinction in the New Testament between God's Old Covenant people, the Jews, and His New Covenant people, Christians.[48] Such a distinction does, of course, exist. The most dramatic example of this is found in the Apostle Paul's discussion of the Jews—as distinct from Christians—in Romans chapters 9, 10, and 11. These chapters begin with some words of lamentation from Paul (Romans 9:1-5):

1   I tell the truth in Christ, I am not lying, my conscience also bearing me witness in the Holy Spirit,
2   that I have great sorrow and continual grief in my heart.
3   For I could wish that I myself were accursed from Christ for my brethren, my countrymen according to the flesh,
4   who are Israelites, to whom pertain the adoption, the glory, the covenants, the giving of the law, the service of God, and the promises;
5   of whom are the fathers and from whom, according to the flesh, Christ came, who is over all, the eternally blessed God. Amen.

Paul confirms Darby's observation: Christians and Jews are two different groups, and they are treated as such throughout the New Testament narrative. But Darby took this to an extreme. He argued that the New Testament writers did not simply talk about these as two separate groups, as Paul does here, but rather that the whole New Testament is comprised of two distinct—albeit interwoven—messages: some verses are meant for Christians and others are addressed to Jews. On its surface, we should see the fallacy of this

---

[47] *The Incredible Cover-Up*, Dave MacPherson (1975; Omega Publications)
[48] *The Roots of Fundamentalism: British and American Millenarianism*, 1800-1930, Ernest R. Sandeen (2008; University Of Chicago Press)

idea. Jews (at least those who have not yet come to the light of the truth about Jesus) reject the New Testament as false doctrine, so no Jew is going to read—let alone take to heart—one word of the New Testament; which would seem like a lot of wasted ink on God's part! More than this, are we as Christians, then, simply to ignore parts of the New Testament—those that are intended not for us but for the Jews? If so, which parts?

Whatever the case—however Darby himself might answer the questions that we raise about his idea, were he alive to do so—his motive for making this claim was this: the Bible makes it clear that God's people will be on Earth throughout the seven-year Great Tribulation, but since Christians will be raptured before the Tribulation (in accordance with Darby's Pre-Tribulation Rapture doctrine) the Bible must be describing God's Old Covenant people, the Jews. The truth, however, is that—especially in matters of End Times prophecy—the people of God who are destined to endure the bad times that are coming are not comprised only of Jews nor only of Christians, but rather *both* groups. When it comes to the last of the Last Days, there is not as much of a distinction between Christians and Jews as a *duality*. All of us—Christians and Jews—are going to go through the Great Tribulation. We may constitute separate groups—the people of the New Covenant and the people of the Old Covenant—but we are inextricably linked and will become more so as we draw nearer to the End.

Nowhere is this duality more evident than in the Book of Revelation itself. Because Revelation is so highly symbolic, it can get a bit tricky identifying the connection between the Old Testament Church and the New Testament Church in its pages. We'll study the following examples in greater depth in later chapters, but a glimpse is in order here. You'll recall that John's vision of the End Times begins with him being called up to Heaven in Revelation chapter 4. Verse 4 of this chapter reads as follows:

> 4   Around the throne were twenty-four thrones, and on the thrones I saw twenty-four elders sitting, clothed in white robes; and they had crowns of gold on their heads.

THE PRE-TRIBULATION RAPTURE

Some Pre-Tribulation Rapture proponents claim that these twenty-four elders represent the raptured Church, but, as we'll see, these twenty-four elders are mentioned much later in the Book of Revelation as being present at the so-called Marriage Supper of the Lamb. There, they are described as *observing* the Bride of Christ, which includes the raptured Church, so they are apparently distinct from it. But who are they? We are given a hint in the Book of Mark (Mark 10:35-45):

> 35 Then James and John, the sons of Zebedee, came to Him, saying, "Teacher, we want You to do for us whatever we ask."
> 36 And He said to them, "What do you want me to do for you?"
> 37 They said to Him, "Grant us that we may sit, one on Your right hand and the other on Your left, in Your glory."
> 38 But Jesus said to them, "You do not know what you ask. Are you able to drink the cup that I drink, and be baptized with the baptism that I am baptized with?"
> 39 They said to Him, "We are able." So Jesus said to them, "You will indeed drink the cup that I drink, and with the baptism I am baptized with you will be baptized;
> 40 "but to sit on My right hand and on My left is not Mine to give, but it is for those for whom it is prepared."
> 41 And when the ten heard it, they began to be greatly displeased with James and John.
> 42 But Jesus called them to Himself and said to them, "You know that those who are considered rulers over the Gentiles lord it over them, and their great ones exercise authority over them.
> 43 "Yet it shall not be so among you; but whoever desires to become great among you shall be your servant.
> 44 "And whoever of you desires to be first shall be slave of all.
> 45 "For even the Son of Man did not come to be served, but to serve, and to give His life a ransom for many."

Here, we see two of Jesus' twelve Disciples making a great request: they want to be seated on either side of Jesus in Heaven (verse 37)—presumably not on wooden stools or recliners or beanbag chairs, but on thrones. Jesus does not deny that these thrones exist, but says simply that the seating arrangement in Heaven is not His to determine. In fact, he implies that the thrones have already been assigned to specific individuals: "it is for those for whom it is prepared" (verse 40). We can assume that it is God that has made these assignments, that there is a finite (limited) number of thrones (otherwise, no such assignments would be necessary), and that the individuals to whom it is granted to sit on the thrones will have met some specific criteria. And Jesus seems to be saying in verses 39 and 43 that His Disciples *will* be among those who fit the bill. This would account for twelve of the twenty-four elders described in Revelation chapter 4 (and mentioned again in chapters 5, 11, and 19), but what about the other twelve? Recall that we're considering the duality of the Old Testament Church and the New Testament Church in End Times prophecy. If such a duality does indeed exist—and this should become apparent in the next few paragraphs—then the other twelve elders are presumably representatives of the twelve tribes of Israel, perhaps the fathers of those tribes, the twelve sons of Jacob.

Another reference to the duality of the old Church and the new is found in Revelation chapter 7, and again in chapter 14. In these chapters, a particular group of people is discussed, referred to cryptically as the 144,000, and these are depicted as being on Earth during the seven-year Great Tribulation. The 144,000 constitutes one of the more controversial topics in the Book of Revelation, so we'll hold off for now on examining this group in detail, but for the purposes of this discussion we should note their number. Many scholars—in fact, entire Christian and even non-Christian sects—insist that the number 144,000 is to be taken literally. But, as we'll see, this number, like so much of Revelation, is symbolic. In this case, notice that the number 144,000 can be arrived at by multiplying 12 x 12 x 1000. The number 1000 in antiquity is symbolic of perfection, in the sense that it represents a perfect cube: 10 x 10 x 10.[49] The two twelves in the equation—again, assuming that our assumption about a duality of Christians and Jews in Bible prophecy is correct—in turn represent the twelve tribes of Israel and the twelve Disciples of Christ; that is, the Old Testament Church and the New Testament Church.

---

[49] *Tales of the End: A Narrative Commentary on the Book of Revelation*, David L. Barr (1998; Polebridge Press)

If all of this number-juggling seems a bit of a stretch, we must remind ourselves that John, in compiling the Book of Revelation, made a concerted attempt to communicate its details using symbolism. In most instances, he does this with words; in some, he does it with numbers. Where he uses numbers for his symbols, we must simply do our best to try to ascertain what he means. Fortunately, as we'll see, John always provides additional clues in the corresponding text to make his true meaning entirely clear. In the case of using numbers to represent the duality of the "old" and "new" people of God, he actually offers us a clue near the end of the Book of Revelation that proves beyond any reasonable doubt that this is, in fact, his intent. In describing the New Jerusalem, John writes (Revelation 21:9-14; emphasis mine):

> 9 Then one of the seven angels who had the seven bowls filled with the seven last plagues came to me and talked with me, saying, "Come, I will show you the bride, the Lamb's wife."
> 10 And he carried me away in the Spirit to a great and high mountain, and showed me the great city, the holy Jerusalem, descending out of heaven from God,
> 11 having the glory of God. Her light was like a most precious stone, like a jasper stone, clear as crystal.
> 12 Also she had a great and high wall with *twelve gates*, and twelve angels at the gates, and names written on them, which are the names of the *twelve tribes of the children of Israel*:
> 13 three gates on the east, three gates on the north, three gates on the south, and three gates on the west.
> 14 Now the wall of the city had *twelve foundations*, and on them were the names of the *twelve apostles of the Lamb*.

Here, we see quite clearly that John makes a distinction *of sorts* between Israel and Christians, but that he regards the two as inextricably joined as well. The New Jerusalem, which represents the Bride of Christ (verse 9), has twelve names adorning its gates: these are the names of the twelve sons of Israel (verse 12). And it has twelve names adorning its foundations: these are the names of the twelve Disciples of Christ (verse 14). Our assumption about the identity of the twenty-four elders is thus supported by this passage, as is our analysis of the 144,000. Taken together, it seems clear: Christians and Jews, while distinct, are represented together throughout the Book of Revelation. Wherever one is, the other is to be found. And, generally speaking, whatever one experiences the other does as well, in particular during the Tribulation's second half, as we'll see.

So, John Darby's observation that the New Testament distinguishes between the Old Testament Church and the New Testament Church is accurate to a degree, but his assertion that End Times prophecy pertains to one group and not the other is simply false. Both groups are equally present in the Book of Revelation and both will be on Earth throughout the Tribulation period, something that will become increasingly apparent to us as our study progresses.

Extensive Use of Old Testament Symbols and Language in Book of Revelation Indicative of Israel, not Christians

The Book of Revelation is rich in images and language derived from the Old Testament. Icons and symbols that seem to point to the people of the Old Covenant, the Jews, appear throughout John's depiction of the End Times. We see very little use of such symbolism in other books of the New Testament, including the other four books written by John (the Gospel of John and 1 John, 2 John, and 3 John), so we're inclined to assume that there is some purpose to his approach here—that by embellishing his account of the Last Days with so much imagery from the Old Testament, John is trying to convey something in particular. This is true in a most extraordinary sense, but not in the way that many scholars have assumed.

A popular argument among End Times teachers is that the reason that so much symbolism pertaining to God's Old Covenant people, as portrayed in the Old Testament, is used in Revelation is that this book is about them (in accordance with John Darby's Pre-Tribulation Rapture doctrine, as we noted in our previous section). In other words, Christians are not portrayed in John's account of the Last Days: Jews are—hence so much symbolic reference to Judaism. However, as we saw in the last section, it is erroneous to make too great a distinction between Judaism and Christianity in this context. Both groups are represented in John's End Times narrative; distinct, yes, but also comprising a single group—God's people—and enduring the same trials (especially during the Tribulation's second half). We should also note that in John's day (much more so than in ours), Christianity was considered an extension—a revelation—of Judaism. There is a saying that goes something like this: "The Old Testament is the New Testament concealed, and the New Testament is the Old Testament revealed." Another way of saying this is that all of the things that took on practical, physical form in the context of the Old Covenant (laws and rituals and sacred objects) were but types and shadows of their full, spiritual manifestation in the New Covenant; and, as such, these things can be said to symbolize *both* paradigms, both Old Testament and New. So, John's heavy utilization of Old Testament symbolism may not merely be a method of identifying his subject. And over-simplifying this device in this way will likely cause one to miss its real purpose—and, consequently, to face serious difficulty in formulating an accurate interpretation of the Book of Revelation.

So, what is the purpose of John's Old Testament symbolism in Revelation, imagery that includes the Tabernacle (precursor to the Temple in Jerusalem), the Ark of the Covenant, the Altar, censers, Menorah (lampstand), etc.? We'll consider the answer to this in a moment, but first let's examine more closely whether reference to these things automatically denotes an Old Testament context; that is, whether such items always symbolize old Israel, as some Pre-Tribulation Rapture proponents claim. We'll focus on the Tabernacle/Temple, since this, for all intents and purposes, encompasses all of the other items.

The Tabernacle of God was introduced to the Israelites through Moses in the Book of Exodus. Its purpose was to provide a "dwelling place" on Earth for the presence of God so that humans might have direct access to Him. As it turned out, though, the innermost part of the sanctuary—known as the "Holy of Holies," the "Most Holy," the "Holiest of All," and like terms, in which the

Spirit of God dwelled—was accessible on only one day per year, only following a very long and intense cleansing ritual, and only by the High Priest. And even he might not survive the encounter with God's presence: the High Priest wore bells on the hem of his garment, and before he passed between the veils and entered the Holy of Holies, the other priests would tie a rope around his leg or ankle; if the bells stopped jingling, they'd know that he'd died and they could pull his body out; or so the story goes.[50]

The Tabernacle formed the very center of the rigid structure of laws and rituals that comprise what we refer to as the Mosaic Law. This is the foundation of traditional Judaism, and one can thus understand how so many references to these things in the Book of Revelation might be interpreted as strictly indicative of Old Testament Israel. But there is, of course, a New Testament version of the Tabernacle—a *spiritual* manifestation of God's Temple on Earth, in the context of the New Covenant—as Paul reveals to us in 1 Corinthians 3:16:

> 16 Do you not know that you are the temple of God and that the Spirit of God dwells in you?

In the context of the New Covenant, it is not a building in Jerusalem that constitutes the Temple; rather, it is the Christian himself. It is no longer just one man (the High Priest) who can enter into God's holy presence and on only one day per year, but, through Christ—our ultimate High Priest[51]—God's holy presence can dwell inside each one of us continually. However, does this mean that with the coming of New Testament times—marked by the crucifixion, resurrection, and ascension of Jesus Christ, God's own Son[52]—all things pertaining to the Old Testament lost their import, and became invalid? Jesus tells us quite the opposite in Matthew 5:17-20:

---

[50] *The Zohar: The First Ever Unabridged English Translation with Commentary (23 Volume Set)*, Rav Shimon Bar (2003; Kabbalah Centre Intl): see Parshas Acharei Mos (67a) and Parshas Emor (102a)
[51] Hebrews 4:14
[52] John 3:16

17 "Do not think that I came to destroy the Law or the Prophets. I did not come to destroy but to fulfill.
18 "For assuredly, I say to you, till heaven and earth pass away, one jot or one tittle will by no means pass from the law till all is fulfilled.
19 "Whoever therefore breaks one of the least of these commandments, and teaches men so, shall be called least in the kingdom of heaven; but whoever does and teaches them, he shall be called great in the kingdom of heaven.
20 "For I say to you, that unless your righteousness exceeds the righteousness of the scribes and Pharisees, you will by no means enter the kingdom of heaven.

Here, Jesus tells us very clearly that even in this new dispensation—in the New Testament paradigm—the Old Testament (referred to here as "the Law and the Prophets"; verse 17) remains completely intact. Nothing that it teaches—at least in essence—was destroyed or invalidated with the New Covenant that He established. Jesus goes on to state in the next verse that "one jot or one tittle [the most miniscule of characters in the Hebrew alphabet] will by no means pass from the law till all is fulfilled" (verse 18; bracketed comment mine). Some argue that Jesus fulfilled everything on the Cross, so all aspects of the pre-Christ religion of Judaism are now obsolete. But note the first part of the same verse: "For assuredly, I say to you, *till heaven and earth pass away…*" (emphasis mine). Have heaven and Earth passed away? No, not yet.

So, the Law, the Prophets, all aspects of the former dispensation—the Old Testament and pre-Christ Judaism—remain. In fact, they are foundational to Christianity. But if this is the case, why don't Christians practice the old Law, like many Jews continue to do to this day? According to Jesus, we should: "Whoever therefore breaks one of the least of these commandments, and teaches men so, shall be called least in the kingdom of heaven; but whoever does and teaches them, he shall be called great in the kingdom of heaven" (verse 19).

But is Jesus referring to all of the ritual and minutiae that comprise the Mosaic Law? On the contrary. Notice in verse 20 that Jesus tells us that our righteousness must *exceed* that of the scribes and

Pharisees. His meaning becomes clear during a particularly impassioned confrontation with these religious leaders that took place just before His arrest and conviction (Matthew 23:25-28):

25 "Woe to you, scribes and Pharisees, hypocrites! For you cleanse the outside of the cup and dish, but inside they are full of extortion and self-indulgence.
26 "Blind Pharisee, first cleanse the inside of the cup and dish, that the outside of them may be clean also.
27 "Woe to you, scribes and Pharisees, hypocrites! For you are like whitewashed tombs which indeed appear beautiful outwardly, but inside are full of dead men's' bones and all uncleanness.
28 "Even so you also outwardly appear righteous to men, but inside you are full of hypocrisy and lawlessness.

Here, Jesus was observing that these—the priests and religious elite of the day—though they apparently followed every detail of the Law, were nonetheless inwardly full of corruption and sin. So, the scribes and Pharisees may have appeared righteous because they did all of the right things, but it was only superficial. Jesus calls His followers to be righteous at a higher level: not in our actions only, but, much more importantly, in our hearts and in our minds. The author of Hebrews summarizes this point nicely for us (Hebrews 10:11-16):

11 And every priest stands ministering daily and offering repeatedly the same sacrifices, which can never take away sins.
12 But this Man, after He had offered one sacrifice for sins forever, sat down at the right hand of God,
13 from that time waiting till His enemies are made His footstool.
14 For by one offering He has perfected forever those who are being sanctified.
15 But the Holy Spirit also witnesses to us; for after He had said before,
16 "This is the covenant that I will make with them after those days, says the Lord: I will put My laws into their hearts, and in their minds I will write them"

Verse 11 here tells us that no amount of human effort pertaining to the old Tabernacle/Temple could achieve man's ultimate need, the forgiveness of sins. But Jesus, offering Himself as a perfect sacrifice, accomplished total forgiveness for those who would accept the sacrifice—even to the point of perfection in God's eyes (verses 12 and 14). So, what becomes of the Law in this dispensation of grace? The author tells us in verse 16, in quoting a prophecy by Jeremiah about the coming Messiah: "This is the covenant that I will make with them after those days, says the Lord: *I will put My laws into their hearts, and in their minds I will write them*" (emphasis mine).

The Law has not passed: it merely has gone from being carved in stone to be written on our hearts. In other words, the Old Testament Law—and all things that pertain to it, including the Tabernacle, the Ark of the Covenant, the Altar, etc.—has a new and powerful manifestation in the New Testament. All things that comprised the Judaism of the Old Testament exist in a different, less physically tangible form in Christianity. Let's examine a profound explanation of this in Hebrews 9:1-12 (emphasis mine):

1. Then indeed, even the first covenant had ordinances of divine service and the earthly sanctuary.
2. For a tabernacle was prepared: the first part, in which was the lampstand, the table, and the showbread, which is called the sanctuary;
3. and behind the second veil, the part of the tabernacle which is called the Holiest of All,
4. which had the golden censer and the ark of the covenant overlaid on all sides with gold, in which were the golden pot that had the manna, Aaron's rod that budded, and the tablets of the covenant;
5. and above it were the cherubim of glory overshadowing the mercy seat. Of these things we cannot now speak in detail.
6. Now when these things had been thus prepared, the priests always went into the first part of the tabernacle, performing the services.

> 7 But into the second part the high priest went alone once a year, not without blood, which he offered for himself and for the people's sins committed in ignorance;
> 8 the Holy Spirit indicating this, that the way into the Holiest of All was not yet made manifest while the first tabernacle was still standing.
> 9 It was symbolic for the present time in which both gifts and sacrifices are offered which cannot make him who performed the service perfect in regard to the conscience—
> 10 concerned only with foods and drinks, various washings, and fleshly ordinances imposed until the time of reformation.
> 11 *But Christ came as High Priest of the good things to come, with the greater and more perfect tabernacle not made with hands, that is, not of this creation.*
> 12 *Not with the blood of goats and calves, but with His own blood He entered the Most Holy Place once for all, having obtained eternal redemption*

Here, the writer of Hebrews reminds us that in the Old Testament manifestation of the Tabernacle, the presence of God was something that could not be experienced by all (verse 7), and that this was only a foreshadow of God's ultimate plan (verse 8), which is to provide a way for everyone to enter into His presence. We are told in verse 9, in fact, that the physical Tabernacle of the Old Testament was merely *symbolic* of its ultimate manifestation, which is established by Christ Himself. We find a beautiful confirmation of this truth in the Book of Revelation (Revelation 21:3):

> 3 And I heard a loud voice from heaven saying, "Behold, the tabernacle of God is with men, and He will dwell with them, and they shall be His people. God Himself will be with them and be their God."

This verse constitutes the end of the prophecy portion of the Book of Revelation, and this declaration—made upon the establishment of the New Heaven, New Earth, and New Jerusalem—constitutes the end of this present age of mankind. This is not about the old Israel, but about the new Israel, the Body of Christ. So, we see quite clearly that in the New Testament—including in Revelation itself—

the use of Old Testament symbols, language and imagery, such as the tabernacle and its contents, is not meant to convey a picture of Old Covenant Israel only, but that these things pertain to the people of God throughout all dispensations.

Which brings us back to our original question: why is John's depiction of the Last Days so rich in images and language from the Old Testament? The answer is quite exciting: He is providing us the key to unlock his prophecy.

Consider the following illustration. Suppose you were my neighbor, and I wrote you the following in a letter:

"And I saw a great sign in the sky, appearing behind four white clouds a dark cloud, and, behold, this latter cloud descended from the sky and stood on the earth. And there was a man on the earth, and in his hand two white sheaves, white as snow, and between the sheaves were many good things, the fruit of the vine and the fruit of the soil. And the cloud deceived the man and enveloped the sheaves, and the sheaves were consumed as in a fire."

At first glance, you wouldn't have a clue about what I was trying to tell you. And even after days or weeks or even years of attempting to figure it out, you might make only minimal progress toward interpreting my meaning. Eventually, you would perhaps form in your mind an image of an ominous black cloud descending from the sky and wreaking great destruction upon the world. You might decide that this is a prophecy about acid rain or some similar phenomenon causing a great famine upon the Earth. But could you ever be certain that your interpretation was correct? In the absence of any supporting information, you could not.

Now, suppose you found some letters that I had written to you earlier, and one of these contained the following text:

"And, behold, a litter was born to my neighbor's dog, four puppies white as clouds, and a fifth puppy, the last to be born, black, like a storm cloud."

And in another writing you found:

"Then I, Ryan, took two pieces of Wonder bread, bleached white like snow, and placed between them the fruit of the vine, grape jelly, and the fruit of the soil, peanut butter."

By simply cross-referencing the first text with my earlier writings, you would be able to quickly, easily and conclusively establish its meaning: your dog ate my peanut butter and jelly sandwich!

Needless to say, nothing in the Book of Revelation is as trivial as pets stealing sandwiches, but this is an illustration of how Revelation can be correctly understood. Revelation is a highly symbolic, richly poetic text that creates what can seem to be an impassable terrain. But we have a road map of sorts in the form of the Old (and, to a lesser degree, New) Testament writings. God intended it to be just this simple when He gave John the prophecy. He never meant for Revelation to be so vague and mysterious that centuries of scholarship could not unlock its secrets—quite the contrary, as one can see by comparing two passages: God's instructions to the Prophet Daniel regarding his prophecy and His instructions to John. God told Daniel (Daniel 12:4):

> 4 "But you, Daniel, shut up the words, and seal the book until the time of the end; many shall run to and fro, and knowledge shall increase."

In other words, the prophecy about the Last Days as recorded by Daniel would be indecipherable to his contemporary audience, and it would remain so until nearly the end of this dispensation of human history, the time that we are living in now. But God made no such statement to John regarding his account of the End Times. On the contrary, in Revelation 22:10 we read (emphasis mine):

> 10 And he said to me, "*Do not seal the words of the prophecy of this book*, for the time is at hand."

Does it sound here like God ever meant John's prophecy to be obscured? Did God intend for the Book of Revelation to be so overwhelmingly cryptic that we are forced to merely speculate about its meaning? Absolutely not. All one needs is the benefit of the Holy Spirit—and maybe a good concordance—and much illumination is waiting for us in John's extraordinary prophecy. The name of John's book is, after all, "Revelation" ("Apocalypse" in the Greek), not "Secret."

It is for this reason that we find such extensive use of Old Testament symbols and language in the Book of Revelation—not because John's book is about Jews only and not Christians, but rather so that we have at our fingertips, in the form of the Word of God itself, the key to decipher this prophecy that is about us all.

Bible Offers No Instructions on How to Live During Great Tribulation

This is perhaps the least challenging of all of the Pre-Tribulation Rapture arguments to refute. The notion here is that if God intended for His people to go through the terrible times that comprise the Great Tribulation, He would have provided us detailed instructions on how to prepare, where to go, what to do, etc. Is this a valid assertion?

There is a somewhat trite, though rather valuable, acronym that someone came up with for the word "BIBLE": "Basic Instructions Before Leaving Earth." The Word of God is so vast and so meaningful, but at its most basic level it is essentially a set of directions on how to live our lives, in good times *and in bad.*

Paul tells us in Philippians 4:11-13:

> 11 ...for I have learned in whatever state I am, to be content:
> 12 I know how to be abased, and I know how to abound. Everywhere and in all things I have learned both to be full and to be hungry, both to abound and to suffer need.
> 13 I can do all things through Christ who strengthens me.

In other words, *through Christ,* Paul tells us, we can have peace and joy in all circumstances in which we find ourselves, whether in abundance and prosperity, or in the trials and tribulations that inevitably come against us as inhabitants of this world. As believers, we should embrace the notion that a life in Christ *can* be one of peace and joy and happiness: God's Word promises as much. Nevertheless, earthquakes may happen under our feet, wars may rage around us, famine and plagues may enter the land—the Word tells us to anticipate these times as well. Recall Jesus' words in His great dissertation on the End Times (Matthew 24:7-9):

> 7 "For nation will rise against nation, and kingdom against kingdom. And there will be famines, pestilences, and earthquakes in various places.
> 8 "All these are the beginning of sorrows.
> 9 "Then they will deliver you up to tribulation and kill you, and you will be hated by all nations for My name's sake.

Remember that Jesus was speaking to His Disciples here, and by extension to us. Despite all of His own efforts in His time here on Earth to feed the hungry, clothe the naked, free the captive, and heal the sick—all manifestations of God's desire that we live a higher life—He does not mince words in telling us that there also will be very hard times in this life, at least for some of us. So, how are we to endure these bad times? Exactly the same way that we endure the good times (Habakkuk 2:4; emphasis mine):

> 4 "Behold the proud, his soul is not upright in him; but *the just shall live by his faith.*"

In all things, in all circumstances, and in all times, we are to live humbly by faith—trusting and believing in God and always prepared to act according to that belief. Paul expands on this point in his second letter to Timothy (2 Timothy 3:12-17):

> 12 Yes, and all who desire to live godly in Christ Jesus will suffer persecution.
> 13 But evil men and impostors will grow worse and worse, deceiving and being deceived.
> 14 But you must continue in the things which you have learned and been assured of, knowing from whom you have learned them,
> 15 and that from childhood you have known the Holy Scriptures, which are able to make you wise for salvation through faith which is in Christ Jesus.

> 16 All Scripture is given by inspiration of God, and is profitable for doctrine, for reproof, for correction, for instruction in righteousness,
> 17 that the man of God may be complete, thoroughly equipped for every good work.

Here, Paul tells us that *all* who live in Christ will suffer persecution, and that the evil men of this world will become more evil as time goes on—ultimately culminating, of course, in the Antichrist himself. But, Paul tells us in verses 14 through 17, we must continue in the Word in spite of persecution and tribulation, keeping our faith in the Lord at all times so that we may abound to every good work, no matter how bad things get around us. In his letter to Titus, Paul reinforces this admonition in the context of our expectation of Christ's Second Coming (Titus 2:11-14):

> 11 For the grace of God that brings salvation has appeared to all men,
> 12 teaching us that, denying ungodliness and worldly lusts, we should live soberly, righteously, and godly in the present age,
> 13 looking for the blessed hope and glorious appearing of our great God and Savior Jesus Christ,
> 14 who gave Himself for us, that He might redeem us from every lawless deed and purify for Himself His own special people, zealous for good works.

As we await Jesus' return and our gathering together to Him, we must continue to conduct ourselves soberly, righteously, and in a godly manner. And the highest form of righteousness is simply believing God and placing our trust in Him.

These general instructions on how to live our lives—in whatever circumstances—should be sufficient to refute the false notion that we as Christians are not equipped to face the Great Tribulation. As it turns out, however, there are some specific directions in the Word of God pertaining to our actions and conduct during the last of the Last Days. Let's consider just a few of these here. First, recall Jesus' detailed imperatives in Matthew chapter 24 (verses 15-18):

15 "Therefore when you see the 'abomination of desolation,' spoken of by Daniel the prophet, standing in the holy place" (whoever reads, let him understand),
16 "then let those who are in Judea flee to the mountains.
17 "Let him who is on the housetop not go down to take anything out of his house.
18 "And let him who is in the field not go back to get his clothes.

Here, Jesus offers very specific instructions to the believers in Israel to flee the region with all urgency when the Antichrist seats himself in the Temple and proclaims himself God (we'll examine this event in great detail later). By "believers," I mean in this context those who would heed Jesus' words; this group will include Christians who are in Israel and Jews who by this point in the Great Tribulation have begun to recognize Jesus for who He truly is. Jesus then goes on to give some brief instructions to us as we endure the period between the Antichrist's self-deification and Jesus' return; that is, the last three-and-a-half years of the seven-year Great Tribulation (Matthew 24:23-27):

23 "Then if anyone says to you, 'Look, here is the Christ!' or 'There!' do not believe it.
24 "For false christs and false prophets will rise and show great signs and wonders to deceive, if possible, even the elect.
25 "See, I have told you beforehand.
26 "Therefore if they say to you, 'Look, He is in the desert!' do not go out; or 'Look, He is in the inner rooms!' do not believe it.
27 "For as the lightning comes from the east and flashes to the west, so also will the coming of the Son of Man be.

Jesus warns us here, no doubt anticipating our expectation of His return—many of us knowing by this point beyond a shadow of a doubt that we are in the last of the Last Days—not to expect Him to arrive in any fashion less spectacular than His departure. As He quite literally ascended up into the clouds at the conclusion of His first term on this Earth, he will likewise return. Only this time, "...all the tribes of the earth will mourn, and they will see the Son of Man coming on the clouds of heaven with power and great glory" (Matthew 24:30). We won't need anyone to point Jesus out to us when He shows up—everyone on Earth, believers and nonbelievers alike, will know. In the meantime, when our expectation is at its peak, we are instructed not to look around us for our Savior, but to look up.

Even in the Book of Revelation, God tells us what His will is for our conduct during the Great Tribulation. In Revelation chapter 13, we find a description of a "beast" (the Antichrist) that "rises from the sea" (ascends to power among the nations) to persecute the people of God (Revelation 13:7-10; emphasis mine):

> 7 It was granted to him to make war with the saints and to overcome them. And authority was given him over every tribe, tongue, and nation.
> 8 All who dwell on the earth will worship him, whose names have not been written in the Book of Life of the Lamb slain from the foundation of the world.
> 9 If anyone has an ear, let him hear.
> 10 *He who leads into captivity shall go into captivity; he who kills with the sword must be killed with the sword. Here is the patience and the faith of the saints.*

Here, we read that the Antichrist is allowed to "make war" with God's people, wherever they may be in the world (verse 7). Not long ago, I was on a high-country retreat with some fellow Christian men, and this topic happened to come up. The group conjured up the usual popular images of troops loyal to the Antichrist's government storming churches and the homes of believers, perhaps shooting Christian men, women, and children on sight, or at least placing them under arrest. In this mountain setting, the air heavy with campfire smoke and the heady scent of pine needles and earth, it was easy to come up with less-than-humble responses to such persecution. Not surprisingly, a few of the guys vowed to defend themselves, their families, and their homes by whatever means necessary—even violent. But here (verse 10), we see that God does not intend for us to respond to the coming persecution in a worldly manner. He explicitly warns us against engaging in an earthly warfare, and relates this mandate to remain outwardly "passive" to our *patience* and our *faith*.

Later in Revelation chapter 13, we read about a second beast (the "False Prophet") that comes "up out of the earth"[53] and introduces something called "the mark" (Revelation 13:15-17):

> 15 He was granted power to give breath to the image of the beast, that the image of the beast should both speak and cause as many as would not worship the image of the beast to be killed.
> 16 He causes all, both small and great, rich and poor, free and slave, to receive a mark on their right hand or on their foreheads,
> 17 and that no one may buy or sell except one who has the mark or the name of the beast, or the number of his name.

Here, we are told that anyone who does not worship the Antichrist will be killed and that "no one may buy or sell except one who has the mark." So, not only will believers face a constant threat of execution under the Antichrist's rule, but we'll also have no (legal) means to obtain food, clothing, and shelter. In the face of such a formidable challenge to survival, some Christians may be tempted to give in to this monumental pressure and surrender to the system. God anticipates this (Revelation 14:9-12; emphasis mine):

> 9 Then a third angel followed them, saying with a loud voice, "If anyone worships the beast and his image, and receives his mark on his forehead or on his hand,
> 10 "he himself shall also drink of the wine of the wrath of God, which is poured out full strength into the cup of His indignation. He shall be tormented with fire and brimstone in the presence of the holy angels and in the presence of the Lamb.
> 11 "And the smoke of their torment ascends forever and ever; and they have no rest day or night, who worship the beast and his image, and whoever receives the mark of his name."
> 12 *Here is the patience of the saints; here are those who keep the commandments of God and the faith of Jesus.*

---

[53] Revelation 13:11

There is much to discuss regarding this passage, but for now let's just note that God gives us a very clear directive regarding the Mark of the Beast: *do not receive it!* Here, our patience and faith is related not to our reaction when confronted with the threat of physical violence, but to our ability to obtain even basic sustenance for ourselves and our families. Rarely in the history of God's people has there been such a need for complete and total dependence on God as there will be in the days that are coming. But don't get nervous—as we'll see, and as we as Christians should presume, God has a plan.

So, we see that the Bible does, in fact, offer us directions on how to live during the Great Tribulation. The ultimate imperative is this: *Trust God.* Our Father no doubt will provide more detailed and specific instructions to His people during the last of the Last Days, but in a period as complex and bewildering as this, these will likely be highly individualized. Our survival will depend on our personal ability to hear the voice of the Holy Spirit, and our willingness to heed His direction. God *does* expect His people to prepare for the Last Days—not by stockpiling food and guns or by digging secret tunnels under our houses, but rather by living in His Word and being filled with His Spirit, growing ever closer to Him so that He can guide us and direct us, in this time and in the time to come.

SECTION II

THE BOOK OF REVELATION: PRELUDE TO THE PROPHECY

Chapter 6

The Book of Revelation

Imagine that you live on a small island somewhere in the South Pacific. You've been hearing your whole life that someday some sort of catastrophe is going to befall the island, and you believe it. But you've also been told that before this disaster comes, an emergency airlift is going to take place, and you've arranged to be on this. You're not too concerned about the details of what's coming, since you're not going to be on the island when everything breaks loose. But it is an interesting topic, and, of course, you're very concerned about your friends and family members who don't yet have their tickets out of here; but you can only warn them so much. Ultimately, you're just glad that you're not going to be around when the catastrophe—whatever it may be—hits.

Now imagine the exact same scenario, only someone got the details of the airlift wrong. There is going to be an airlift, but it's not going to be before the disaster—it's going to come afterward. This changes everything. Now the details of the coming catastrophe suddenly are much more interesting to you: What is the exact nature of the disaster—is it a typhoon? A tsunami? A volcanic eruption? Maybe an invasion by a neighboring island? And what should you do to prepare—move to higher ground? Find shelter on the far side of the island? Maybe store up food or make weapons? In short, once you realize that you're not going anywhere—that you're going to be on the island along with everyone else for the duration of the troubled times that are coming—it becomes imperative that you set yourself to learning as much as you possibly can about what's ahead.

Just as in this analogy, the truth is that we Christians are not going anywhere prior to the catastrophe that is soon going to befall our planet. We are destined to remain here on Earth for the duration of the seven-year Great Tribulation along with the rest of our world's inhabitants. As disconcerting—even disappointing—as this news may be for some among us, we must realize in light of this that it behooves us as believers to learn as much as we possibly can about the times that are coming. We need to understand and we need to be prepared. Fortunately—and not at all surprisingly—our Father does not leave us at a loss. In His Word, God offers an enormous amount of information about our world's future—not for entertainment purposes, but so that we, the Body of Christ, will know what we are going to be facing in the years ahead; what we will one day soon be challenged to endure and overcome.

Every book of the Bible, in one form or another, touches on the End Times. But the richest compendium of the last of the Last Days—by far— is the one book that is solely dedicated to the topic, the Bible's last book, the Book of Revelation. And so—in order to grasp to the full extent possible the times that are soon coming— we will embark on a careful, in-depth, and thorough analysis of this, God's parting written words to mankind. Revelation is beautiful and mysterious, poetic and cryptic, offering us a glimpse of the future of our species and our world. It is a message from God, who instructed His servant John to record it for his own and later generations, not to confuse or frighten, but to encourage with a vision of a common destiny wherein the Kingdom of God will be fully manifest. Many of us avoid this magnificent text because on the surface it seems complicated and foreboding. And yet the book itself pronounces a blessing on all who read and receive it (Revelation 1:3):

> 3 Blessed is he who reads and those who hear the words of this prophecy, and keep those things which are written in it; for the time is near.

Revelation is not to be shunned, but should be embraced by every believer. It is devoted to a topic that is touched on, to one degree or another, by every other book of the Bible, Old Testament and New. The events that comprise the last of the Last Days can be challenging to comprehend, but, apparently, God wants to impart this knowledge to us. And there is no more comprehensive source of this knowledge than the Book of Revelation.

One of our main tasks will be to use Revelation as a tool to confirm what we've already determined about the timing of the Rapture. Again, most scholars do not believe that this book presents End Times events in the order in which they occur, but, as we've seen, this perspective is erroneous and only neutralizes much of what God wants to reveal to us. Revelation does, in fact, provide us a chronology of the Last Days. But, like any volume describing a complex period in history (recall my earlier analogy about a chronicle on World War II), many events overlap and some require significant auxiliary information to be completely understood. In the Book of Revelation we also encounter a literary style that is common in Hebrew texts, but that can be confounding to Western readers (Revelation was penned in Greek, but its writer, John, was Jewish and thus of a Hebrew mindset). Specifically, narratives that are, in fact, chronological often contain parts that appear to be out of order. An example of this appears very early in the New Testament, where God's supernatural protection of His infant Son, Jesus, is chronicled (Matthew 2:13-16; this book, too, was written in Greek but by a Jewish writer):

> 13 Now when they had departed, behold, an angel of the Lord appeared to Joseph in a dream, saying, "Arise, take the young Child and His mother, flee to Egypt, and stay there until I bring you word; for Herod will seek the young Child to destroy Him."
> 14 When he arose, he took the young Child and His mother by night and departed for Egypt,

15 and was there until the death of Herod, that it might be fulfilled which was spoken by the Lord through the prophet, saying, "Out of Egypt I called My Son."

16 Then Herod, when he saw that he was deceived by the wise men, was exceedingly angry; and he sent forth and put to death all the male children who were in Bethlehem and in all its districts, from two years old and under, according to the time which he had determined from the wise men.

In verse 13, we see that Joseph is instructed by God to take Mary and Jesus to Egypt to hide from King Herod, who seeks to kill the newborn Messiah. In verse 14, Joseph does so and he and his family remain in Egypt until the death of Herod, which occurs in verse 15. But in verse 16, we see that suddenly Herod is alive again, ordering the mass execution of hundreds of babies in and around Bethlehem. Was Herod resurrected so that he could commit this heinous act? Of course not. A more pertinent question: is the Book of Matthew a random assortment of events recorded in no particular order? Again, of course not. Matthew, like many other books of the Bible, constitutes a perfect chronology that happens to employ a literary mechanism that confuses many Western readers—that is, jumping forward or backward in time to make a particular point. Revelation is another such chronology.

In order to concretely establish the Rapture in the timetable that is the Book of Revelation, a comprehensive tour of the entire text, from Revelation 1:1 to Revelation 22:21, is in order. This approach will also seek to address the inevitable concern: if God's people really are to endure the Great Tribulation, what can we expect during that time? What are we in for?

But before we immerse ourselves, there's just one more bit of foundation that I'd like to lay. In order to understand the true message of the Book of Revelation, we need to briefly acquaint ourselves with the man who wrote it.

About the Author

The Old Testament is rich in books written by men who we refer to as "minor prophets" because of their relative obscurity outside of their texts. None of us would argue against the statement that individuals such as Obadiah, Micah, Nahum, and Zephaniah, at least on some level, hold more personal import than any of us do. After all, none of us have written words that made it into the Bible! However, this is about the limit of their distinction in the grand scheme of things. (I say this with the greatest respect, of course.)

The Book of Revelation might likewise have been written by someone who, beyond this great call, was relatively undistinguished. This would certainly help those who are uncomfortable with the book to marginalize it. But this is not the case—not by a long shot. God gave His great and final prophecy about the last of the Last Days not to a mysterious someone whose name we wouldn't otherwise know, but to one of the twelve Disciples of Christ, the Apostle John, son of Zebedee.

John is credited with the authorship of more books of the New Testament than any other of Jesus' twelve Disciples, second only to the Apostle Paul in count. He wrote the same number of books as Moses is credited with; though, admittedly, two of John's five books are quite short (2 John and 3 John constitute barely a page of text each).

Interestingly, those of John's books that precede the Book of Revelation deal very little with the End Times, which demonstrates that this topic, at least during the majority of his life and ministry, was not foremost in his mind. In fact, John's primary concern seemed to be the topic of love, and he is often referred to as the "disciple of love." He even refers to himself as the "beloved disciple" and the one "whom Jesus loved."[54] John was part of Jesus' "Inner Circle" of Disciples (the other two being Peter and James), and only these three were present on the so-called Mount of Transfiguration when Jesus encountered Moses and Elijah; John was the one who laid his head on Jesus' bosom at the Last Supper; John was the only Disciple present at Jesus' crucifixion, where Jesus commended His mother, Mary, to him; and John was the only one of the twelve Disciples not to die a violent death. Though he was severely persecuted for his beliefs, he survived to a ripe old age,

---

[54] John 13:23; 20:2; 21:7; 21:20

long enough to record God's final message to mankind while a prisoner on the Island of Patmos, some sixty years after the death, resurrection, and ascension of Jesus.

Revelation was not written by some obscure prophet, but by one who in many ways may be considered the most significant of Jesus' confidants. God appointed John to write Revelation because he was intimately trusted by His Son, and because the true message of Revelation is one of hope and love.

With that, let's begin our journey...

Chapter 7

The Introduction

Revelation 1:1-1:3 ~ The Vision Begins

1 The Revelation of Jesus Christ, which God gave Him to show His servants—things which must shortly take place. And He sent and signified it by His angel to His servant John,
2 who bore witness to the word of God, and to the testimony of Jesus Christ, to all things that he saw.
3 Blessed is he who reads and those who hear the words of this prophecy, and keep those things which are written in it; for the time is near.

The Book of Revelation begins by identifying its source as Jesus, who was given the information contained therein by God. Revelation is the only text in the Bible that claims origination with Jesus. Thus the importance of its content is underscored, as well as the fact that it is a message that pertains directly to Christians, who here are referred to as His "servants" (like "saints," a term that is found throughout the Book of Revelation).

We also see in verse 1 that the prophecy is described as "things which must shortly take place." This implies an imminence that convinced many in the early church that they would not taste death, but would be raptured at Christ's impending Second Coming. Indeed, every generation of Christians since the first has suspected that they might be the last. Jesus' own words inspired such expectancy. After describing the Antichrist, the Great Tribulation, His Second Coming, and the Resurrection/Rapture in Matthew 24, Jesus instructed His listeners to anticipate His soon return (Matthew 24:42-44):

> 42 "Watch therefore, for you do not know what hour your Lord is coming.
> 43 "But know this, that if the master of the house had known what hour the thief would come, he would have watched and not allowed his house to be broken into.
> 44 "Therefore you also be ready, for the Son of Man is coming at an hour you do not expect.

Here, Jesus advises every Christian to constantly be prepared for His Second Coming, and to continually watch for the signs that will precede it. This is not a call to live our lives in a state of limbo, blankly staring at the sky, awaiting our rescue from this planet. Rather, it is an emphasis on the Great Commission—an imperative to bring as many into the Kingdom of God as possible, before it's too late. And it is an admonition to be ready ourselves, to not be presumptuous about tomorrow but to seek after righteousness today—to push forward and stay on track to the very end. Every generation of Christians is to be deeply rooted in the things of God. And for the one that is slated to see Christ's return and to endure the times that immediately precede it, this will be a matter of life and death—perhaps physically, and certainly spiritually. As we await His Coming, Jesus instructs each of us to remain faithful to Him and true in our service to others (Matthew 24:45-51):

> 45 "Who then is a faithful and wise servant, whom his master made ruler over his household, to give them food in due season?
> 46 "Blessed is that servant whom his master, when he comes, will find so doing.

> 47 "Assuredly, I say to you that he will make him ruler over all his goods.
> 48 "But if that evil servant says in his heart, 'My master is delaying his coming,'
> 49 "and begins to beat his fellow servants, and to eat and drink with the drunkards,
> 50 "the master of that servant will come on a day when he is not looking for him and at an hour that he is not aware of,
> 51 "and will cut him in two and appoint him his portion with the hypocrites. There shall be weeping and gnashing of teeth.

Jesus bids us to conduct our lives as if He might return at any time, and this call to expectancy is apparent in writings throughout the New Testament. Even in our quintessential Rapture passage, we read, "Then we who are alive and remain shall be caught up together with them in the clouds to meet the Lord in the air" (1 Thessalonians 4:17). Paul does not say, "Then *they* who are alive and remain," but "*we*"—Paul, like many of us, believed that he would live to see Jesus come back.

Today, I don't doubt any more than Paul did that Jesus will return in my lifetime. After a hundred generations of Christians who were mistakenly convinced likewise, this mindset may seem foolish. Admittedly, it began to seem foolish to me in my early adult years. As a kid, I'd become quite convinced by all the films and sermons on the subject that Jesus was even then packing his bags for His return trip to Earth, but as I got older I started to wonder, "Well, where is He?" As my reasoning and critical thinking skills developed, I began to think more and more that it could be another thousand years before the Second Coming of Christ. I thought that I was being objective, but, in fact, the Word admonishes us not to be flippant about—not to question or doubt the immediacy of—Christ's return. In 2 Peter 3:3-9, the Apostle Peter tells us:

> 3 knowing this first: that scoffers will come in the last days, walking according to their own lusts,

4 and saying, "Where is the promise of His coming? For since the fathers fell asleep, all things continue as they were from the beginning of creation."
5 For this they willfully forget: that by the word of God the heavens were of old, and the earth standing out of water and in the water,
6 by which the world that then existed perished, being flooded with water.
7 But the heavens and the earth which are now preserved by the same word, are reserved for fire until the day of judgment and perdition of ungodly men.
8 But, beloved, do not forget this one thing, that with the Lord one day is as a thousand years, and a thousand years as one day.
9 The Lord is not slack concerning His promise, as some count slackness, but is longsuffering toward us, not willing that any should perish but that all should come to repentance.

Here, Peter tells us that in the Last Days there will be those who question whether Jesus is really coming back because life has continued on normally for so long since His departure. Similar to Jesus' analogy about the "days of Noah" in Matthew 24:37-39, Peter compares the Second Coming to the Great Flood—Jesus' return, as was that event, is imminent, even if the apparent normalcy of life causes our expectancy to wane. We are assured in verse 7 of our passage that the Day of the Lord is coming, ready or not; and, ultimately, it will culminate in a fiery judgment. In verses 8 and 9, Peter reminds us that our concept of time is different from God's, and that what seems like an inexplicably long wait to us is explained most simply by God's love: He is allowing ample time for the world to hear His Word, come to repentance, and be saved. More than anything else, Jesus' delay is a clarion call to get His message preached to a lost and dying world before it's too late.

Finally, we see in Revelation 1:1 that the Book of Revelation tells us about "things which must shortly take place" that were "signified" to John by an angel of the Lord. Merriam-Webster's Collegiate Dictionary defines the word "signify" as "to show especially by a conventional token (as word, signal, or gesture)."[55] In other words, to signify something means to describe it symbolically. And so, in the very first verse of Revelation, we are given a critical piece of information about how to properly approach this amazingly complex text. Those who attempt to interpret this book using a strictly literal approach unavoidably come up short, and those who assume that Revelation is strictly symbolic likewise miss its true meaning. Revelation is neither purely literal *nor* purely symbolic. Correctly interpreting John's words begins with an understanding that the Book of Revelation depicts actual *things* that are presented using *symbolic language and images*. It is about real people and places and events that comprise our near future, much of which is illuminated in the light of the whole rest of the Word of God, as we've discussed[56] and as we'll see as our study progresses.

Revelation 1:4-1:8 ~ Salutations

4   John, to the seven churches which are in Asia: Grace to you and peace from Him who is and who was and who is to come, and from the seven Spirits who are before His throne,

5   and from Jesus Christ, the faithful witness, the firstborn from the dead, and the ruler over the kings of the earth. To Him who loved us and washed us from our sins in His own blood,

6   and has made us kings and priests to His God and Father, to Him be glory and dominion forever and ever. Amen.

7   Behold, He is coming with clouds, and every eye will see Him, even they who pierced Him. And all the tribes of the earth will mourn because of Him. Even so, Amen.

8   "I am the Alpha and the Omega, the Beginning and the End," says the Lord, "who is and who was and who is to come, the Almighty."

---

[55] *Merriam-Webster's Collegiate Dictionary* (2008; Merriam-Webster, Inc.)
[56] Discussed in Chapter 5 "The Pre-Tribulation Rapture", in the section "Extensive Use of Old Testament Symbols and Language in Book of Revelation Indicative of Israel, not Christians"

Chapters 2 and 3 of the Book of Revelation are comprised of seven letters to seven churches, which we'll study in depth shortly. These letters have stirred up much debate over the centuries: what is their purpose in the context of Revelation? Are we to consider the letters as messages literally for the seven churches to whom they are addressed, or is a much broader audience intended? If it is the latter, the churches specified must be representative of something or someone else, but what or whom? Many modern scholars have adopted the notion that the Seven Churches are symbolic of seven "Church ages" that have comprised the two millennia since the establishment of Christianity.

We won't review these presumed ages here, primarily because this interpretation is awkward and unnecessary. An understanding of the seven letters simply does not require a contrived delineation of periods in Christianity, nor any such complex and arbitrary approach. On the contrary, these letters are simply a message to the Church as a whole, from the time that they were written to the time of Christ's return. Verse 4 of the above passage supports this position. Here, in his introduction, John establishes that it is not only the seven personal messages in chapters 2 and 3 that are addressed to the "seven churches which are in Asia," but, in fact, the whole Book of Revelation is. Would we therefore argue that this entire book is meant only for seven small churches in Asia Minor that no longer even exist; or, equally problematic, that the Book of Revelation is to be somehow divvied up among seven different periods of Church history? Of course not. John is merely utilizing a literary device that is common in the New Testament—that is, addressing a text that is meant for the whole Body of Christ to a particular group or even to an individual. We first encounter this in the introduction to the Gospel of Luke (Luke 1:1-4; emphasis mine):

1. Inasmuch as many have taken in hand to set in order a narrative of those things which have been fulfilled among us,
2. just as those who from the beginning were eyewitnesses and ministers of the word delivered them to us,

> 3 it seemed good to me also, having had perfect understanding of all things from the very first, *to write to you an orderly account, most excellent Theophilus,*
> 4 that you may know the certainty of those things in which you were instructed.

It should be clear to us that the Book of Luke was not intended for Theophilus only: he just happened to be the addressee. Theophilus was also the recipient of the message that we know as the Book of Acts. All of the Apostle Paul's books bear the names of the communities or individuals to whom they were originally written. The Book of James was written to "the twelve tribes which are scattered abroad," the two books of Peter were addressed to specific groups of Gentile Christians, and the three letters of John and the Book of Jude all specify particular original recipients. Knowing a Biblical book's intended audience can be helpful—context is important—but all of us understand that the books of the Bible constitute a general message to the Church as a whole. The Book of Revelation is no exception. It may be addressed to seven churches that once existed in a small region of Asia Minor, but, like the rest of the Word of God, it is to be received as a word for all Christians. That's why it's in the Bible.

Also in verse 4 of our Revelation passage, we notice that the Seven Churches are greeted not only by Jesus ("Him who is and who was and who is to come") but also by "the seven Spirits who are before His throne." With this, we are introduced at the outset to John's utilization of symbolic speech to convey his message to us. Few of us would claim to know the identity and nature of these "seven Spirits" at first glance since this is not a term that occurs anywhere else in the Bible; rather, it is used only in the Book of Revelation. As mentioned, much of John's imagery can be deciphered by directly referencing other parts of Scripture, but this is an early exception to this. So, let's establish two other types of symbolism that we can expect to encounter as we explore John's text. First, we will run across some symbols that are interpreted for us by John; that is, their meaning is given to us, either directly or indirectly, within the Book of Revelation itself. Second, we will find terms and images that lack a simple interpretation; in other words, a superficial search of the Bible will not reveal their meaning. The term "seven

Spirits" is of the former type, to a degree: John gives us clues to its definition later in Revelation, as we'll see.

In verses 5 and 6, John refers to Jesus as the "firstborn from the dead" and the "ruler over the kings of the earth," and refers to us as "kings and priests." The first term, "firstborn from the dead," is a reference to the resurrection which will take place at Christ's return (recall 1 Corinthians 15:22-23: "For as in Adam all die, even so in Christ all shall be made alive. But each one in his own order: Christ the firstfruits, afterward those who are Christ's at His coming."). The second term, "ruler over the kings of the earth," refers to Jesus' earthly reign following His return (1 Corinthians 15:24-25: "Then comes the end, when He delivers the kingdom to God the Father, when He puts an end to all rule and all authority and power. For He must reign till He has put all enemies under His feet."). The last term, which identifies us as "kings and priests," certainly has a spiritual connotation in the present but ultimately anticipates the role of believers during Jesus' Millennial Reign. Before John even begins to record the prophecy, he presents all three of these things as if they've already taken place, though of course they have not. This introduces yet another important literary approach that we should note at this early stage: future events—things that are not to be interpreted as having already occurred—are sometimes presented, perhaps prophetically, in the past or present tense.[57] This style can be confusing and can contribute to the misinterpretation of the Book of Revelation, but it needn't be a pitfall for us. We simply need to understand in advance this and other mechanisms that John uses to present his message.

In verse 7 of our Revelation passage, John writes that Jesus "is coming with clouds, and every eye will see Him, even they who pierced Him. And all the tribes of the earth will mourn because of Him." This correlates with Jesus' description of His return in Matthew 24:30: "Then the sign of the Son of Man will appear in heaven, and then all the tribes of the earth will mourn, and they will see the Son of Man coming on the clouds of heaven with power and great glory." And recall that we've already related this verse

---

[57] As discussed in the introduction to Chapter 6 "The Book of Revelation"

THE INTRODUCTION

from Matthew to our quintessential Rapture passage: "For the Lord Himself will descend from heaven with a shout, with the voice of an archangel, and with the trumpet of God. And the dead in Christ will rise first. Then we who are alive and remain shall be caught up together with them in the clouds to meet the Lord in the air..." (1 Thessalonians 4:16-17). So, we see that very early on, John establishes the Second Coming/Resurrection/Rapture event as a central theme in Revelation, contrary to modern popular belief. John also confirms what we've already learned—that the Second Coming/Resurrection/Rapture will not be a covert operation in which millions of Christians mysteriously disappear, but will be a very visible phenomenon that corresponds with God's judgment; hence the mourning among the unbelieving world.

One other interesting thing to notice in verse 7 is that John says that when Jesus returns everyone will see Him, including "they who pierced Him." On the surface, this seems to be a reference to the Crucifixion. As most of us know, after Jesus died on the cross a Roman soldier pierced His side with a sword to confirm that He was dead. But by the time that John penned the Book of Revelation, most of those who had instituted and overseen Jesus' crucifixion had almost certainly died of old age, and the younger of those who had participated were, like John—who was now a very old man—nearing a similar fate. So, John is not likely to have believed that "they who (literally) pierced Him"—that is, the Roman soldiers who officiated over His crucifixion—would be present at the Second Coming. And if we believe in the infallibility of the Bible, we know that John would not have made such a mistake in his narrative. This term must therefore be meant to refer to someone else. Indeed, this constitutes an early example of John's most important literary mechanism, as we established earlier: that is, the embedding of specific references to other parts of Scripture in order to convey a broader meaning. In this case, the reference is to the Book of Zechariah, which John had quoted once before in his Gospel when recounting the Crucifixion event (John 19:31-37; emphasis mine):

> 31 Therefore, because it was the Preparation Day, that the bodies should not remain on the cross on the Sabbath (for that Sabbath was a high day), the Jews asked Pilate that

their legs might be broken, and that they might be taken away.
32 Then the soldiers came and broke the legs of the first and of the other who was crucified with Him.
33 But when they came to Jesus and saw that He was already dead, they did not break His legs.
34 But one of the soldiers pierced His side with a spear, and immediately blood and water came out.
35 And he who has seen has testified, and his testimony is true; and he knows that he is telling the truth, so that you may believe.
36 For these things were done that the Scripture should be fulfilled, "Not one of His bones shall be broken."
37 *And again another Scripture says, "They shall look on Him whom they pierced."*

Verse 37, the quote from Zechariah, demonstrates that John is not averse to referencing other Scripture in his own work and, equally important, that he finds it appropriate to relate Old Testament concepts to New. But in order to establish John's meaning when he uses this phrase again in Revelation, we must go all the way back to the original Scripture (Zechariah 12:10-14; emphasis mine):

10 "And I will pour on the house of David and on the inhabitants of Jerusalem the Spirit of grace and supplication; then they will look on Me *whom they pierced.* Yes, they will mourn for Him as one mourns for his only son, and grieve for Him as one grieves for a firstborn.
11 "In that day there shall be a great mourning in Jerusalem, like the mourning at Hadad Rimmon in the plain of Megiddo.
12 "And the land shall mourn, every family by itself: the family of the house of David by itself, and their wives by themselves; the family of the house of Nathan by itself, and their wives by themselves;
13 "the family of the house of Levi by itself, and their wives by themselves; the family of Shimei by itself, and their wives by themselves;
14 "all the families that remain, every family by itself, and their wives by themselves.

Upon tracing John's reference back to Zechariah, we can conclude that the "they" in "they who pierced Him" in Revelation 1:7 does not refer to the Roman soldiers who actually committed the deed or even more broadly to the Jewish religious elite who had influenced them, but to Israel as a nation. Furthermore, Zechariah prophesies that when the nation of Israel (that is, modern Jews) sees Jesus at His Second Coming they will mourn because they will know Him as their "only son" and their "firstborn"—that is, they will at last *en masse* recognize Jesus as the Messiah.

If Zechariah's prophecy is true (and, of course, it is), does this mean that all of Israel will be saved when Jesus returns? In Matthew 8:11-12, Jesus seems to suggest otherwise:

> 11 "And I say to you that many will come from east and west, and sit down with Abraham, Isaac, and Jacob in the kingdom of heaven.
> 12 "But the sons of the kingdom will be cast out into outer darkness. There will be weeping and gnashing of teeth."

And, in Matthew 21:43 (speaking to the Jewish religious leaders):

> 43 "Therefore I say to you, the kingdom of God will be taken from you and given to a nation bearing the fruits of it."

The "nation" Jesus speaks of here is the spiritual Israel, comprised of Jews and Gentiles alike who acknowledge Jesus as Lord and Savior. Every human being, regardless of national origin, must receive Jesus in order to be saved. This is not yet the case for the vast majority of Jews in the modern state of Israel. However, this does not mean that God does not have an ultimate plan of redemption for His original Chosen People. He does, and this plan—which, of course, must include the acceptance of His Son as their true Messiah—will manifest in the Last Days. The Apostle Paul, a former Pharisee (Jewish religious leader) himself, has much to say on this topic in the Book of Romans. He describes the current lost condition of Israel in Romans 10:1-9:

1   Brethren, my heart's desire and prayer to God for Israel is that they may be saved.
2   For I bear them witness that they have a zeal for God, but not according to knowledge.
3   For they being ignorant of God's righteousness, and seeking to establish their own righteousness, have not submitted to the righteousness of God.
4   For Christ is the end of the law for righteousness to everyone who believes.
5   For Moses writes about the righteousness which is of the law, "The man who does those things shall live by them."
6   But the righteousness of faith speak in this way, "Do not say in your heart, 'Who will ascend into heaven?'" (that is, to bring Christ down from above)
7   or, "'Who will descend into the abyss?'" (that is, to bring Christ up from the dead).
8   But what does it say? "The word is near you, in your mouth and in your heart" (that is, the word of faith which we preach):
9   that if you confess with your mouth the Lord Jesus and believe in your heart that God has raised Him from the dead, you will be saved.

Paul acknowledges that those of the Jewish faith are seeking after the righteousness of God, but he points out that they are doing so ignorantly, according to their own works under the old form of the Law. They do not recognize that salvation can be achieved only by grace through Christ Jesus, and therefore salvation eludes them. But, according to Paul, all is not lost (Romans 10:19—11:5):

19 But I say, did Israel not know? First Moses says: "I will provoke you to jealousy by those who are not a nation, I will move you to anger by a foolish nation."
20 But Isaiah is very bold and says: "I was found by those who did not seek Me; I was made manifest to those who did not ask for Me."
21 But to Israel he says: "All day long I have stretched out My hands to a disobedient and contrary people."

THE INTRODUCTION

> 1 I say then, has God cast away His people? Certainly not! For I also am an Israelite, of the seed of Abraham, of the tribe of Benjamin.
> 2 God has not cast away His people whom He foreknew. Or do you not know what the Scripture says of Elijah, how he pleads with God against Israel, saying,
> 3 "Lord, they have killed Your prophets and torn down Your altars, and I alone am left, and they seek my life"?
> 4 But what does the divine response say to him? "I have reserved for Myself seven thousand men who have not bowed the knee to Baal."
> 5 Even so then, at this present time there is a remnant according to the election of grace.

In verse 19, Paul relates a statement by Moses to the concept of Jews being displaced by Gentiles in the Kingdom of God and the frustration that such a notion may provoke. Paul underscores his point with some quotes from Isaiah in verses 20 and 21. But in verses 1 through 5, he explains that Israel's present unsaved state is not indicative of a complete and permanent severing of God's relationship with the Jews, and even in Paul's day a "remnant"—some small percentage of Jews, including Paul—had come to the light of the truth of salvation through Jesus Christ. Even this, though, is only a glimpse of the ultimate plan of redemption that God has in store for His original Chosen People, as Paul explains a few verses later in Romans 11:25-27 (emphasis and bracketed comment mine):

> 25 For I do not desire, brethren, that you should be ignorant of this mystery, lest you should be wise in your own opinion, that blindness in part has happened to Israel *until the fullness of the Gentiles has come in.*
> 26 *And so all Israel will be saved,* as it is written: "The Deliverer will come out of Zion, and He will turn away ungodliness from Jacob [Israel];
> 27 For this is My covenant with them, when I take away their sins."

In this passage, Paul explains that, ultimately, "*all* Israel will be saved" (verse 26). The Jews will at last come into salvation when the time of the Gentiles—the span of time that began with Christ's First Coming—has reached its conclusion. This is marked by Christ's return, which Paul confirms in verse 26 by quoting Isaiah's prophecy about the coming of the "Deliverer" (when Paul wrote this Jesus had already come once, so, of course, he is referring to His Second Coming). At this point, according to Paul and Isaiah, "all Israel" will repent and will be saved. But does Paul really mean "*all* Israel"; that is, every Jew who is alive at that time, perhaps even all Jews from all time? This one statement has been the subject of much debate among scholars, but if we are to reconcile what Paul is saying to what Jesus said in Matthew 8:12 ("But the sons of the kingdom will be cast out into outer darkness. There will be weeping and gnashing of teeth"), the answer is clearly no. Paul does not mean that literally every single Jew will be saved, any more than he means in 1 Corinthians 15:22 that literally all of humankind will be saved: "For as in Adam all die, even so in Christ *all* shall be made alive." In this verse, Paul is merely speaking from a deep faith that everyone on Earth, including his Jewish brethren, *can* be saved. As we work to fulfill the Great Commission in these Last Days, our faith can be no less than Paul's. And we can count on the prophecies concerning Israel to come true: many—most?—of God's original Chosen People will come to repentance and accept Jesus of Nazareth as their Messiah in the final days leading up to His return (a point that we will explore in-depth in Book Two of this series, *These Final Days, Part 2—The Truth About How the Great Tribulation Begins, the Third Temple, and Jerusalem*).

Finally, in verse 8 of our passage, we get our first direct quote from Jesus, who identifies Himself as "the Alpha and the Omega, the Beginning and the End." What an awesome description of our Lord, and Revelation is the only book of the Bible where it occurs. We know from John's Gospel that "In the beginning was the Word [Jesus], and the Word was with God, and the Word was God" (John 1:1). Jesus comprised the beginning of our world, and in the Book of Revelation we are told that He will likewise constitute its end. However, as we'll see, a New Heaven and a New Earth are to come, and those of us who are in Christ will have no end.

Revelation 1:9-1:20 ~ The Seven Golden Lampstands

THE INTRODUCTION

9 I, John, both your brother and companion in the tribulation and kingdom and patience of Jesus Christ, was on the island that is called Patmos for the word of God and for the testimony of Jesus Christ.

10 I was in the Spirit on the Lord's Day, and I heard behind me a loud voice, as of a trumpet,

11 saying, "I am the Alpha and the Omega, the First and the Last," and, "What you see, write in a book and send it to the seven churches which are in Asia: to Ephesus, to Smyrna, to Pergamos, to Thyatira, to Sardis, to Philadelphia, and to Laodicea."

12 Then I turned to see the voice that spoke with me. And having turned I saw seven golden lampstands.

13 and in the midst of the seven lampstands One like the Son of Man, clothed with a garment down to the feet and girded about the chest with a golden band.

14 His head and hair were white like wool, as white as snow, and His eyes like a flame of fire;

15 His feet were like fine brass, as if refined in a furnace, and His voice as the sound of many waters;

16 He had in His right hand seven stars, out of His mouth went a sharp two-edged sword, and His countenance was like the sun shining in its strength.

17 And when I saw Him, I fell at His feet as dead. But He laid His right hand on me, saying to me, "Do not be afraid; I am the First and the Last.

18 "I am He who lives, and was dead, and behold, I am alive forevermore. Amen. And I have the keys of Hades and of Death.

19 "Write the things which you have seen, and the things which are, and the things which will take place after this.

20 "The mystery of the seven stars which you saw in My right hand, and the seven golden lampstands: The seven stars are the angels of the seven churches, and the seven lampstands which you saw are the seven churches.

In verse 9 of this passage, John establishes his physical location during his authoring of the Book of Revelation. He reports that he is on the island of Patmos, to which he has been exiled "for the word of God and for the testimony of Jesus Christ." Patmos, located some 60 miles from the seaport of Ephesus, one of the Seven Churches to which John is instructed to write, was a Roman penal colony where prisoners were forced to do hard labor in the island's granite quarries. At the time John is given the vision that constitutes the Book of Revelation, he is suffering serious persecution for his proclamation of Christianity. He does not consider himself unique in this suffering, but refers to himself as "your brother and companion in the tribulation and kingdom and patience of Jesus Christ." So, barely halfway through his introduction, John establishes a theme that is central to the message of Revelation and that supports our analysis about the timing of the Rapture: Christians must be prepared to patiently endure *tribulation* as the Kingdom of God manifests. In this, John offers us no sense of the escapism that is inherent in the Pre-Tribulation Rapture view.

In verses 10 and 11 of our passage, John writes that he was "in the Spirit." This suggests a deep, meditative state that is familiar to many of us and that opens the believer to revelation from God. And, of course, the revelation that John is about to receive is quite extraordinary: it will define the destiny of our entire planet. But even more than this, "in the Spirit" means that John was tuned in to (filled with) the Holy Spirit in order to receive his vision; and, in turn, the Holy Spirit is *our* ultimate, indispensable key to understanding all that John writes. John goes on to say that the vision he is about to convey took place on "the Lord's Day." This is the first known occurrence of this term in Christian literature, and it demonstrates John's propensity for inventing terminology; which, of course, adds somewhat to the challenge of deciphering his narrative. John's vision is initiated by Jesus, who instructs John to record what he is about to be shown and to send this to seven specific churches located in close proximity to one another in what is today western Turkey. These were not the only Christian churches in Asia Minor, but they were the major ones, located within a key transportation network that ensured that John's text would be quickly disseminated throughout the Body of Christ. This may at least in part explain why these seven churches were the specified recipients—John (or, more accurately, God) wanted to ensure that the message of Revelation would reach its ultimate intended audience: you and me.

THE INTRODUCTION

Verses 12 through 16 of our passage reemphasize an important truth about the Book of Revelation. These verses are extremely rich in symbolic imagery: we find seven golden lampstands, seven stars, and a detailed description of Jesus that includes a long garment, a golden band about the chest, snow-white hair, eyes like flames of fire, feet like refined brass, a voice like many waters, and a sharp two-edged sword coming from His mouth. Many take this description of Jesus to be literal, and it may be to some extent: some who claim to have been visited by Jesus in the modern era have reported that His hair is completely white, for example. But certainly much of this is poetic imagery, such as the sword protruding from Jesus' mouth. And as for the seven golden lampstands among which Jesus is standing and the seven stars in His right hand, we find that this is indeed symbolic, of the self-interpreting type. Their meaning is clearly explained by Jesus in Revelation 1:20: "The mystery of the seven stars which you saw in My right hand, and the seven golden lampstands: The seven stars are the angels of the seven churches, and the seven lampstands which you saw are the seven churches." Some modern prophecy scholars insist on a literal interpretation of the strange and exotic images that John describes in his vision, but, as we noted earlier, this is a wrong approach, and here in Revelation's first chapter this approach is plainly refuted: John sees and records seven lampstands and seven stars; but Jesus, while not denying that this is indeed what John saw, explains that these images are merely representative of the churches being addressed and the seven angels who were assigned to watch over those churches.

As we're seeing more and more—and we're only through its first chapter—Revelation is an incredibly rich, and incredibly complex, book. To fully comprehend it requires that we approach it soberly and, most importantly, with an ear to the Holy Spirit. This grounding will come in very handy later on when we read, for example, about a seven-headed, ten-horned beast rising up out of the sea.

Chapter 8

The Letters to the Seven Churches

And so we arrive at the seven letters to the seven churches addressed in the first chapter of the Book of Revelation. Again, while many scholars have developed impressively elaborate theories on what the Seven Churches represent (the "seven Church ages" model being the most popular today), the assumption that we made in the last chapter—that the Book of Revelation is a message to the Body of Christ as a whole, throughout the centuries—is by far the most useful. Revelation is about the End Times, but it was never meant to be a message *only* to the End Times Church. And if its message were dependent on a hindsight view of the history of Christianity since the time of Jesus—as the "seven Church ages" approach demands—then Revelation would have no meaning to anyone except the very last generation of Christians. And we know that this can't be God's intent, since, again, this book was addressed to seven churches that existed in John's day. Furthermore, the "seven Church ages" interpretation of Revelation is so complex—so scholarly—that it implies that Revelation's message is intended only for those with Ph.D.s in historical theology. This is by no means the case. Revelation may seem mysterious, even inaccessible, to many readers—especially at first glance—but God's purpose in sometimes communicating in challenging ways is not to build intellectual and educational barriers. Jesus frequently taught using parables, and while these sometimes bewildered His listeners, including His Disciples, Jesus offers a perfectly sound reason for this approach in Matthew 13:10-13:

> 10 And the disciples came and said to Him, "Why do You speak to them in parables?"
> 11 He answered and said to them, "Because it has been given to you to know the mysteries of the kingdom of heaven, but to them it has not been given.
> 12 "For whoever has, to him more will be given and he will have abundance; but whoever does not have, even what he has will be taken away from him.
> 13 "Therefore I speak to them in parables, because seeing they do not see, and hearing they do not hear, nor do they understand.

A parable is a metaphoric, or symbolic, story designed to convey a particular truth without just coming out and saying it. Some are more difficult to decipher than others, and it sometimes takes an experienced Christian to derive a parable's deeper meaning—that is, where Jesus doesn't provide His own explanation, as He occasionally did. The purpose of teaching in this way, as Jesus explains to His Disciples in the passage above, is not to confuse or hide something from the believer, but to confound those who are wise in their own eyes apart from God. Jesus had some important things to teach God's children during His short ministry here on Earth and He didn't want to waste words on deaf ears. He says it this way in Matthew 7:6:

> 6 "Do not give what is holy to the dogs; nor cast your pearls before swine, lest they trample them under their feet, and turn and tear you in pieces.

We might say that God often speaks to His people "in code" so as not to expose His holy Word—and those for whom it is meant—to more scorn than we are already subject to. We can understand the heavy use of metaphor, analogy and simile—that is, symbolism—in the Book of Revelation in this light. Especially in this critical text—which defines the ultimate fate of mankind, this world, and our enemy—we might expect God to create a bit of a challenge for those who would search its pages. Jesus offers a one-verse parable along these lines in Matthew 13:44:

> 44 "Again, the kingdom of heaven is like treasure hidden in a field, which a man found and hid; and for joy over it he goes and sells all that he has and buys that field.

In other words, this Kingdom, these truths, that we are seeking are like buried treasure that we have to work to dig out, but it's more than worth the effort in the long run. And the treasure is not buried so deep and in such stony ground that most of us could not possibly ever get to it. On the contrary, Jesus tells us in Matthew 7:7-8:

> 7 "Ask, and it will be given to you; seek, and you will find; knock, and it will be opened to you.
> 8 "For everyone who asks receives, and he who seeks finds, and to him who knocks it will be opened.

Not only are the answers that we seek right there in God's Word, waiting to be found, but *every* believer who seeks them will find them. This fact should alleviate some of our apprehension in approaching the more difficult books of the Bible. And we can rest assured that all of Revelation's secrets—including the real meaning of the Seven Letters to the Seven Churches—while perhaps a bit challenging, are not so difficult to unlock.

The Seven Churches in Revelation may be labeled as follows:

1. The Loveless Church
2. The Persecuted Church
3. The Compromising Church
4. The Corrupt Church
5. The Dead Church
6. The Faithful Church
7. The Lukewarm Church

One hardly needs to explore the past two thousand years of Church history to find churches that fit these definitions. For most of us, we don't even need to leave the borders of our own towns. In fact, we can reduce these labels even further, to within the individual church. Your congregation may include representatives of each of these definitions. And, ultimately, we can apply these even to our own selves: the true Christian endeavors daily to walk in love, to endure whatever persecutions may come, to avoid compromise, to shun corruption (sin), to choose life, to remain faithful, and to stay on fire for God. So, while the "Church ages" interpretation of the messages to the Seven Churches is impressive from an academic point of view, these seven messages are for *me* (and you).

With that, let's take a look at the letters. And, along the way, we'll see what light they shed on our principal topic, the timing of the Rapture.

Revelation 2:1-2:7 ~ The First Letter: The Loveless Church

1 "To the angel of the church of Ephesus write, 'These things says He who holds the seven stars in His right hand, who walks in the midst of the seven golden lampstands:
2 "I know your works, your labor, your patience, and that you cannot bear those who are evil. And you have tested those who say they are apostles and are not, and have found them liars;
3 "and you have persevered and have patience, and have labored for My name's sake and have not become weary.
4 "Nevertheless I have this against you, that you have left your first love.
5 "Remember therefore from where you have fallen; repent and do the first works, or else I will come to you quickly and remove your lampstand from its place—unless you repent.
6 "But this you have, that you hate the deeds of the Nicolaitans, which I also hate.
7 "He who has an ear, let him hear what the Spirit says to the churches. To him who overcomes I will give to eat from the tree of life, which is in the midst of the Paradise of God.'"

The first letter begins in verse 1 with a poetic description of Jesus. We know that this describes Jesus because this picture was given and explained to us in Revelation chapter 1. Of course, instead of using symbolism, Jesus could simply have said to John here, "These things says Jesus…," but this would break with the style that is used throughout the Book of Revelation: few things are simply stated; nearly all are described with imagery and metaphor instead.[58]

In the verses that follow (verses 2 through 6), Jesus commends the Ephesians for their perseverance, but He also criticizes them for slipping into religiosity. Instead of remaining focused on the reason for their Christianity—their love for Jesus and the Father, and for other people—apparently they'd fallen into routine and mediocrity. He admonishes them to get back to the root of their faith, to humility and love—good advice for us all. Finally, Jesus warns them that failure to return to true Christianity could cost them their status in the Kingdom of God. He may be speaking even to matters of spiritual life or death, but it's a bit premature in our study to discuss the issue of the permanency (or impermanency) of salvation. For now, let's at least acknowledge that there are great benefits to believers who walk in the ways of God and great costs to those who do not.

With these verses, a pattern is established that we will see repeated throughout the remaining six letters. Jesus introduces Himself using poetic imagery—imagery that communicates something about His character and who He is to the Body of Christ—and this is followed by a commendation (a word of encouragement) and/or an admonition (a chastening and a warning). Finally, in verse 7, we find two more elements that occur in all seven of the letters. First, Jesus says (through the Apostle John), "He who has an ear, let him hear what the Spirit says to the churches." This phrase is repeated verbatim throughout the Seven Letters, so we must assume that it is a particularly important point. As we've noted several times so far, it is only *by the Holy Spirit* that we are able to truly comprehend the Word of God. It is only he who is *filled with the Spirit* and able

---

[58] As we discussed in the introduction to Chapter 8 "The Letters to the Seven Churches"

to hear from Him directly who has a chance of understanding the Book of Revelation, and of surviving the times that it tells us about.

Lastly, Jesus tells us that "him who overcomes I will give to eat from the tree of life, which is in the midst of the Paradise of God." The "tree of life," which many of us will identify with the Garden of Eden in the Book of Genesis,[59] appears again in the final chapter of the Book of Revelation where the New Heaven and the New Earth—the ultimate manifestation in this Universe of the Kingdom of God, and our ultimate destination—are described. Here, Jesus promises that whoever *overcomes* will find himself enjoying this paradise that awaits in Earth's future. We might ask what happens to him who does not overcome; but, for now, let's simply ask, "He who overcomes *what?*" We know that this letter is addressed to a specific church that was having some specific problems in its day that it needed to overcome. But we also know that this is a message to the Church as a whole and ultimately to that generation of believers who will experience the last of the Last Days. If Christians are to be whisked away to Heaven before facing any real threat to our spiritual survival, why would Jesus feel the need here (and in the six letters that follow) to place this condition—that we must *overcome*—on our spiritual future? Far from the easy escapism that the Pre-Tribulation Rapture doctrine offers, Jesus' words here instead line up with what we've already discovered about the extraordinary trials that we are destined to face as the Body of Christ…which lines up perfectly with Jesus' words in the Book of Matthew, in His great End Times dissertation (Matthew 24:13):

> 13 "But he who endures to the end shall be saved."

Revelation 2:8-2:11 ~ The Second Letter: The Persecuted Church

> 8 "And to the angel of the church in Smyrna write, 'These things says the First and the Last, who was dead, and came to life:

---

[59] Genesis 2:8-9

> 9 "I know your works, tribulation, and poverty (but you are rich); and I know the blasphemy of those who say they are Jews and are not, but are a synagogue of Satan.
> 10 "Do not fear any of those things which you are about to suffer. Indeed, the devil is about to throw some of you into prison, that you may be tested, and you will have tribulation ten days. Be faithful until death, and I will give you the crown of life.
> 11 "He who has an ear, let him hear what the Spirit says to the churches. He who overcomes shall not be hurt by the second death.'"

Here, Jesus is introduced in terms of His comprising the beginning of this world and its end: He was before creation, and He will continue through eternity in the new creation. We also see a reference to Jesus' resurrection, an experience that is promised to all deceased believers in the mass resurrection that will coincide with the Rapture at His Second Coming.

In verses 9 and 10, Jesus acknowledges the efforts, and the suffering, of the Smyrnites, and He tells them to expect even more trouble. Far from promising an easy road, as so many modern Christians expect (as per the "God loves us too much to ever let us go through times of trial and tribulation" argument that we discussed earlier[60]), Jesus says that this group of believers would suffer "tribulation"; indeed, even unto death. This is one of only two of the Seven Churches for which Jesus offers no chastisement, but He nonetheless admonishes these believers to remain faithful—to endure—to the very end. Again, we should perceive this message to be not for the church in Smyrna only, but for the Body of Christ as a whole and, arguably, to the End Times Church in particular. Here, as in the previous letter, we see no indication of a sudden rescue from troubles, no underlying theme that suggests that Christians do not sometimes go through bad, maybe the worst of, times. Verse 9 also introduces us to an interesting term, "synagogue of Satan." Jesus uses this term again in His Sixth Letter,

---

[60] Chapter 5 "The Pre-Tribulation Rapture"; section "The 'Loving Father' Argument"

to the church in Philadelphia.[61] We'll discuss this in detail when we get to that letter.

In verse 11 we again see the imperative to overcome, this time with a promise to the overcomer that he will be spared the "second death," a reference to the Final Judgment, which we'll see described in Revelation's latter chapters. This is a concept that is fundamental to Christianity: not only can our Christian walk include trials and tribulations such as most modern Christians—at least those in the United States and other Christian-tolerant nations—have never experienced, but the believer may even face an untimely death. It is not this physical death that we should fear, however, but the eternal death that will come upon many at the Final Judgment. Jesus says it this way in Matthew 10:28:

> 28 "And do not fear those who kill the body but cannot kill the soul. But rather fear Him who is able to destroy both soul and body in hell.

And just a few verses later in Matthew 10:39, Jesus tells us:

> 39 "He who finds his life will lose it, and he who loses his life for My sake will find it.

We know that the early Church lived daily with the threat of physical death because of their beliefs, and yet the Body of Christ thrived to survive to this day. As you read these words, there are many Christians in troubled parts of the world—such as China and North Korea, and throughout the Middle East—who even today must embrace this concept. We should be equally strong, equally bold in our faith. There will be Christian martyrs during the Great Tribulation, but they will not have been the first. Jesus was willing to come in the flesh to die for us. How many of us today would have the courage to die for Him? Do we possess the strength of spirit to be as faithful to Him as He was to us? An entire generation of us will one day soon face these questions in their extreme.

---

[61] Revelation 3:7—3:13

Revelation 2:12-2:17 ~ The Third Letter: The Compromising Church

> 12 "And to the angel of the church in Pergamos write, 'These things says He who has the sharp two-edged sword:
> 13 "I know your works, and where you dwell, where Satan's throne is. And you hold fast to My name, and did not deny My faith even in the days in which Antipas was My faithful martyr, who was killed among you, where Satan dwells.
> 14 "But I have a few things against you, because you have there those who hold the doctrine of Balaam, who taught Balak to put a stumbling block before the children of Israel, to eat things sacrificed to idols, and to commit sexual immorality.
> 15 "Thus you also have those who hold the doctrine of the Nicolaitans, which thing I hate.
> 16 "Repent, or else I will come to you quickly and will fight against them with the sword of My mouth.
> 17 "He who has an ear, let him hear what the Spirit says to the churches. To him who overcomes I will give some of the hidden manna to eat. And I will give him a white stone, and on the stone a new name written which no one knows except him who receives it.'"

Here, we again see the concept of Christians enduring in the midst of great opposition. Scholars are unsure what exactly "Satan's throne" (verse 13) refers to, but a likely candidate is the Altar of Zeus (Zeus was the father and king of all of the gods, according to ancient Greek religion), upon which was sacrificed Antipas, the bishop of Pergamos, who refused to renounce Christianity and bow down in worship to the Roman emperor.[62] Whatever the case, it is clear that the Pergamites were attempting to follow Christ in an environment that was antithetical to Christianity. And yet Jesus' focus is not on the trials that this body of believers was facing, but rather on the fact that they'd allowed sin and idolatry—devotion to things other than God—to creep in among them. In keeping with the pattern of most of the other letters, Jesus admonishes these believers to change their ways or suffer the consequences. Under similar circumstances, so many of us would cry to God to rescue us,

---

[62] *A Light in Darkness*, Rick Renner (2010; Teach All Nations)

but His concern is that we repent and endeavor toward righteousness. Sometimes, we might say, tribulation even facilitates this. The Apostle Peter supports this notion (1 Peter 1:6-7):

> 6   In this you greatly rejoice, though now for a little while, if need be, you have been grieved by various trials,
> 7   that the genuineness of your faith, being much more precious than gold that perishes, though it is tested by fire, may be found to praise, honor, and glory at the revelation of Jesus Christ...

We don't enjoy tests and trials, but through them our faith is confirmed and strengthened. It is refined as gold is refined by fire. Jesus is coming back for His Church in its most refined state ever...but only after our faith has been perfected by the greatest time of tribulation that the world has even seen.

In the previous two letters, Jesus concludes by promising that the Christian who overcomes will experience some blessing that pertains to concepts that are explored later in Revelation: the first letter mentions the Tree of Life that will stand in the new creation, and the second letter describes the overcomer receiving amnesty on Judgment Day. In this third letter, we find in verse 17 a promise of "hidden manna" to eat. Manna, as many will recall from the Exodus story, was a bread-like substance that God miraculously provided to the Israelites each day to sustain them in the Wilderness.[63] This, then, may be a reference to the fact that God is going to miraculously provide for His original Chosen People in such a way again, after the Holy Spirit leads them into "the wilderness," during the time of the Antichrist,[64] as we'll see. Another possibility is that Jesus is referring to the manna that was placed inside the Ark of the Covenant,[65] which has been missing (hidden inside Jerusalem's Temple Mount; we'll discuss this later) for some 2,600 years, and which will be recovered during the Great Tribulation. Jesus also promises we who overcome a "white stone" with "a new name" written on it, which may allude to an ancient

---

[63] Exodus chapter 16
[64] Revelation 12:13-14
[65] Hebrews 9:4

practice of giving a white stone to someone who has been acquitted of a crime: in Christ, the guilt of our sins is washed away, and we will be proclaimed innocent on the Great Day of Judgment.[66]

Revelation 2:18-2:29 ~ The Fourth Letter: The Corrupt Church

18 "And to the angel of the church in Thyatira write, 'These things says the Son of God, who has eyes like a flame of fire, and His feet like fine brass:

19 "I know your works, love, service, faith, and your patience; and as for your works, the last are more than the first.

20 "Nevertheless I have a few things against you, because you allow that woman Jezebel, who calls herself a prophetess, to teach and seduce My servants to commit sexual immorality and eat things sacrificed to idols.

21 "And I gave her time to repent of her sexual immorality, and she did not repent.

22 "Indeed I will cast her into a sickbed, and those who commit adultery with her into great tribulation, unless they repent of their deeds.

23 "I will kill her children with death, and all the churches shall know that I am He who searches the minds and hearts. And I will give to each one of you according to your works.

24 "Now to you I say, and to the rest in Thyatira, as many as do not have this doctrine, who have not known the depths of Satan, as they say, I will put on you no other burden.

25 "But hold fast what you have till I come.

26 "And he who overcomes, and keeps My works until the end, to him I will give power over the nations—

27 'He shall rule them with a rod of iron; They shall be dashed to pieces like the potter's vessels'—

28 "and I will give him the morning star.

29 "He who has an ear, let him hear what the Spirit says to the churches.'"

With this letter, we begin to get a better grasp of the most important application of the letters to the Seven Churches of

---

[66] Revelation 20:11-15

Revelation. We begin to see that they are, in fact, meant not only for the churches in antiquity to whom they are addressed, but for all of us and, ultimately, for the End Times Church. This letter's main content is similar to most of the others. The Thyatirans are commended, then chastised, then warned to repent. But notice how Jesus concludes this letter. In verse 25, He says, "But hold fast what you have *till I come.*" Since the church of Thyatira no longer even exists—the ancient city is today a ruin—this letter clearly has a broader intended audience, namely the whole Body of Christ up to the time of Jesus' return. This also further weakens the "Church ages" theory. The "fourth Church age" supposedly began around A.D. 600 and ended around A.D. 1500,[67] but Jesus did not return in that time. Since Jesus' instructions are to hold fast to what we have *until He comes*, this is clearly not a message for Medieval Christians only, but for the whole Church in general and the End Times Church in particular.

In the next verse, Jesus adds a new component to the concept of the overcomer. Here, as in the previous letters, He refers to "he who overcomes," but this time He adds "and keeps My works *until the end.*" We may reasonably ask, the end of what? It wouldn't seem errant, particularly if we relate this verse to the prior one which makes reference to the Second Coming, to assume that Jesus is referring to the end of this age—the so-called time of the Gentiles—which culminates in the reign of the Antichrist. In other words, Jesus is speaking of the end of the Great Tribulation. After all, the beginning of the Tribulation doesn't mark the end of anything, only the beginning of the end. Both of these verses are instructing believers to continue in good works until a particular event: in one verse, Jesus' return; in the next, the end of this age. Taken together, they offer yet another piece of evidence that our model is correct. Christians are going to remain on Earth until Christ's return at the end of the seven-year Tribulation. The concept of overcoming is so stressed throughout the Seven Letters because the Body of Christ is ultimately going to have to overcome the greatest possible test of our faith, the Great Tribulation itself.

---

[67] *Revelation Unveiled*, Tim LaHaye (1999; Zondervan)

Finally, in verses 26 through 28, Jesus promises those believers who endure to the end "power over the nations" and "the morning star." These, like the promises of the other letters, pertain to End Times concepts that we'll explore in depth as we progress through Revelation. In brief, the first is a reference to the Millennial Reign. Recall in chapter 1 of Revelation that we are referred to as "kings and priests," and, indeed, we will reign with Christ during the Millennial Reign, that period wherein God's Kingdom is consummated here on Earth. The second term refers to Jesus Himself. In the final chapter of Revelation, Jesus identifies Himself as "the Root and the Offspring of David, the Bright and Morning Star" (Revelation 22:16). Jesus, of course, is our greatest reward of all.

Revelation 3:1-3:6 ~ The Fifth Letter: The Dead Church

1   "And to the angel of the church in Sardis write, 'These things says He who has the seven Spirits of God and the seven stars: "I know your works, that you have a name that you are alive, but you are dead.
2   "Be watchful, and strengthen the things which remain, that are ready to die, for I have not found your works perfect before God.
3   "Remember therefore how you have received and heard; hold fast and repent. Therefore if you will not watch, I will come upon you as a thief, and you will not know what hour I will come upon you.
4   "You have a few names even in Sardis who have not defiled their garments; and they shall walk with Me in white, for they are worthy.
5   "He who overcomes shall be clothed in white garments, and I will not blot out his name from the Book of Life; but I will confess his name before My Father and before His angels.
6   "He who has an ear, let him hear what the Spirit says to the churches."'

This letter follows the pattern of the previous ones, though, tragically for the Sardisians, Jesus seems to have little praise to give to them as a body. He tells them that as a church they are spiritually dead, a fact underscored not by their presumed sin or some other such shortcoming, but by the deficiency of their "works" (verses 1 and 2). What we *do* as believers is more important than many Christians—those of us who may emphasize things like grace and faith—sometimes realize. It is true that a man is not saved by his works but by his faith in Christ alone. And yet these two things—our works and our faith—are inextricably linked. James, the brother of Jesus, tells us as much in James 2:14-17:

> 14 What does it profit, my brethren, if someone says he has faith but does not have works? Can faith save him?
> 15 If a brother or sister is naked and destitute of daily food,
> 16 and one of you says to them, "Depart in peace, be warmed and filled," but you do not give them the things which are needed for the body, what does it profit?
> 17 Thus also faith by itself, if it does not have works, is dead.

We may be saved by grace through faith, but without works—and not just any works, but works that derive from the Holy Spirit[68]—perhaps our very salvation becomes precarious. Jesus seems to imply this in His letter to the Sardisians. In verse 3 he warns them that if they do not remain in a righteous state of readiness, His return will be to them as a thief comes; that is, they won't be prepared for Him. The obverse must be true as well: those of us who *are* watching—those of us who hear the voice of the Spirit and who have a correct understanding of what the Bible teaches about the End Times—*will*, when the time comes, "know what hour (Jesus) will come upon (us)." This, of course, is contrary to the Pre-Tribulation Rapture model, which posits a sudden catching away of the Church that takes us all by surprise. And, it lines up perfectly with the words of the Apostle Paul that we studied in Chapter 3 (1 Thessalonians 5:1-6; emphasis mine):

> 1 But concerning the times and the seasons, brethren, you have no need that I should write to you.
> 2 For you yourselves know perfectly that the day of the Lord so comes as a thief in the night.

---

[68] See Galatians 5:22-23

3   For when they say, "Peace and safety!" then sudden destruction comes upon them, as labor pains upon a pregnant woman. And they shall not escape.
4   *But you, brethren, are not in darkness, so that this Day should overtake you as a thief.*
5   You are all sons of light and sons of the day. We are not of the night nor of darkness.
6   Therefore let us not sleep, as other do, but *let us watch* and be sober.

In verse 4 of our letter, Jesus tells the Sardisians that only a few of them had clean garments and were worthy to walk with Him in white; this is a reference to the Bride of Christ, the perfected Church for whom Christ will one day soon return. Finally, and most compellingly, in verse 5 Jesus refers again to "he who overcomes" (as He does in the other letters) and proclaims that not only will the overcomer "be clothed in white garments," but he will also not have his name removed from the "Book of Life." Jesus also says in this verse that He will confess this individual's name "before My Father and before His angels." Consider this statement in the light of Matthew 10:32-33:

32   "Therefore whoever confesses Me before men, him I will also confess before My Father who is in heaven.
33   "But whoever denies Me before men, him I will also deny before My Father who is in heaven.

So, we can conclude from this letter to the church in Sardis that Christians are susceptible to falling away, and that this can result in layers of consequences in the Last Days. Jesus' return will find them unready. They will not be counted among the Bride of Christ (the raptured and resurrected believers at the Second Coming). They will, in effect, have lost their salvation. And the individual's faith and conduct will have been the measure. Paul underscores this point in Philippians 2:12-13:

12   Therefore, my beloved, as you have always obeyed, not as in my presence only, but now much more in my absence, work out your own salvation with fear and trembling;

13 for it is God who works in you both to will and to do for His good pleasure.

When I was four years old I said the prayer of salvation, and for many years after that, throughout my childhood and teen years, I believed that that little prayer was my Golden Ticket into Heaven. But in my adult years I've matured more and more as a believer, and the more that I get to know God and His Word, the less convinced I am that salvation is immutable. Jesus died once and for all for my sins, but I must *walk* in that free gift. Salvation is a lifelong process, not a singular event. This question of the permanency of salvation is an issue that may seem beyond the scope of this book, but it is in fact critical to its core message. Indeed, the issue of the timing of the Rapture may relate quite directly to the salvation of End Times Christians, as we'll see.

Revelation 3:7-3:13 ~ The Sixth Letter: The Faithful Church

7 "And to the angel of the church in Philadelphia write, 'These things says He who is holy, He who is true, "He who has the key of David, He who opens and no one shuts, and shuts and no one opens":

8 "I know your works. See, I have set before you an open door, and no one can shut it; for you have a little strength, have kept My word, and have not denied My name.

9 "Indeed I will make those of the synagogue of Satan, who say they are Jews and are not, but lie—indeed I will make them come and worship before your feet, and to know that I have loved you.

10 "Because you have kept My command to persevere, I also will keep you from the hour of trial which shall come upon the whole world, to test those who dwell on the earth.

11 "Behold, I am coming quickly! Hold fast what you have, that no one may take your crown.

12 "He who overcomes, I will make him a pillar in the temple of My God, and he shall go out no more. I will write on him the name of My God and the name of the city of My God, the New Jerusalem, which comes down out of heaven from My God. And I will write on him my new name.

13 "He who has an ear, let him hear what the Spirit says to the churches.'"

For this church, the Philadelphians, Jesus offers only praise for their faithfulness and their perseverance. Apparently, this body had remained consistent in their walk, and had not fallen away into sin or mediocrity. We might say that this simple description defines the nature of the Bride of Christ for whom Jesus is returning. This is the state to which all believers must aspire. It does not take superhuman effort to achieve this—Jesus says that this group of believers had only "a little strength" (verse 8). But the key is consistency. They stayed on track and remained focused on their walk with God, even when their circumstances made it difficult to do so. Tribulation—small or great—provides us no excuse to compromise, a point that is especially crucial for the Last Days Church.

In verse 9, we encounter a concept that Jesus mentioned in an earlier letter, as well—the second letter, to the Church in Smyrna.[69] He promises strong correction for a "synagogue of Satan" that is comprised of people "who say they are Jews and are not" (verse 9). During the first decades of Christianity, Christians—who were, after all, simply Jews (or Gentile converts) who had recognized Jesus of Nazareth as the promised Jewish Messiah—were in many instances allowed to present the Christian message in traditional (non-Christian) Jewish synagogues. Indeed, Jesus Himself often taught there, as did the Apostles, as the Gospels and the Book of Acts bear out.[70] Of course, extreme opposition—and sometimes violent persecution—by some Jews was typically encountered. But generally speaking, Christians were tolerated in Jewish houses of worship. But in A.D. 80—just a few years before John penned the Book of Revelation—that changed. Christians were officially banned from entering any synagogue by the Jewish religious authorities.[71] It is almost certainly these—the scribes and Pharisees who sought to quash Christianity—to whom Jesus is referring when He uses the

---

[69] Revelation 2:9
[70] Examples: Matthew 4:23, 9:35, 12:9, 13:54; John 18:20; Acts 9:20, 13:5, 14:1, 18:26, 19:8
[71] *The Apocalypse of John*, Charles C. Torrey (1958; Yale University Press)

term "synagogue of Satan." Even during His earthly ministry, it was this group who posed the greatest opposition to Jesus, and it was they who provoked the Romans to crucify Him. In his Gospel, John records a particularly heated exchange between the Pharisees and Jesus (John 8:39-44):

> 39 They answered and said to Him, "Abraham is our father." Jesus said to them, "If you were Abraham's children, you would do the works of Abraham.
> 40 "But now you seek to kill Me, a Man who has told you the truth which I heard from God. Abraham did not do this.
> 41 "You do the deeds of your father." Then they said to Him, "We were not born of fornication; we have one Father—God."
> 42 Jesus said to them, "If God were your Father, you would love Me, for I proceeded forth and came from God; nor have I come of Myself, but He sent Me.
> 43 "Why do you not understand My speech? Because you are not able to listen to My word.
> 44 "You are of your father the devil, and the desires of your father you want to do. He was a murderer from the beginning, and does not stand in the truth, because there is no truth in him. When he speaks a lie, he speaks from his own resources, for he is a liar and the father of it."

Here, Jesus confronts the Jewish religious leaders who violently oppose Him, and He states that because of this—because they "seek to kill (Him)" (verse 40)—they are not really Jews: "If you were Abraham's children, you would do the works of Abraham" (verse 39). Instead, Jesus says, these Pharisees "are of (their) father the devil" (verse 44). This lines up perfectly with Jesus' words in our Revelation letters: "the synagogue of Satan, who say they are Jews and are not" (Revelation 2:9 and verse 9 of our current passage). This highlights for us a particularly nefarious tactic of the enemy that he has been using against God's people—those of the Old Covenant and those of the New Covenant—from the very beginning: inciting both groups to hate and to persecute one another. As we discussed at length in Chapter 5 of this book,[72] God's ultimate intent is to bring Jews and Christians together as the New Jerusalem, the Bride of Christ. And Satan has, in an attempt to frustrate God's plan, been driving a spirit of anti-Christianity on one side and a spirit of anti-Semitism on the other from the very start. Those Jews and Christians who surrender to this are only playing into Satan's hand. In fact, just as Jesus plainly states that Jews who despise and persecute Christians are not really Jews at all, can we not likewise say that Christians who despise and persecute Jews are not really Christians? At present, we may not see eye-to-eye on the true identity of the Messiah, but we are both awaiting the same One. And, in the end, as the Apostle Paul tells us, we will come into full agreement. The Jews will at last recognize Jesus of Nazareth as God's promised Savior. Let's look again at Paul's words in Romans 11:25-27 (emphasis and bracketed comments mine):

> 25 For I do not desire, brethren, that you should be ignorant of this mystery, lest you should be wise in your own opinion, that blindness in part has happened to Israel until the fullness of the Gentiles has come in.
> 26 *And so all Israel will be saved,* as it is written: "The Deliverer [Messiah] will come out of Zion, and He will turn away ungodliness from Jacob [the Jews];
> 27 For this is My covenant with them, when I take away their sins."

In the meantime—while we await the day when Jews and Christians at last come together in Christ—it behooves us to love, support, and respect one another. In the great spiritual war that defines the history of mankind in this world, we are truly on the same side. We are, all of us, God's Chosen People.

In Chapter 5 of this book,[73] we briefly examined the true meaning of Jesus' promise in verse 10 of our current passage: "Because you have kept My command to persevere, I also will keep you from the

---

[72] Chapter 5 "The Pre-Tribulation Rapture"; section "Church Not Mentioned During Depiction of Tribulation in Book of Revelation"
[73] Chapter 5 "The Pre-Tribulation Rapture"; section "The 'Loving Father' Argument"

hour of trial which shall come upon the whole world, to test those who dwell on the earth." As we discussed, this statement is often pointed to as evidence of a Pre-Tribulation Rapture. That is, Jesus assures us that He will keep us from the "hour of trial," a term that some scholars believe refers to the seven-year Great Tribulation. Thus, the argument goes, Jesus is promising us that He will rescue us from Earth before that period of time begins. This term does not appear anywhere else in Scripture, however. So, in order to analyze it—to determine what Jesus really means by "hour of trial"—we must break it down. The word "trial" in singular form (as it is here) appears only six other times in the Bible, and never in the context of the End Times. It therefore *could* refer to the Great Tribulation in our Revelation verse, or it could mean something else. The word "hour" sheds a bit more light on the subject: This word appears 89 times in Scripture, and in virtually every instance it refers to a brief period of time, from literally one hour (most common meaning) to some unspecified, but in any event short, time span (as opposed to a long period such as the seven-year Tribulation). John uses the word "hour" only one other time in the context of Revelation's Seven Letters, and, as we've seen, it plainly refers to a very brief period of time, a singular moment: in the letter just prior to this one (to the church in Sardis), Jesus warned: "Therefore if you will not watch, I will come upon you as a thief, and you will not know what *hour* I will come upon you" (Revelation 3:3). As we discussed, the "hour" that Jesus is referring to here is the moment of His Second Coming—His return to Earth—at the end of the Great Tribulation. It seems logical to surmise, then, that the "hour" that He mentions in our current passage, the letter to the Philadelphians, is referring to precisely the same event: a moment that, for the unrighteous, will indeed be one of severe trial. It seems clear—Revelation 3:10 does not constitute a promise that we will be whisked away to Heaven before the seven-year Great Tribulation begins, but rather that we will be spared from the wrath and judgment that accompany our Lord's return at its end.

Revelation 3:14-3:22 ~ The Seventh Letter: The Lukewarm Church

14 "And to the angel of the church of the Laodiceans write, 'These things says the Amen, the Faithful and True Witness, the Beginning of the creation of God:

15 "I know your works, that you are neither cold nor hot. I could wish you were cold or hot.

16 "So then, because you are lukewarm, and neither cold nor hot, I will vomit you out of My mouth.

17 "Because you say, 'I am rich, have become wealthy, and have need of nothing'—and do not know that you are wretched, miserable, poor, blind, and naked—

18 "I counsel you to buy from Me gold refined in the fire, that you may be rich; and white garments, that you may be clothed, that the shame of your nakedness may not be revealed; and anoint your eyes with eye salve, that you may see.

19 "As many as I love, I rebuke and chasten. Therefore be zealous and repent.

20 "Behold, I stand at the door and knock. If anyone hears My voice and opens the door, I will come in to him and dine with him, and he with Me.

21 "To him who overcomes I will grant to sit with Me on My throne, as I also overcame and sat down with My Father on His throne.

22 "He who has an ear, let him hear what the Spirit says to the churches."'"

And so we arrive at the last letter, the one that according to the "Church ages" theory represents our generation, the modern Church. Supposedly, many Christians in our time have come to be comfortable enough in their material well-being that they have become mediocre—lukewarm—in their walk with God. But this is by no means a new phenomenon—we can safely assume that this tendency existed even in John's time. It certainly did in the case of the particular body to which he is conveying Jesus' words here, the church in Laodicea. In fact, Jesus, during His earthly ministry, had issued a warning to John and the others about the pitfall of trusting in one's own material wealth (Mark 10:23-27):

23 Then Jesus looked around and said to His disciples, "How hard it is for those who have riches to enter the kingdom of God!"
24 And the disciples were astonished at His words. But Jesus answered again and said to them, "Children, how hard it is for those who trust in riches to enter the kingdom of God!
25 "It is easier for a camel to go through the eye of a needle than for a rich man to enter the kingdom of God."
26 And they were greatly astonished, saying among themselves, "Who then can be saved?"
27 But Jesus looked at them and said, "With men it is impossible, but not with God; for with God all things are possible."

Here, Jesus is describing the same condition that He associates with the Laodiceans in our current Revelation letter. But there is no hint that this temptation—to rely on one's own resources and abilities—posed less of a challenge to believers in that time than to Christians in our time. On the contrary, in verse 26 even the Disciples seem troubled by Jesus' words, which suggests that this was a mindset that even they struggled with. Admittedly, the culture of self-sufficiency and apathy grows stronger as we near the last of the Last Days, particularly in affluent nations like the United States. But this is true of all of the sins that Jesus warns against, throughout the letters to the churches of Revelation chapters 2 and 3.

Of course, we should note that Jesus is not saying here that a financially comfortable person cannot be part of the Kingdom of God—He had friends who were wealthy, such as Jairus, whose daughter He revived from a coma,[74] and Joseph of Arimathea, a wealthy Pharisee who donated a family tomb for Jesus' burial[75] (likely without realizing that Jesus would only need it for a few days). Jesus is simply warning that the Christian walk can be particularly difficult for such an individual, as personal wealth may lead to such things as selfishness and independence from God, traits that are antithetical to Christianity. In other words, while hard times tend to refine the true believer and make him pure, lack of

---

[74] Mark 5:35-43
[75] Luke 23:50—56

hardship can easily have the opposite effect. This is the theme of all seven letters, as we've seen, and, again, is much more compatible with our notion that God is not averse to His people experiencing trials and tribulations—it is such times that make us strong in our faith in Him. Like the gold that Jesus instructs us to buy from Him in our current letter, it is "fire"—not comfort and ease—that refines us (verse 18). And it is those of us who, at His return, have overcome—who have endured to the end, who have been purified, whose garments are white (verse 18)—to whom Jesus "will grant to sit with [Him] on [His] throne" (verse 21); that is, to rule and reign with Him for a thousand years in the earthly Kingdom that is to come.

The Seven Letters to the Seven Churches of Revelation—messages to us, to the Last Days Body of Christ—are unanimous in their imperative. Stay on track with God and remain consistent in our walk with Him, or be in danger of suffering the consequences that the world will face when His Son returns. The clue as how to accomplish this is found in the very symbolism used to depict the Seven Churches. They are presented as "seven golden lampstands,"[76] which is a picture of the seven-branched candelabra—the golden Menorah—that once stood just outside the veil of the Holy of Holies in the Tabernacle and the First and Second Temples. The Menorah symbolized the function of the Holy Spirit: as long as it was continuously replenished with oil, its flames burned brightly. Likewise, as long as we are continually filled with the anointing of the Holy Spirit, our lamps will shine and we will be a light to the whole world.[77]

The reward for this—for remaining filled and persevering to the end, no matter how formidable the circumstances between now and then—will be great.

---

[76] Revelation 1:20
[77] Matthew 5:14-16; see also Matthew 25:1-13

Chapter 9

John Prepared to Receive the Prophecy

John's vision began in Revelation chapter 1 with, appropriately, an encounter with Jesus, whom John describes in His present glorified state. Chapters 2 and 3 subsequently presented a message that is ultimately meant to prepare us, the last generation of God's people, the Last Days Body of Christ, for the times that we are destined to face. Chapter 4 in effect initiates the prophecy that will describe this period. It begins as follows:

Revelation 4:1 ~ John Summoned to Heaven

1 After these things I looked, and behold, a door standing open in heaven. And the first voice which I heard was like a trumpet speaking with me, saying, "Come up here, and I will show you things which must take place after this."

As we studied in Chapter 5 of this book[78], this verse is popular among many Pre-Tribulation Rapture proponents, who claim that

---

[78] See Chapter 5 "The Pre-Tribulation Rapture"; section "Rapture Depicted Prior to Great Tribulation in Book of Revelation"

the incident described is a symbolic depiction of the Rapture of the Church. We've already established the weakness of this position. Simply stated, John's location changes several times as he is shown the prophecy in Revelation, and never does this coincide with a reasonable assumption about the location of the Church during the Last Days, according to anyone's model. In fact, only one element of this verse might relate it to our primary Rapture scriptures: the trumpet. But there is a notable distinction between this trumpet and the trumpet in our Rapture passages. Let's review 1 Thessalonians 4:16:

> 16 For the Lord Himself will descend from heaven with a shout, with the voice of an archangel, and with the trumpet of God. And the dead in Christ will rise first.

And Matthew 24:31:

> 31 "And He will send His angels with a great sound of a trumpet, and they will gather together His elect from the four winds, from one end of heaven to the other.

In these verses, we are told that Jesus' return will be accompanied by "the trumpet of God" and "a great sound of a trumpet." Both of these suggest that a *literal* trumpet of some kind is involved. But in verse 1 of our Revelation passage, John is not suggesting a literal trumpet at all—rather, he conveys that he heard a voice that was "*like* a trumpet," just as in Revelation 1:10 when he first encounters Jesus (emphasis mine):

> 10 I was in the Spirit on the Lord's Day, and I heard behind me a loud voice, *as of* a trumpet...

This may seem a small grammatical point, but there is a significant difference between a noun ("trumpet") and a simile ("like a trumpet" or "as of a trumpet"). Of course, all of this splitting of hairs will have seemed unnecessary when we find the Rapture given proper treatment—described quite extensively, in fact—later in Revelation; depicted, as we should by now expect, not before, but at the end of the Great Tribulation.

Once Jesus calls John up to Heaven, which is the vantage point from which he'll be shown much of the vision of the Great Tribulation, he finds himself in the throne room of God, which he describes for us in wonderful—and, of course, largely symbolic—detail:

Revelation 4:2-4:11 ~ The Throne Room Described

2   Immediately I was in the Spirit; and behold, a throne set in heaven, and One sat on the throne.
3   And He who sat there was like a jasper and a sardius stone in appearance; and there was a rainbow around the throne, in appearance like an emerald.
4   Around the throne were twenty-four thrones, and on the thrones I saw twenty-four elders sitting, clothed in white robes; and they had crowns of gold on their heads.
5   And from the throne proceeded lightnings, thunderings, and voices. Seven lamps of fire were burning before the throne, which are the seven Spirits of God.
6   Before the throne there was a sea of glass, like crystal. And in the midst of the throne, and around the throne, were four living creatures full of eyes in front and in back.
7   The first living creature was like a lion, the second living creature like a calf, the third living creature had a face like a man, and the fourth living creature was like a flying eagle.
8   The four living creatures, each having six wings, were full of eyes around and within. And they do not rest day or night, saying: "Holy, holy, holy, Lord God Almighty, who was and is and is to come!"
9   Whenever the living creatures give glory and honor and thanks to Him who sits on the throne, who lives forever and ever,
10 the twenty-four elders fall down before Him who sits on the throne and worship Him who lives forever and ever, and cast their crowns before the throne, saying:
11 "You are worthy, O Lord, to receive glory and honor and power; for You created all things, and by Your will they exist and were created."

Here, John gives us a fantastic portrayal of the dwelling place of the Almighty. He describes God using rich imagery that is meant to convey His holiness, glory, and omnipotence. There are also several entities described who are in God's presence and engaged in continuous worship of Him. These all are mentioned several times in Revelation and are worth brief examination here. As promised, we won't spend too much time attempting to understand every minute detail in Revelation. However, we also don't want to be too neglectful in this regard, as this could cause us to miss some important information, which, in turn, could weaken the veracity our overall interpretation of this book. Every aspect of Revelation contributes to its total message, so we'll devote at least some time and effort to its more substantial points.

Verse 4 describes twenty-four elders, arrayed in white and wearing gold crowns, sitting on twenty-four thrones. Some Pre-Tribulation Rapture proponents posit that these elders represent the raptured Church, but you'll recall in Chapter 5 of this book that we identified these individuals as the twelve apostles of Jesus and representatives of the twelve tribes of Israel, perhaps the fathers of those tribes, Jacob's twelve sons. This seems by far the soundest interpretation. The word "elder" appears more than two hundred times in the Bible, and in all cases (where it forms a noun) it is used to describe specific persons of the highest level of human authority, most commonly in the context of God's people. So, John here is most likely describing a select group of individuals who have achieved a patriarchal role over the entire Church. You'll recall that Jesus' Disciples petitioned Him for this station in Mark 10:35-45, and that Jesus acknowledged that this would be granted to them.[79] Indeed, John, the author of Revelation, introduces himself as "The Elder" in two of his three epistles (see the opening verses of 2 John and 3 John). Most compelling of all, Jesus, while speaking to His Disciples, states in no uncertain terms that John and his brethren would be occupying, alongside His, twelve thrones (Matthew 19:28):

---

[79] See Chapter 5 "The Pre-Tribulation Rapture"; section "Church Not Mentioned During Depiction of Tribulation in Book of Revelation"

> 28 So Jesus said to them, "Assuredly I say to you, that in the regeneration, when the Son of Man sits on the throne of His glory, you who have followed Me will also sit on twelve thrones, judging the twelve tribes of Israel."

The idea that in his vision in Revelation John might be seeing himself among the elders in God's throne room may seem a bit bizarre, but remember that he is seeing himself in the future and in glorified form. I suspect, though, that he recognizes himself. In any event, we can be confident that John and the other Disciples account for twelve of the twenty-four elders depicted in our current passage. As for the other twelve, recall John's continuing emphasis on the duality of Old Testament Israel and the New Testament Body of Christ throughout the Book of Revelation. If such a duality exists, it is only fair to assume that twelve representatives of the Old Covenant will join those of the New in judging "the twelve tribes of Israel," a reference to the people of God as a whole—Jews and Christians alike (keeping in mind that, as we've seen, Jews *en masse* are going to enter into the New Covenant in the last of the Last Days[80]).

In verse 5 of our Revelation passage, John mentions another group of entities who are in God's presence in the throne room, "the seven Spirits of God." You may recall that John introduced us to the term "seven Spirits" in Revelation 1:4. We avoided spending time trying to decipher it at that point, but we now have enough information to make an educated guess about what—or, more precisely, who—John is describing. In Revelation 3:1, the fifth church letter's introduction, John coupled these seven Spirits with "the seven stars." In his introduction to the seven letters, he explained that these seven stars represent "the angels of the seven churches" (Revelation 1:20). In that same passage, he coupled the seven stars with the "seven golden lampstands," identified as the churches themselves. This seems to correlate the seven Spirits and the seven lampstands, and, sure enough, in our current verse, John confirms this connection: "Seven lamps of fire were burning before the throne, *which are* the seven Spirits of God" (emphasis mine). So, the seven lamps (or lampstands) are a metaphor for the Seven

---

[80] See Chapter 7 "The Introduction"; section "Revelation 1:4–1:8 ~ Salutations"

Churches *and* for the seven Spirits. We've already established that the Seven Churches are in turn a metaphor for the Church as a whole, so it seems plausible that the seven Spirits are likewise a metaphor for some spiritual entity that is very closely linked to the Church. Who might this be? Our best first guess, of course, would be the Holy Spirit... but how do we reconcile John's vision of "*seven* Spirits" with just *one* Holy Spirit? For starters, let's remind ourselves that John's text is highly symbolic, and it often draws on Old (and sometimes New) Testament imagery to formulate depictions of persons, places, and things. So, one Holy Spirit symbolized by seven Spirits should not be unduly difficult for us to accept. That said, let's explore further to see if we can substantiate this notion.

Again, in our current passage, the "seven lamps (or lampstands)" are equated to "the seven Spirits of God" (verse 5). In the last chapter[81], we saw that the seven lampstands are a picture of the Menorah—the seven-branched candelabra—that symbolized the presence of the Spirit of God in the Tabernacle and Temples.[82] The Prophet Zechariah confirms this connection between the Menorah and the Holy Spirit in Zechariah 4:1-2, 5-6; bracketed comments mine):

1   Now the angel who talked with me came back and wakened me, as a man who is wakened out of his sleep.
2   And he said to me, "What do you see?" So I said, "I am looking, and there is a lampstand of solid gold with a bowl on top of it, and on the stand seven lamps with seven pipes to the seven lamps [the Menorah]."

5   Then the angel who talked with me answered and said to me, "Do you not know what these are?" And I said, "No, my lord."

---

[81] See Chapter 8 "The Letters to the Seven Churches"; section "Revelation 3:14-3:22 ~ The Seventh Letter: The Lukewarm Church"
[82] See Chapter 8 "The Letters to the Seven Churches"; section "Revelation 3:14-3:22 ~ The Seventh Letter: The Lukewarm Church"

> 6 So he answered and said to me: "This is the word of the Lord to Zerubbabel: 'Not by might nor by power, but by My Spirit [the Holy Spirit],' says the Lord of hosts."

In this passage, Zechariah is shown a Menorah in a vision (verse 2), and then the angel who is showing him this vision explains that this is a symbol of the Holy Spirit (verse 6). So, if in John's vision the seven lampstands are equivalent to the seven Spirits and in Zechariah's the seven lampstands are analogous to the Holy Spirit, our idea that the seven Spirits are simply a symbol of the Holy Spirit is greatly strengthened. Still more evidence for this is found in the Book of Revelation itself. In Revelation's salutations, we read (Revelation 1:4-5a):

> 4 John, to the seven churches which are in Asia: Grace to you and peace from Him who is and who was and who is to come, and from the seven Spirits who are before His throne,
> 5 and from Jesus Christ, the faithful witness, the firstborn from the dead, and the ruler over the kings of the earth...

Notice who Revelation's greetings to the "seven churches" (verse 4) are from:

1. "Him who is and who was and who is to come" (verse 4)
2. "the seven Spirits who are before His throne" (verse 4)
3. "Jesus Christ, the faithful witness" (verse 5)

In this, the presentation of Revelation's true source of authorship, we should not expect to find sandwiched between God and Jesus – our divine Creator(s) – some obscure group of otherwise unidentifiable created spiritual beings. Simply put, the three entities in John's list represent the whole of the Godhead, the Holy Trinity: God, the Holy Spirit, and Jesus. Later, in Revelation 5:6, we find the seven Spirits again inextricably linked to Christ (bracketed comment mine):

> 6 And I looked, and behold, in the midst of the throne and of the four living creatures, and in the midst of the elders, stood a Lamb as though it had been slain [Jesus Christ],

having seven horns and seven eyes, which are the seven Spirits of God sent out into all the earth.

Here, two metaphors are presented for the seven Spirits: "seven horns" and "seven eyes". These denote total power and complete knowledge, two attributes that can only belong to a divine being like the Holy Spirit.

Let's look at one final piece of evidence that the seven Spirits seen by John in the throne room of God indeed represent the Holy Spirit. Most of us are familiar with the story of Jesus being baptized by His cousin, John the Baptist, in preparation for His earthly ministry, and many of us will recall the highlight of this event (Matthew 3:16-17):

> 16 When He had been baptized, Jesus came up immediately from the water; and behold, the heavens were opened to Him, and He saw the Spirit of God descending like a dove and alighting upon Him.
> 17 And suddenly a voice came from heaven, saying, "This is My beloved Son, in whom I am well pleased."

This—the alighting of the Holy Spirit upon the coming Messiah—had been prophesied by the Prophet Isaiah some 700 years earlier (Isaiah 11:1-2):

> 1 There shall come forth a Rod from the stem of Jesse, and a Branch shall grow out of his roots.
> 2 The Spirit of the Lord shall rest upon Him, the Spirit of wisdom and understanding, the Spirit of counsel and might, the Spirit of knowledge and of the fear of the Lord.

Matthew's account makes it plain that there was only one Spirit—the Holy Spirit—who alighted upon Jesus, but notice that Isaiah's wording seems to imply multiple Spirits. And, sure enough, if we count these, we find that the prophet has enumerated precisely seven:

1. The Spirit of the Lord
2. The Spirit of wisdom

3. The Spirit of understanding
4. The Spirit of counsel
5. The Spirit of might
6. The Spirit of knowledge
7. The Spirit of the fear of the Lord

We see, then, that the Holy Spirit is, in fact, comprised of seven distinct functions or offices that may be depicted as several different "Spirits". In effect, *one* Holy Spirit is equal to *seven* Spirits, just as John describes Him in the Book of Revelation.

This analysis may seem complex, but it helps to establish an important point about the Book of Revelation: sometimes in his text John not only uses symbolism but *multiple layers* of symbolism that may span multiple books of the Bible in order to describe a concept that is otherwise rather simple. We should not be intimidated by the strange creatures and events that are presented, a point that we might especially want to embrace as we approach John's next group of beings.

Following his description of the twenty-four elders and the seven Spirits, John tells us that surrounding God's throne are "four living creatures" (verse 6). He then paints a very strange picture of these entities. They have multiple eyes all around and within, each is adorned with six wings, and each has a unique appearance: one like a lion, one a calf, one a man, and one a flying eagle. Verse 9 tells us that these creatures "give glory and honor and thanks" to God. Although their description might seem unnerving, they are obviously welcome in God's throne room. Can these beings possibly be ones that the reader would recognize if all of this were replaced by a straightforward identification? We know that John is speaking in similes: he says that the first creature's appearance is *like* a lion, the second *like* a calf, and so forth. John's description of these "creatures" is purely symbolic. "Full of eyes" indicates unceasing watchfulness, and the creatures' individual descriptions may denote courage, strength, intelligence, and speed. But who are they? To answer this, we must turn to perhaps the strangest of all biblical books, that of the Prophet Ezekiel. Ezekiel himself had a fantastic vision of the future that we'll be referring to many times throughout our study. His book—which records a series of visions conveyed to him by God—begins as follows (Ezekiel 1:1-14):

1. Now it came to pass in the thirtieth year, in the fourth month, on the fifth day of the month, as I was among the captives by the River Chebar, that the heavens were opened and I saw visions of God.
2. On the fifth day of the month, which was in the fifth year of King Jehoiachin's captivity,
3. the word of the Lord came expressly to Ezekiel the priest, the son of Buzi, in the land of the Chaldeans by the River Chebar; and the hand of the Lord was upon him there.
4. Then I looked, and behold, a whirlwind was coming out of the north, a great cloud with raging fire engulfing itself; and brightness was all around it and radiating out of its midst like the color of amber, out of the midst of the fire.
5. Also from within it came the likeness of four living creatures. And this was their appearance: they had the likeness of a man.
6. Each one had four faces, and each one had four wings.
7. Their legs were straight, and the soles of their feet were like the soles of calves' feet. They sparkled like the color of burnished bronze.
8. The hands of a man were under their wings on their four sides; and each of the four had faces and wings.
9. Their wings touched one another. The creatures did not turn when they went, but each one went straight forward.
10. As for the likeness of their faces, each had the face of a man; each of the four had the face of a lion on the right side, each of the four had the face of an ox on the left side, and each of the four had the face of an eagle.
11. Thus were their faces. Their wings stretched upward; two wings of each one touched one another, and two covered their bodies.
12. And each one went straight forward; they went wherever the spirit wanted to go, and they did not turn when they went.
13. As for the likeness of the living creatures, their appearance was like burning coals of fire, like the appearance of torches going back and forth among the living creatures. The fire was bright, and out of the fire went lightning.

> 14 And the living creatures ran back and forth, in appearance like a flash of lightning.

And people think that the Book of Revelation is challenging! Ezekiel goes on to describe a scene that is very much like John's description of the throne room of God in our Revelation passage. We are left with the impression that the throne of God itself descended from Heaven to deliver Ezekiel's vision.

The careful reader may immediately notice that John's four living creatures and those of Ezekiel's don't seem to be *exactly* identical, but perhaps we shouldn't get too caught up in the differences. Remember that both men are describing these beings using highly symbolic speech. In both texts there are four of them, they are depicted as "living creatures," they have multiple wings, the various faces (human and otherwise) are mentioned, and they are described in the context of the throne of God; this should provide a satisfactory enough correlation for us to conclude that, at minimum, they are the same *kind* of beings. Which brings us back to our question. Who, or what, are they? Happily, Ezekiel gives us the very simple answer when he describes these entities again later in his vision (Ezekiel 10:9-14, 21-22):

> 9 And when I looked, there were four wheels by the cherubim, one wheel by one cherub and another wheel by each other cherub; the wheels appeared to have the color of a beryl stone.
> 10 As for their appearance, all four looked alike—as it were, a wheel in the middle of a wheel.
> 11 When they went, they went toward any of their four directions; they did not turn aside when they went, but followed in the direction the head was facing. They did not turn aside when they went.
> 12 And their whole body, with their back, their hands, their wings, and the wheels that the four had, were full of eyes all around.
> 13 As for the wheels, they were called in my hearing, "Wheel."
> 14 Each one had four faces: the first face was the face of a cherub, the second face the face of a man, the third the face of a lion, and the fourth the face of an eagle.

21 Each one had four faces and each one four wings, and the likeness of the hands of a man was under their wings.
22 And the likeness of their faces was the same as the faces which I had seen by the River Chebar, their appearance and their persons. They each went straight forward.

Here, Ezekiel deviates a bit even from his own previous description of the four living creatures in Ezekiel chapter 1, but in verse 22 he confirms that he is describing the same beings. Most importantly, he uses a different term for the creatures here, thus revealing to us their true identity. They are "cherubim," a particular class of angels whose sole purpose is to attend on God. One difference worth pointing out between the creatures depicted in Revelation and Ezekiel's creatures is that each of John's has six wings, while Ezekiel's have only four. Isaiah, in his own vision of the throne room of God, has this to offer us (Isaiah 6:1-3; emphasis mine):

1 In the year that King Uzziah died, I saw *the Lord sitting on a throne*, high and lifted up, and the train of His robe filled the temple.
2 Above it stood *seraphim*; each one had *six wings*: with two he covered his face, with two he covered his feet, and with two he flew.
3 And one cried to another and said: "Holy, holy, holy is the Lord of hosts; the whole earth is full of His glory!"

Let's not try too hard to reconcile the visions of the three men—John, Ezekiel, and Isaiah are all describing, in similar enough terms, heavenly beings that attend to God as He sits on His throne. Whatever their specific type—whether cherubim or seraphim (a higher class of angelic being, and with a similar purpose)—the four living creatures of Revelation simply represent a high-ranking order of angels. This may seem a bit of a letdown—that so extraordinary a description can depict something as "ordinary" as angels—but this is an important realization that should comfort us as we endeavor to understand John's vision of the End Times. Again, we are going to encounter many unusual beings and events as we proceed through Revelation, but all of these—if approached soberly—will prove to be well within the realm of the comprehensible.

JOHN PREPARED TO RECEIVE THE PROPHECY

With this—a visit to the very throne room of God—the stage is set for the prophecy portion of John's vision to begin.

SECTION III

The Book of Revelation: The Prelude to the Great Tribulation

Chapter 10

The Scroll with the Seven Seals: Prelude to the Great Tribulation

Some six thousand years ago[83], God breathed His spirit into a being that He'd created called man. His plan was to bring into existence a creature that, unlike all of His previous creation, was capable of loving Him and communing with Him on His level. In other words, He desired not servants nor pets, but children. Like His other creatures, this new being was given a measure of free will, but more importantly—and, potentially, more dangerously—man was granted that special aspect of which God Himself had until that time been the sole possessor: the ability to create. This would be a powerful creature indeed, one that would hopefully choose to remain in the presence—and the will—of God. As we all know, things didn't quite work out that way. Since God is omniscient—He knows all things across all time—we can assume that He knew that man would make the wrong choice when confronted in the Garden of Eden with the temptation to "be like

---

[83] Or perhaps much longer: some estimates place the dawn of human civilization at 12,000 years ago or more; we won't take time to explore this here.

God,"[84] presented by another creature that had made a similarly wrong choice. But before Eve, and then her husband Adam, ever bit into that apple,[85] God had a blueprint for man's redemption and, ultimately, for the redemption of the entire realm over which He'd given him dominion, the planet Earth. This would prove to be a very extravagant plan indeed, involving thousands of years of human history, choices by billions of individuals to either follow God or follow in the footsteps of Adam, and the eventual arrival on Earth of God's only begotten Son[86]—God in the flesh, in a sense—to present Himself a perfect sacrifice so that those who choose rightly can achieve righteousness and salvation, and can regain God's presence and His will. But because inevitably there would be a majority of humans who would choose to serve themselves (or, more precisely, the "god of this world," Satan[87]) rather than their Creator, God's plan also needed to include an ultimate "house-cleaning" on Earth. Man's version of creation must be judged, and when it is it will be found lacking.

A key component of God's plan for final redemption pertains to His system of authority. God granted man dominion over this world, and, generally speaking, He will not supersede our authority here. It is ours to use or to give away, and as a race we gave it away to that tempter, Satan, long ago. Humankind—at least some of us—have been gradually inviting God's authority back into this world since that time, through righteous men that followed Adam; through a nation—Israel—that would, albeit imperfectly and inconsistently, submit to God's Law; and finally through the faith of countless millions in His Son whom God sent in order to allow us to be fully reconciled to Him. But there is a flip side to this. As God works His will back into this world through the obedience of some, those who are perpetuating Satan's opposing plan for this world—also in steady progression since the Garden—continue to slip deeper into lawlessness, moving toward that time when at last all rights and authority will be *legally* stripped from them (according to God's own Law), and from the one whom they follow.

---

[84] Genesis 3:5
[85] Genesis 3:6-7
[86] John 3:16
[87] 2 Corinthians 4:4

But while it's true that God won't bend or break His own Law—He won't, without precise cause, override a being's authority once it's been granted—He has always, and will always, influence people and events toward the destiny that He's predetermined for this planet. We see the hand of God working throughout history, and He will continue to maneuver the world as we know it toward its inevitable end. He does this by every means that are "legally" (again, according to His own Law) at His disposal, ranging from setting choices before individuals to driving entire peoples in particular directions. Indeed, contrary to some popular conceptions about God not violating humans' freedom of choice, He sometimes will impel certain persons, and even nations, toward fulfilling His will without their awareness or consent. At its heart, this is what the Great Tribulation is all about. Ultimately, God is still sovereign, still in control, and His plan is going to come to pass—and come to pass in His timing. Some of the events that comprise the Great Tribulation, as well as those that usher in this period, are by God's own hand; all of the rest nonetheless align perfectly with His plan for the fate of our planet. The ultimate act of lawlessness that will "allow" God to commence His judgment on this world and usher in the Millennial Reign of His Son on this Earth will occur only after God has paved the way.

We may reasonably ask, why the delay? Why has God not yet pushed this world toward its cataclysmic conclusion so that Satan may be deposed, and God's Son, Jesus Christ, inaugurated as the rightful King of this realm? We might speculate that the Church is not yet ready to don the garments of the Bride of Christ, perfect before God, without spot or wrinkle. Conversely, we might assume that the world system has not yet reached its ultimate fallen state, the one that will accommodate its ultimate leader, the Antichrist. But the simplest answer is that, all other considerations aside, God in His great mercy is delaying the end so that as many as possible may be saved before it's too late. The Apostle Peter confirms this notion in his second epistle (2 Peter 3:9):

> 9   The Lord is not slack concerning His promise, as some count slackness, but is longsuffering toward us, not willing

that any should perish but that all should come to repentance.

Whatever the case, remember Paul's words about the coming of the Antichrist in 2 Thessalonians 2:6-8 (bracketed comment mine):

6   And now you know what is restraining, that he [the Antichrist] may be revealed in his own time.
7   For the mystery of lawlessness is already at work; only He who now restrains will do so until He is taken out of the way.
8   And then the lawless one will be revealed, whom the Lord will consume with the breath of His mouth and destroy with the brightness of His coming.

Whoever "He who now restrains" is—there are varied interpretations of this, but I think a safe guess is that this is the Holy Spirit—make no mistake about it: the end will come when God is ready. And it will begin with a scroll, the first page of God's plan for Earth's final redemption.

Revelation 5:1-5:14 ~ God's Decree of Judgment

1   And I saw in the right hand of Him who sat on the throne a scroll written inside and on the back, sealed with seven seals.
2   Then I saw a strong angel proclaiming with a loud voice, "Who is worthy to open the scroll and to loose its seals?"
3   And no one in heaven or on the earth or under the earth was able to open the scroll, or to look at it.
4   So I wept much, because no one was found worthy to open and read the scroll, or to look at it.
5   But one of the elders said to me, "Do not weep. Behold, the Lion of the tribe of Judah, the Root of David, has prevailed to open the scroll and to loose its seven seals."
6   And I looked, and behold, in the midst of the throne and of the four living creatures, and in the midst of the elders, stood a Lamb as though it had been slain, having seven horns and seven eyes, which are the seven Spirits of God sent out into all the earth.

THE SCROLL WITH THE SEVEN SEALS: PRELUDE TO THE GREAT TRIBULATION

7 Then He came and took the scroll out of the right hand of Him who sat on the throne.

8 Now when He had taken the scroll, the four living creatures and the twenty-four elders fell down before the Lamb, each having a harp, and golden bowls full of incense, which are the prayers of the saints.

9 And they sang a new song, saying: "You are worthy to take the scroll, and to open its seals; for You were slain, and have redeemed us to God by Your blood out of every tribe and tongue and people and nation,

10 And have made us kings and priests to our God; and we shall reign on the earth."

11 Then I looked, and I heard the voice of many angels around the throne, the living creatures, and the elders; and the number of them was ten thousand times ten thousand, and thousands of thousands,

12 saying with a loud voice: "Worthy is the Lamb who was slain to receive power and riches and wisdom, and strength and honor and glory and blessing!"

13 And every creature which is in heaven and on the earth and under the earth and such as are in the sea, and all that are in them, I heard saying: "Blessing and honor and glory and power be to Him who sits on the throne, and to the Lamb, forever and ever!"

14 Then the four living creatures said, "Amen!" And the twenty-four elders fell down and worshiped Him who lives forever and ever.

In Revelation chapter 4, as we saw, John found himself in the throne room of God, which he described in awesome detail. We might assume that his depiction revealed the normal state of things there: God is seated on His throne, surrounded by a multitude of beings who are engaged in continuous service to, and worship of, the Creator of all things. But John was summoned to this place not to observe the usual, but to bear witness to an extraordinary period in human history. This period begins in Revelation 5:1. Here, John sees that God is holding in His right hand a scroll, written on the front and the back and sealed with seven seals. This is not unusual in prophetic visions—we find similar depictions of heavenly scrolls in the prophecies of Isaiah, Jeremiah, Ezekiel, and Zechariah.

These scrolls are to denote written law, the immutable dictates of God, to decree His present and future plans. But there is a difference between the scroll that John sees and the ones described by the others. The one in John's vision apparently cannot legally be opened by anyone "in heaven or on the earth or under the earth" (verse 3)—or so it seems at first. This is obviously a very special edict, the most pivotal ever issued by God. Fortunately, as one of the elders tells John, there is, in fact, One who is worthy to open this scroll: Jesus. In this context, Jesus is described as a "Lamb" who "had been slain" (verse 6) and the One who has prevailed (verse 5). These descriptions offer us clues as to why Jesus is the only One in all of God's creation who can legally usher in the events that will bring about the end of this age and restore God's authority over our world. He came into this world as a man, but denied His sin nature and remained obedient to God, achieving an unprecedented level of righteousness. He offered Himself up as a perfect sacrifice to atone for the sins of the rest of us. He overcame death and was resurrected from the dead. And He continues to overcome through us, His Church. God gave full authority over this world to the human race, so only a member of the human race could submit this authority to God—and only if that individual did not first give His authority over to Satan by surrendering to sin. Jesus was the first to accomplish this, and many of the rest of us have followed suit in the centuries since by accepting Jesus' total atonement for our sins and, in turn, recouping our own God-given authority in this world. In a way, all of us as believers are partakers in Jesus' right to unfurl that final scroll.

In verse 7, Jesus takes the Scroll. In it are written the plans to unleash horrific events upon our world. We might therefore expect a less-than-enthusiastic reaction—at least some apprehension—from those present in God's throne room as they brace themselves for what is about to take place. But quite the contrary occurs. The four living creatures and the twenty-four elders begin to sing a "new song" of praise to Jesus, acknowledging His right to take the Scroll, His redemptive power, and His impending reign on Earth. In short order, an immeasurable multitude of angels join in with their own praise of the Lamb. Perhaps this is not so hard to swallow—after all, these beings are all in Heaven, and will have the luxury of watching the terrible events that are to come upon the Earth from a distance. But notice in verse 13 who joins next in the excitement: "every creature" which is "on the earth and under the earth and such as are in the sea." As we read what happens to their realm when the Seven Seals are opened, one by one, we might find it difficult to understand what all the creatures on the Earth are so happy about. But the answer is simple, as Paul explains in Romans 8:18-22:

> 18 For I consider that the sufferings of this present time are not worthy to be compared with the glory which shall be revealed in us.
> 19 For the earnest expectation of the creation eagerly waits for the revealing of the sons of God.
> 20 For the creation was subjected to futility, not willingly, but because of Him who subjected it in hope;
> 21 because the creation itself also will be delivered from the bondage of corruption into the glorious liberty of the children of God.
> 22 For we know that the whole creation groans and labors with birth pangs together until now.

So, the birds and the bees and the fish and the trees all have the right perspective regarding the Great Tribulation. They don't fear it or hope to escape it, but simply embrace it as a necessary step on the path to our planet's ultimate redemption. How much more should we, as the children of God, who presumably know and trust Him, do likewise? Indeed, John implies in verse 8 of our Revelation passage that the "prayers of the saints" are to be in earnest anticipation of the opening of the Scroll. But how many of us pray for the Great Tribulation? In the current mainstream Christian culture, saturated with the Pre-Tribulation Rapture doctrine, most of us long not for God's plan for the end but for our complete exemption from that plan. We pray for the Rapture to come while life is still comfortable. We don't want to be here when the real trouble starts. One major reason for this, of course, is that most believers think that if we are on Earth for the Great Tribulation, we will be subject to all of the horrors of it; that is, that we will suffer alongside all those in rebellion against God for whom His wrath is really intended. As it turns out, however, this is a monumental misconception. God always has, and will again, make provision for the protection of His people, as we will see.

But first, the End must begin...

Revelation 6:1-6:8 ~ The Four Horsemen

1. Now I saw when the Lamb opened one of the seals; and I heard one of the four living creatures saying with a voice like thunder, "Come and see."
2. And I looked, and behold, a white horse. He who sat on it had a bow; and a crown was given to him, and he went out conquering and to conquer.
3. When He opened the second seal, I heard the second living creature saying, "Come and see."
4. Another horse, fiery red, went out. And it was granted to the one who sat on it to take peace from the earth, and that people should kill one another; and there was given to him a great sword.
5. When He opened the third seal, I heard the third living creature say, "Come and see." So I looked, and behold, a black horse, and he who sat on it had a pair of scales in his hand.
6. And I heard a voice in the midst of the four living creatures saying, "A quart of wheat for a denarius, and three quarts of barley for a denarius; and do not harm the oil and the wine."
7. When He opened the fourth seal, I heard the voice of the fourth living creature saying, "Come and see."
8. So I looked, and behold, a pale horse. And the name of him who sat on it was Death, and Hades followed with him. And power was given to them over a fourth of the earth, to kill with sword, with hunger, with death, and by the beasts of the earth.

Welcome to the beginning of the End—sort of. Most scholars align the start of the Great Tribulation with this, the first four seals, which depict what have come to be known as the "Four Horsemen of the Apocalypse." However, this period arguably begins not here, but when God releases His plagues upon the Earth—the first phase of His wrath—with the "Seven Trumpets" that are introduced in Revelation chapter 8. The Four Horsemen, conversely, seem to describe man-made conditions on Earth, which lead up to a precipitating event that prompts the ushering in of the Tribulation period. But before we explore this idea, it will be useful to consider how the period of the Great Tribulation is defined.

Daniel's "70-Weeks Prophecy"

According to Jesus, the end of human history as we know it will be marked by a brief span of time that will include various natural disasters and a treacherous, self-deifying world leader, and which will culminate and conclude with Jesus' return (recall Matthew chapter 24). Others, like John, likewise define the End Times as a set of specific events that will lead up to the collapse of a rebellious world system and usher in the Kingdom of God on Earth. As we'll see, this period begins with a natural catastrophe of immense proportions that sets off a series of events and a set of conditions that pave the way for the Antichrist and his government. This regime, after a time, will begin to fall apart under pressure—from God and, somewhat surprisingly, from the world system itself—and final destruction will come at the climax of the War of Armageddon. Scripture gives the impression that all of this takes place over the course of just a few years, and indeed, though the Bible doesn't explicitly tell us, we have good reason to believe that the Great Tribulation comprises a period of approximately seven calendar years. This generally held notion is derived from a vision given to the Prophet Daniel by the Archangel Gabriel (Daniel 9:24-27):

> 24 "Seventy weeks are determined for your people and for your holy city, to finish the transgression, to make an end of sins, to make reconciliation for iniquity, to bring in everlasting righteousness, to seal up vision and prophecy, and to anoint the Most Holy.
> 25 "Know therefore and understand, that from the going forth of the command to restore and build Jerusalem until Messiah the Prince, there shall be seven weeks and sixty-two weeks; the street shall be built again, and the wall, even in troublesome times.

26 "And after the sixty-two weeks Messiah shall be cut off, but not for Himself; and the people of the prince who is to come shall destroy the city and the sanctuary. The end of it shall be with a flood, and till the end of the war desolations are determined.

27 "Then he shall confirm a covenant with many for one week; but in the middle of the week he shall bring an end to sacrifice and offering. And on the wing of abominations shall be one who makes desolate, even until the consummation, which is determined, is poured out on the desolate."

Most scholars would agree that this—Daniel's so-called "70-weeks prophecy"—is among the most challenging in Scripture. To begin to understand this prophecy, we need first to establish its context. In 586 B.C., the Babylonians had invaded Jerusalem. They sacked and burned the city and destroyed the Holy Temple (the first of the two Jewish Temples that occupied a precise spot on Jerusalem's Temple Mount). The Babylonians had also taken many of the surviving Jews into captivity in their own country. Daniel was among these.

For nearly 50 years, the Jews were forbidden to return to their homeland. Then in 538 B.C., King Cyrus of Persia conquered the Babylonian Empire,[88] and one of his first acts was to issue a decree that allowed the Jews to return to the land of Israel. By the time that Gabriel conveyed the above prophecy to Daniel ("In the first year of Darius the son of Ahasuerus";[89] that is, 522 B.C.[90]), the Jews had been in the process of returning to Israel under Cyrus' decree for some 16 years. Temple reconstruction had begun, but Jerusalem remained in ruins: the Jews had not yet received official permission to rebuild their Holy City.

---

[88] *Zarathustra, Philo, the Achaemenids and Israel*, Lawrence Heyworth Mills (1906; Open Court Publishing Company)
[89] Daniel 9:1
[90] *History Of Darius The Great*, Jacob Abbott (2012; Nabu Press)

Then one day in 446 B.C., Artaxerxes I (who had become ruler of the Persian Empire in 465 B.C.[91]) noticed that the countenance of his royal cupbearer, a Jew named Nehemiah, was down. Nehemiah explained that his heart ached to see the city of his fathers restored and he requested that the king send him to his homeland to begin the project. Artaxerxes agreed and issued a decree to rebuild the city of Jerusalem and the wall that surrounded it. And so we are provided a clear point of reference in our prophecy, which tells us that the clock will start ticking "from the going forth of the command to restore and build Jerusalem," even making reference to the details of Nehemiah's task (verse 25; bracketed comments mine): "the street [the Tyropoeon Valley street, the main street of Jerusalem that ran from the city's northernmost gate, along the base of the Temple Mount's western wall, and south through what is today known as the City of David to the city's southernmost gate[92]] shall be built again, and the wall [the wall that surrounded the ancient city of Jerusalem]."

Daniel's prophecy tells us that from this year—446 B.C., the year of Artaxerxes' decree—there will be "seven weeks and sixty-two weeks...until Messiah the Prince" (verse 25). As Christians, we should interpret this to mean that from the time that the decree to rebuild Jerusalem was issued there would be sixty-nine "weeks"—some sort of unit of time, obviously—until Jesus would be "officially" revealed as the Messiah.

To test this, our next task must be to determine what the Archangel Gabriel meant by "weeks." The Hebrew word for "weeks" in this passage is *shabuah*, which translates as "seven" and indicates a period of either seven days or seven years.[93] Most scholars agree that Daniel is using this word in the latter sense (seven years), and this certainly places events on a timescale closer to what we would expect given the details of the prophecy. But if this is the case, why didn't Gabriel just convey the prophecy in terms of years? We

---

[91] *History of the Persian Empire*, A.T. Olmstead (1959; University Of Chicago Press)
[92] *The Quest: Revealing the Temple Mount in Jerusalem*, Leen Ritmeyer (2012; Carta)
[93] *Enhanced Strong's Lexicon*, James Strong (1996; Woodside Bible Fellowship)

might guess that by "weeks" Gabriel doesn't mean to indicate seven-year blocks of time by our normal reckoning—but rather a time period similar to seven years, perhaps, but different somehow.

This brings us to the somewhat challenging concept of a "prophetic year." Often in Biblical prophecy, we encounter a term that seems to indicate a period of years, but when we run the numbers (by cross-referencing, where possible, other descriptions of the same period expressed in other terms, like months or days), we find that things don't quite add up. A "year" in a prophetic context doesn't seem to equal precisely 365 days. Our best examples of this can be found in the Bible's ultimate prophetic text, the Book of Revelation. For instance, in Revelation chapter 11, which describes two individuals (referred to as the "Two Witnesses") who prophesy during the first half of the Great Tribulation (as we'll see later in our study), we read (Revelation 11:2b; bracketed comment mine):

> 2 "...And they [Gentiles] will tread the holy city underfoot for forty-two months."

"Forty-two months," of course, equals exactly three-and-a-half years (42 months divided by a 12-month year equals 3.5). But in the next verse, wherein the Archangel Gabriel (the same Gabriel who prophesied to Daniel in our current passage) describes for John another detail of this same time period, we read (Revelation 11:3):

> 3 "And I will give power to my two witnesses, and they will prophesy one thousand two hundred and sixty days, clothed in sackcloth."

"One thousand two hundred and sixty days" sounds close to three-and-a-half years, but when we check this, we discover that the number is slightly off: 1,260 days equals only 3.45 years by our normal reckoning (1,260 days divided by a 365-day year equals 3.45), while 3.5 (three-and-a-half) years multiplied by a 365-day year actually comes to about 1,277 days. Why the disparity? A good approach to figuring out the answer might begin with figuring out what kind of a year Gabriel's "one thousand two hundred and sixty days" produces. Again, we know from verse 2 above (which specifies 42 months) that this number must equal three-and-a-half of these

THE SCROLL WITH THE SEVEN SEALS: PRELUDE TO THE GREAT TRIBULATION

"years." This said, we find that 1,260 days produces a 360-day "year": 1,260 divided by 3.5 equals 360. In turn, a "prophetic month" must be equal to 30 days; and, sure enough, 42 months multiplied by 30 days per month equals 1,260 days, which perfectly reconciles the above two verses from Revelation chapter 11. And so, we discover that a prophetic year—the kind that is used in apocalyptic literature like the Book of Daniel and the Book of Revelation—consists not of 365 days (like a "normal" calendar year) but 360 days.

Looking further in Revelation, we find another example of the prophetic year concept. Revelation chapter 12 describes what is often referred to as the "Woman in the Wilderness." This story comprises a somewhat symbolic depiction of the Holy Spirit hiding and protecting Jews (and the Antichrist making war against both Jews and Christians) during the last half of the Great Tribulation. In Revelation 12:6, we read:

> 6 Then the woman fled into the wilderness, where she has a place prepared by God, that they should feed her there one thousand two hundred and sixty days.

Here again, we see the time period in question specified as "one thousand two hundred and sixty days." Later in the same passage we read (Revelation 12:14):

> 14 But the woman was given two wings of a great eagle, that she might fly into the wilderness to her place, where she is nourished for a time and times and half a time, from the presence of the serpent.

In this verse, we encounter another unusual term—"times"—that obviously denotes a specific period of time, and, from the context, seems to suggest years ("a time and times and half a time" is typically interpreted as a year, two years and half a year; that is, three-and-a-half years). But, like "weeks" in our Daniel prophecy, the word "years" is not used here, and for the same reason: A year by our normal reckoning (that is, a 365-day time period) is not what's meant. And here again (as in our previous Revelation passage), we are, fortunately, given the benefit of a key of sorts to unlock the meaning of "times": A corresponding description of the same time period is given in days (verse 6). Running a similar calculation as above, we confirm our conclusion: A prophetic year consists of 360 days.

So, now that we understand what a prophetic year is—which will, of course, help us tremendously in deciphering prophecy wherever this time period is specified—we might ask, where did this concept come from? Is this—a 360-day year—completely arbitrary? Maybe not. As the reader probably knows, one year by our normal reckoning (according to the calendar that is most commonly used throughout the world today, the Gregorian calendar) is equal to 365 days. This is approximately equal to the number of days that it takes for the Earth to complete one orbit around the Sun; the more precise number is 365.25 days (which is why our calendar requires occasional adjustments, such as leap years). A solar month, then, is equal to approximately 30.44 days (one solar year [365.25 days] divided by twelve months). However, a lunar month—that is, the time that it takes for the moon to complete one full cycle from new moon to full moon and back again—is equal to approximately 29.53 days. Interestingly, when we add a solar month and lunar month and then divide the sum by two, we find that an "average month"—we might say, at the risk of sounding overly poetic, the perfect harmony between sun and moon—is equal to 29.99 days, almost precisely our prophetic month of 30 days. Of course, extrapolating this (by adding our solar year of 365.25 days to a "lunar year" of 354.37 days and dividing the sum by two), we arrive at our prophetic year of 360 days (359.81 days rounded up).

Now that we know how to count—we now understand that one "week" in Daniel's prophecy is equal to 2,520 days (7 prophetic years multiplied by 360 days)—let's run the numbers and see if we find anything interesting. To begin with, let's figure out the exact date that we're counting from. Again, the clock in Daniel's prophecy started ticking when Artaxerxes I, king of the Persian Empire, issued the decree to rebuild the city of Jerusalem. The Book of Nehemiah tells us the exact day on which this took place (Nehemiah 2:1a):

THE SCROLL WITH THE SEVEN SEALS: PRELUDE TO THE GREAT TRIBULATION

1   And it came to pass in the month of Nisan, in the twentieth year of King Artaxerxes...

In Hebrew writing, whenever the day of the month is omitted, as we see here, the first day of the month is typically meant. As mentioned, the twentieth year of Artaxerxes' reign was 446 B.C. So, the decree to rebuild Jerusalem was issued on the first day of Nisan, 446 B.C. Many attempts have been made in recent times to determine which date this corresponds to on the Gregorian calendar,[94] but we won't try this here, for two reasons: First, Hebrew dates in Biblical times were influenced by such things as whether or not the skies over Jerusalem were cloudy on a particular night (that is, whether or not the moon in a particular phase was visible)[95]— things for which there is no historical record. So, it simply is not feasible to determine when Nisan 1 occurred in 446 B.C. Second, since we're actually dealing with a hybrid date—our month and day are Hebrew, but the year is Gregorian—we're in a good enough position as-is to run our numbers and see if we find anything interesting (you'll see what I mean in a moment).

Let's begin. Since, as we'll see, we're still awaiting the last week of Daniel's 70-weeks prophecy—the seven-year Great Tribulation—we'll only be counting from the beginning of Daniel's first week to the end of his 69th week. Our first step is to figure out how many days this period spans, so let's multiply 69 prophetic weeks times 7 (since there are 7 prophetic years in one prophetic week). This gives us a total of 483 prophetic years. Now let's multiply this number by 360 (since there are 360 days in one prophetic year). This equals exactly 173,880 days. Now, to arrive at an actual date, we'll need to convert 173,880 days into true years. This isn't as straightforward as it sounds. All calendars—Hebrew, Gregorian, Julian, etc.—resolve over time to actual solar years, but this is accomplished through somewhat complicated systems of adjustment: Additional months are added on occasion to the

---

[94] For example: *The Coming Prince or The Seventy Weeks of Daniel with an Answer to the Higher Criticism*, Sir Robert Anderson (1915; London: James Nisbet and Co., Limited)
[95] *Calendar and Community: A History of the Jewish Calendar, 2nd Century BCE to 10th Century CE*, Sacha Stern (2001; Oxford University Press)

Hebrew calendar (in the Metonic cycle of 19 years used today, 12 years are non-leap years of 12 months and 7 are leap years consisting of 13 months);[96] leap days are added every four years to the Gregorian calendar (unless the leap year is an integer multiple of 100, with the exception of years that are at the same time integer multiples of 400),[97] etc. To keep our calculation as simple as possible, we'll forget all of that and simply divide our 173,880 days by an actual solar year, which (to be slightly more precise than we were earlier) is approximately 365.2425 days. The result is 476.0673 years; that is, 476 years and change.

Now, let's see what year this brings us to. To keep it simple, we'll simply subtract 446 (as in, the year of Artaxerxes' decree, 446 B.C.) from 476. The result is 30. Since there was no year zero (that is, when the year 1 B.C. concluded, the year A.D. 1 began), we'll need to add 1 to arrive at our year. We now find ourselves in the year A.D. 31.

The Christian might immediately recognize this as a potentially significant year: Most scholars believe that Jesus began His ministry sometime around A.D. 30 and was crucified sometime around A.D. 33. However, there is no consensus on the precise years of these events, and estimates range in five years in either direction. As it turns out, though, the Bible—and other historical records—may provide us enough information to make a surprisingly educated guess. Luke 3:1-3 tells us:

> 1 Now in the fifteenth year of the reign of Tiberius Caesar, Pontius Pilate being governor of Judea, Herod being tetrarch of Galilee, his brother Philip tetrarch of Iturea and the region of Trachonitis, and Lysanias tetrarch of Abilene,
> 2 while Annas and Caiaphas were high priests, the word of God came to John the son of Zacharias in the wilderness.
> 3 And he went into all the region around the Jordan, preaching a baptism of repentance for the remission of sins...

---

[96] *Ibid.*
[97] http://en.wikipedia.org/wiki/Leap_year

Here, Luke supplies us with a substantial amount of historical context within which John the Baptist began his ministry. The most useful detail is the one listed first: "in the fifteenth year of the reign of Tiberius Caesar" (verse 1). There is ample recorded history about Rome and its emperors, so we can confidently assign a precise year to the beginning of John's ministry. Tiberius Julius Caesar Augustus became emperor in A.D. 14.[98] So, John the Baptist's ministry began in A.D. 28. Reading further in Luke chapter 3, we see that another significant event happened shortly thereafter (Luke 3:21-23a):

> 21 When all the people were baptized, it came to pass that Jesus also was baptized; and while He prayed, the heaven was opened.
> 22 And the Holy Spirit descended in bodily form like a dove upon Him, and a voice came from heaven which said, "You are My beloved Son; in You I am well pleased."
> 23 Now Jesus Himself began His ministry at about thirty years of age...

From this, it seems reasonable to suggest that Jesus began His ministry, at the age of 30, in the same year that John the Baptist began his; that is, A.D. 28. Most scholars believe that Jesus' ministry commenced over a span of three-and-a-half years and that He was crucified at the age of 33. This is mainly derived by studying the chronologies laid out in the four Gospels. Unfortunately, the first three—the Synoptic Gospels of Matthew, Mark, and Luke—turn out not to be very helpful in this regard. These only mention one Passover (an annual Jewish holiday, and therefore a good point of reference for distinguishing years). The Gospel of John, on the other hand, is a bit more thorough in presenting a historical record of Jesus' ministry. John's account clearly describes three separate Passovers[99] (including the one around the time of Jesus' crucifixion and resurrection), strongly suggesting that Jesus' ministry did indeed equal a period of three years and change. This, then, would

---

[98] *The Lives of the Twelve Caesars*, Gaius Suetonius Tranquillus (2012; CreateSpace Independent Publishing Platform)
[99] John 2:13-25; John 6:4; John 12:1-13:1, 18:28-19:14

place Jesus' death, burial, and resurrection in the year A.D. 31—the exact year to which Daniel's 69 prophetic weeks brought us!

Let's extrapolate even further and see how much more interesting Daniel's prophecy may be. Again, running the numbers on Daniel's 69 prophetic weeks (173,880 days divided by the 365.2425 days of a solar year) gives us a result of 476.0673 calendar years. We've seen what year the whole part of this number brings us to and the events that may correspond to that year (Jesus' death, burial, and resurrection). Now, let's look at the remainder. One solar year multiplied by the remainder (365.2425 times 0.0673) gives us about 24 days. Assuming that our forward trek of 476 years has landed us on the same month and day from which we started—the first day of Nisan—we'll continue onward from this date: Nisan 1, A.D. 31. Adding 24 days, we arrive at Nisan 25. This is ostensibly a significant date. Passover begins each year on Nisan 15 and continues for one week, and Jesus was crucified during the time of Passover. However, when we assign the significant events of this time to their corresponding dates given our current assumption—again, that we're counting from Nisan 1—do we really find anything interesting? Let's try. As we'll see later in our study, the Passover that corresponded with Jesus' crucifixion took place on a Friday. Jesus entered Jerusalem and was greeted with much fanfare on the Sunday before, which would have been Nisan 10 according to our assumption. Jesus was crucified on the following Thursday, which would be Nisan 14. Passover, again, began the next day, Friday, Nisan 15. And Jesus was resurrected from the dead two days later on Sunday, Nisan 17. Given this, Daniel's prophecy takes us—assuming that we're counting correctly—to exactly eight days past Jesus' resurrection; that is, to Monday, Nisan 25. Did anything important happen on this day? Not really: at this point, Jesus had been alive in His resurrected body and interacting (at various intervals) with His Disciples for a little over a week. The next truly significant event wouldn't occur until Jesus' ascension to Heaven some 32 days later.[100]

So, what's happened here? Is Daniel's prophecy imprecise, or did we just miss our mark somehow? Let's not give up yet. It may help

---

[100] Acts 1:1-3

to consider exactly what we're looking for. Looking again at Daniel's prophecy, we read (Daniel 9:25-26; emphasis mine):

> 25 "Know therefore and understand, that from the going forth of the command to restore and build Jerusalem *until Messiah the Prince*, there shall be seven weeks and sixty-two weeks; the street shall be built again, and the wall, even in troublesome times.
> 26 "And after the sixty-two weeks Messiah shall be cut off, but not for Himself; and the people of the prince who is to come shall destroy the city and the sanctuary. The end of it shall be with a flood, and till the end of the war desolations are determined."

Verse 25 identifies our target event: "Messiah the Prince." But what does this mean exactly? Does this refer to the day that Jesus was conceived in His mother's womb by the Holy Spirit? The day that He was born? The day that John baptized Him and the Holy Spirit alighted upon Him? Was Jesus "officially" inaugurated as Messiah when He rode into Jerusalem on Palm Sunday? When He was crucified? Resurrected? When He ascended to Heaven? There are so many significant moments in Jesus' life. Which is the one that we're looking for? The Archangel Gabriel (who, again, delivered this prophecy to Daniel) gives us at least one clue. In verse 26, we read (emphasis and bracketed comment mine) that "*after* the sixty-two weeks [that is, sometime after the end of the 69th week of Daniel's 70-weeks prophecy] Messiah shall be cut off, but not for Himself." In other words, the event that we're looking for—whatever it is—is either the Crucifixion (when Jesus was "cut off") or an event that preceded it. So, our current assumption—that once we arrive at A.D. 31 we are to continue counting from Nisan 1, thereby arriving at Nisan 25, some 11 days after the Crucifixion—is clearly wrong.

There may be one more thing we can try. Recall from above that the Hebrew calendar follows a Metonic cycle of 19 years (wherein 12 years are non-leap years of 12 months and 7 are leap years consisting of 13 months).[101] The Hebrew calendar has been standardized on this cycle since about the fourth century,[102] thereby fixing dates mathematically and allowing us to more confidently locate past events. But in the time of Christ, the calendar was a bit more fluid. Passover is a spring festival, and to ensure that it did not take place before the spring, various tests were applied. Was the barley ripe? Had the fruit crops grown properly? Had the winter rains stopped? Were the roads for Passover pilgrims sufficiently dry to allow passage? Had the young pigeons matured enough to fly? If two or more of these conditions were not met, the Jews applied a simple solution: they simply added an extra ("intercalary") month, called Adar (or "Adar II" in a leap year), to the calendar, thereby postponing Nisan 1 for that year by 30 days.[103]

If this was the case with our year in question—if by the ancient Jewish standard spring had not yet begun, and so an extra month was added to the calendar to delay the Passover holiday—then Daniel's 69 weeks of prophetic years takes us not to Nisan 25, but to Adar 25. There are 29 days in Adar, so, counting forward, we find that Adar 25 would place us 14 days before Jesus' triumphal entry into Jerusalem (which, again, took place on Nisan 10 and was followed several days later by Jesus' crucifixion [Nisan 14], Passover [Nisan 15], and then the Resurrection [Nisan 17]).

So, what happened precisely two weeks prior to the day that we Christians celebrate as Palm Sunday, the day that Jesus arrived in Jerusalem? The truth is, we can't say for sure. Not only does the Bible not offer us specific dates for the significant events in Jesus' life; it provides only a very weak chronology. The Gospel narratives move from account to account and rarely tell us the number of days, months, or years between these. So, we are left to simply guess. However, this isn't as bad as it sounds. A fairly simple approach to the problem may be simply to look back over all of the

---

[101] *Calendar and Community: A History of the Jewish Calendar, 2nd Century BCE to 10th Century CE*, Sacha Stern (2001; Oxford University Press)
[102] *The Comprehensive Hebrew Calendar: Its Structure, History, and One Hundred Years of Corresponding Dates: 5660-5760, 1900-2000*, Arthur Spier (1952; Behrman House, Inc.)
[103] *Ibid.*

events that could have taken place during the last month or so of Jesus' life and simply formulate a hypothesis. Which event might have been the one that Daniel's prophecy points to, the one that "officially" established Jesus as "Messiah the Prince"?—and then decide whether this could have occurred on the date in question, Adar 25.

This is a subjective exercise, to be sure, but looking through all of the events that comprise the final weeks of Jesus' ministry here on Earth—all of His miracles, all of His teachings, all of His interactions with the religious authorities—one event in particular stands out as supremely unique. This is Jesus' supernatural encounter and physical transformation on top of the so-called Mount of Transfiguration. All three Synoptic Gospels provide an account of this event. Let's take a look at Matthew's version (Matthew 17:1-9):

1 Now after six days Jesus took Peter, James, and John his brother, led them up on a high mountain by themselves;
2 and He was transfigured before them. His face shone like the sun, and His clothes became as white as the light.
3 And behold, Moses and Elijah appeared to them, talking with Him.
4 Then Peter answered and said to Jesus, "Lord, it is good for us to be here; if You wish, let us make here three tabernacles: one for You, one for Moses, and one for Elijah."
5 While he was still speaking, behold, a bright cloud overshadowed them; and suddenly a voice came out of the cloud, saying, "This is My beloved Son, in whom I am well pleased. Hear Him!"
6 And when the disciples heard it, they fell on their faces and were greatly afraid.
7 But Jesus came and touched them and said, "Arise, and do not be afraid."
8 When they had lifted up their eyes, they saw no one but Jesus only.
9 Now as they came down from the mountain, Jesus commanded them, saying, "Tell the vision to no one until the Son of Man is risen from the dead."

The reader should immediately recognize this as an important event. In the course of Jesus' ministry leading up to His crucifixion, this occurrence is rivaled—in terms of establishing Jesus' true identity—perhaps only by His baptism at the hands of John the Baptist. For comparison, let's take a look at that event (Mark 1:9-11):

> 9   It came to pass in those days that Jesus came from Nazareth of Galilee, and was baptized by John in the Jordan.
> 10 And immediately, coming up from the water, He saw the heavens parting and the Spirit descending upon Him like a dove.
> 11 Then a voice came from heaven, "You are My beloved Son, in whom I am well pleased."

Here, Jesus likewise receives a supernatural visitation. The Holy Spirit alights upon Him—signifying the act of anointing—and He is empowered to begin His three-and-a-half-year-long earthly ministry. We also see words spoken from Heaven similar to those that would later be spoken on the Mount of Transfiguration: "You are My beloved Son, in whom I am well pleased" (verse 11). On the Mount of Transfiguration, however, not only does Jesus have a supernatural encounter—this time not with the Holy Spirit but with two Old Testament prophets, Moses and Elijah—but He is physically altered by the interaction: "He was transfigured before them. His face shone like the sun, and His clothes became as white as the light" (verse 2 of our Matthew passage). Similarly, when Jesus was baptized, the words spoken from Heaven were for Him alone: "*You* are My beloved Son"; verse 11. But the words spoken on the Mount were to Jesus' Disciples: "*This* is My beloved Son," and concluded with a command to submit to Jesus' authority: "Hear Him!" (verse 5 of our Matthew passage). Could this—Jesus' transfiguration on the Mount—be the singular moment that "officially" inaugurated Jesus as Messiah the Prince?[104] Could this be our target event, the one that fulfills—to the very day!—Daniel's 69-weeks prophecy? To fully test this, let's plug the Mount of

---

[104] Daniel 9:25

Transfiguration event into our current hypothesis—that is, by assigning it the date of Sunday, Adar 25—and see if it fits.

Although the Bible doesn't offer a clear timeline of Jesus' ministry here on Earth, the Gospel accounts do provide details about what transpired following the Mount of Transfiguration. From these, we can create a hypothetical timeline. In Luke 9:37, we read:

> 37 Now it happened on the next day, when they had come down from the mountain, that a great multitude met Him.

This, then, would bring us to Monday, Adar 26. From here, the Gospels describe—interwoven with accounts of Jesus performing miracles, interacting with His Disciples, etc.—a fairly linear journey to Jerusalem. Jesus and His Disciples stay briefly "in Galilee" (Matthew 17:22), a region that includes Mount Tabor, the strongest candidate for the Biblical Mount of Transfiguration.[105] Next, they travel to Capernaum (Matthew 17:24), a town situated on the northern shore of the Sea of Galilee, about one day's walk from Mount Tabor. Assuming that they took their time traveling there (perhaps they lingered for a couple of nights somewhere along the way), this might place us on Adar 28. From here, the Bible records—again, intermingled with various incidents—Jesus' journey from Capernaum south through Samaria along the so-called Jericho Road, through "Judea beyond the Jordan" (a.k.a. "Perea," an area considered part of Israel at the time[106]), through the town of Jericho and finally on to Jerusalem. This was the most direct route, about 120 miles walking distance. Without stops, such a journey—assuming progress of 20 miles per day, which was not uncommon for travelers in those days—would have only taken Jesus' party seven days (six days travel plus one day of Sabbath rest), placing them in Jerusalem on Nisan 6, well in advance of Jesus' triumphal entry into Jerusalem on Sunday, Nisan 10. In other words, following the Mount of Transfiguration event, Jesus would have had more than enough time to journey to Jerusalem—ministering and teaching in towns along the way—and still arrive in

---

[105] Based on early Christian tradition, its proximity to the Sea of Galilee, and other factors.
[106] Matthew 19:1

time to fulfill His ultimate act as Messiah the Prince: His death on the Cross, at the time of Passover, our perfect Passover sacrifice.[107]

We should note here that many scholars place a lot more time—up to a year—between the Mount of Transfiguration event and Jesus' last week on Earth. But there is no Biblical reason to assume that this is accurate. On the contrary, in Luke's account of the Transfiguration, we read (Luke 9:30-31):

> 30 And behold, two men talked with Him, who were Moses and Elijah,
> 31 who appeared in glory and spoke of His decease which He was about to accomplish at Jerusalem.

Luke tells us that the core topic of conversation between Jesus and the two Old Testament prophets was His death on the Cross in Jerusalem, and they make it sound like an imminent—soon to occur—event: "which He was about to accomplish" (verse 31). So, not only is our presumed timeline not incompatible with Scripture, but, as we see here, it seems to fit quite well. It makes perfect sense that immediately following His meeting with Moses and Elijah about His destiny as Messiah the Prince, He would set out toward the place where this destiny would be fulfilled.

Many scholars have attempted to analyze Daniel's 70-weeks prophecy, and, of course, we can't be sure that our analysis is the right one. Are our dates accurate? Have we honed in on the correct events? But regardless of the precise details, it's hard to deny that the prophecy given to Daniel by the Archangel Gabriel almost certainly correctly predicts—as our hypothesis shows, perhaps even to the exact day!—the timespan between Artaxerxes' decree to rebuild the city of Jerusalem and the moment that Jesus "officially" stepped into the office of Messiah. The astounding accuracy of this prophecy should be apparent, and on this basis we should be confident in presuming that the final week of the prophecy—which has yet to occur—can be defined according to the same terms as the first 69 weeks. Daniel's seventieth week, the period that we refer

---

[107] 1 Corinthians 5:7

to as the Great Tribulation, will span precisely seven prophetic years; that is, 2,520 days, 35 days shy of seven calendar years.

The Gap in the 70-Weeks Prophecy

As of the date of this writing, it's been some two thousand years since the end of Daniel's sixty-ninth week. We may reasonably ask, why the gap between the end of the sixty-ninth week and the beginning of the seventieth? As we've seen, the first sixty-nine weeks of Daniel's 70-weeks prophecy are comprised of 173,880 consecutive days, and then suddenly we encounter a millennia-long delay which continues to this very day. Why? We are given a clue that this gap is indeed integral to Daniel's prophecy in the prophecy itself. Let's look again at the last two verses of the 70-weeks prophecy (Daniel 9:26-27; paraphrase in brackets and emphasis mine):

> 26 "And *after* the sixty-[nine] weeks Messiah shall be cut off, but not for Himself; and the people of the prince who is to come shall destroy the city and the sanctuary. The end of it shall be with a flood, and till the end of the war desolations are determined.
> 27 "*Then* he shall confirm a covenant with many for one week; but in the middle of the week he shall bring an end to sacrifice and offering. And on the wing of abominations shall be one who makes desolate, even until the consummation, which is determined, is poured out on the desolate."

Recall from our analysis that Daniel's sixty-ninth week concludes with the anointing of Jesus as Messiah on the Mount of Transfiguration. According to verse 26 above, sometime *after* this, Jesus was to be crucified ("Messiah shall be cut off"), and sometime later "the people of the prince who is to come shall destroy the city and the sanctuary." You'll recall that, just before delivering His great dissertation on the Last Days, Jesus reiterated this latter prediction (Matthew 24:1-2):

> 1   Then Jesus went out and departed from the temple, and His disciples came up to show Him the buildings of the temple.
> 2   And Jesus said to them, "Do you not see all these things? Assuredly, I say to you, not one stone shall be left here upon another, that shall not be thrown down."

This prophecy was fulfilled some thirty-eight years after Jesus' death and resurrection, in A.D. 70. In that year, as I mentioned in Chapter 2[108], the Roman general Titus invaded Jerusalem and destroyed the city and the Temple. And, according to Daniel's prophecy, it is sometime after this—the destruction of the Temple in A.D. 70—that the seventieth and final week would begin: "*Then he shall confirm a covenant with many for one week*" (verse 27). And so, we see that an unspecified span of time between the sixty-ninth and seventieth weeks is indeed part of the timeline that Daniel lays out.

Presumably, there is a reason for this long gap of time. Can we gain some insight into its significance, its purpose? We can. The event described in verse 26 above—"the people of the prince who is to come shall destroy the city and the sanctuary"—should be understood as the defining moment of this millennia-long interim period. This—the destruction of the Jews' Holy City and Temple—resulted in the scattering of the Jews throughout the world for the next two millennia. This tragedy befell the Jews for one simple reason: they had rejected Jesus Christ as their long-promised Messiah. What has been happening since that time—in the interim between Jesus' First Coming, when He was rejected *en masse* by the primary people for which He'd come[109], and His Second Coming, when the Jews will at last anoint Him their King and Messiah—is described in much detail in Romans chapter 11. Here, the Apostle Paul explains (Romans 11:11-15; bracketed comments mine):

> 11 I say then, have they [the Jews] stumbled that they should fall? Certainly not! But through their fall, to provoke them to jealousy, salvation has come to the Gentiles [non-Jews].

---

[108] Chapter 2 "Finding a Model for the Timing of the Rapture"
[109] See Romans 1:16

THE SCROLL WITH THE SEVEN SEALS: PRELUDE TO THE GREAT TRIBULATION

12 Now if their fall is riches for the world, and their failure riches for the Gentiles, how much more their fullness!
13 For I speak to you Gentiles; inasmuch as I am an apostle to the Gentiles, I magnify my ministry,
14 if by any means I may provoke to jealousy those who are my flesh and save some of them.
15 For if their being cast away is the reconciling of the world, what will their acceptance be but life from the dead?

So, it is within this gap between Daniel's sixty-ninth and seventieth weeks that the "reconciling of the world" (verse 15) would take place: salvation, as it turns out, would not be for the Jews alone, but would be available to everyone who would receive it, Jew and Gentile alike. This is a promise that dates back to the very moment that God promised that He would enter into covenant with what would become the nation of Israel, the Jewish people (Genesis 12:1-3):

1 Now the Lord had said to Abram: "Get out of your country, from your family and from your father's house, to a land that I will show you.
2 I will make you a great nation; I will bless you and make your name great; and you shall be a blessing.
3 I will bless those who bless you, and I will curse him who curses you; and in you all the families of the earth shall be blessed."

Here, God tells Abram—who He would later rename Abraham—that He would "make [him] a great nation" and would "bless [him] and make [his] name great" (verse 2; bracketed comments mine). But notice that this blessing would not be limited to Abraham's nation—Israel, the Jewish people—alone. Ultimately, God tells Abram, "in you all the families of the earth shall be blessed" (verse 3). God's plan all along was to extend His covenant to this whole world, at least to all of us who would partake of it. And this is precisely what has been taking place between Jesus' First Coming and His Second (Daniel's sixty-ninth and seventieth weeks): even as the Jews are being reconciled to God, a process that truly began to manifest only within the last century or so[110], Gentiles—non-Jews—have been entering into covenant with God—receiving the salvation offered through His Son's sacrifice on the Cross.

Still, two thousand years seems like an awfully long time. But, if anything, we should be grateful for this. As the Apostle Peter tells us in 2 Peter 3:3-4, 9):

> 3 knowing this first: that scoffers will come in the last days, walking according to their own lusts,
> 4 and saying, "Where is the promise of His coming? For since the fathers fell asleep, all things continue as they were from the beginning of creation."
>
> 9 The Lord is not slack concerning His promise, as some count slackness, but is longsuffering toward us, not willing that any should perish but that all should come to repentance.

It is because of God's great mercy on this world—on all of us—that the gap between Daniel's sixty-ninth and seventieth weeks—the timespan between Jesus' First Coming and His Second Coming—has been so long. God wants to save as many of us—Jews and Gentiles—as possible before it's too late. Let's look again at Paul's words in Romans 11:25-27[111] (emphasis and bracketed comments mine):

> 25 For I do not desire, brethren, that you should be ignorant of this mystery, lest you should be wise in your own opinion, that blindness in part has happened to Israel *until the fullness of the Gentiles [non-Jews] has come in.*
> 26 And so all Israel will be saved, as it is written: "The Deliverer [Messiah] will come out of Zion, and He will turn away ungodliness from Jacob [the Jews];

---

[110] Key events that we can point to include the reestablishment of the State of Israel on May 14th, 1948 and the recapturing of the Temple Mount in Jerusalem on June 7th, 1967.

[111] Discussed in Chapter 7 "The Introduction" (section "Revelation 1:4-1:8 ~ Salutations") and Chapter 8 "The Letters to the Seven Churches" (section "Revelation 3:7-3:13 ~ The Sixth Letter: The Faithful Church")

THE SCROLL WITH THE SEVEN SEALS: PRELUDE TO THE GREAT TRIBULATION

27 For this is My covenant with them, when I take away their sins."

When God is satisfied that "the fullness of the Gentiles has come in" (verse 25)—that as many of us that may be saved in this interim between Daniel's sixty-ninth and seventieth weeks have been saved—the final week of Daniel's 70-weeks prophecy will begin.

In conveying the last part of the vision to Daniel, the Archangel Gabriel begins, "Then he shall confirm a covenant with many for one week." Who is "he"?: he is the one whom Gabriel described in the prior verse, "the prince who is to come." Some scholars contend that the "prince" of Daniel 9:27 describes Antiochus Epiphanes, a Syrian king who persecuted the inhabitants of Jerusalem in the second century B.C., some 150 years before Jesus' birth. This would mean, of course, that Daniel's seventieth week has already occurred, and the entire prophecy of Daniel chapter 9 is thus fulfilled. However, let's recall Jesus' words in Matthew 24:15-21:

15 "Therefore when you see the 'abomination of desolation,' spoken of by Daniel the prophet, standing in the holy place" (whoever reads, let him understand),
16 "then let those who are in Judea flee to the mountains.
17 "Let him who is on the housetop not go down to take anything out of his house.
18 "And let him who is in the field not go back to get his clothes.
19 "But woe to those who are pregnant and to those who are nursing babies in those days!
20 "And pray that your flight may not be in winter or on the Sabbath.
21 "For then there will be great tribulation, such as has not been since the beginning of the world until this time, no, nor ever shall be.

Here, in verse 15, Jesus quotes the Book of Daniel explicitly and paraphrases his description of the "prince" in Daniel 9:27: "and on the wing of abominations shall be one who makes desolate." But Jesus is not recounting some event that took place a century and a half before His birth. This is His dissertation on the End Times, and He is speaking in the future tense, of one who is to come later; namely, the Antichrist. Antiochus Epiphanes was undeniably an archetype of the Antichrist—there have been many over the centuries—but Daniel is describing *the* Antichrist, and Jesus and Daniel both are describing the wrapping up of world history. Daniel goes on to give us some important details about the Antichrist's activities during this period, but we'll examine these later. For now, let's be content that Daniel's seventieth week is, in fact, describing some future period of time and that this period, which we refer to as the Great Tribulation, will—in harmony with that portion of the prophecy that has already been fulfilled (the other sixty-nine weeks)—span approximately seven calendar years.

Back to the Four Horsemen

Now that we understand that the Great Tribulation does, in fact, constitute a period of seven years—the last seven years of this world's history—let's get back to our look at the events and conditions that lead up to this time, the first four of the Seven Seals, the so-called Four Horsemen of the Apocalypse. When Jesus opens the First Seal on the Scroll in verse 1 of our Revelation passage,[112] John is directed by one of the four living creatures to observe an individual on a white horse who is carrying a bow, symbolizing militarism, and wearing a crown, which represents authority. John writes that this horseman "went out conquering and to conquer" (verse 2). Some scholars have identified this horseman as none other than Jesus Himself, no doubt based on a comparison of this scripture to a later description of Jesus in Revelation 19:11-12 (emphasis mine):

> 11 Now I saw heaven opened, and behold, *a white horse*. And he who sat on him was called Faithful and True, and in righteousness He judges and *makes war*.
> 12 His eyes were like a flame of fire, and *on His head were many crowns*. He had a name written that no one knew except Himself.

---

[112] Revelation 6:1--6:8

THE SCROLL WITH THE SEVEN SEALS: PRELUDE TO THE GREAT TRIBULATION

This is a depiction of Christ returning to Earth for the conclusion of the so-called Battle of Armageddon at the end of the Tribulation. Admittedly, this passage correlates very well with John's description of the First Seal, but there are some points to consider before we conclude that he is talking about the same thing in both places. First, and most compelling, we know that even now Jesus sits at the right hand of His Father in Heaven. His return to Earth—the Second Coming—is going to be a triumphant occasion that will be witnessed by all. Jesus Himself told us this, as you'll recall, in Matthew 24:30:

> 30 "Then the sign of the Son of Man will appear in heaven, and then all the tribes of the earth will mourn, and they will see the Son of Man coming on the clouds of heaven with power and great glory.

The horseman in question hardly seems to portray this monumental event. On the contrary, he is one of several horsemen, and he appears to have but one simple task: to establish a particular condition on Earth; that is, a global spirit of military conquest. This aligns well with the descriptions of his three companions, the other horsemen. The one on the red horse (represented by the Second Seal) generates an environment of strife and conflict. The rider of the black horse (the Third Seal) spreads scarcity and economic disparity. And the Fourth Horseman (the Fourth Seal), on a pale horse, ushers in widespread death by famine, disease, and violence. These are not single, specific events, but together comprise a frightening and unprecedented paradigm, a set of conditions necessary to create, over time, an environment that is conducive to the coming Great Tribulation period. So, if the rider on the white horse is not Jesus, who is he, and who are the others? For the answer, let's turn again to the Old Testament prophet Zechariah (Zechariah 1:7-11):

> 7 On the twenty-fourth day of the eleventh month, which is the month Shebat, in the second year of Darius, the word of the Lord came to Zechariah the son of Berechiah, the son of Iddo the prophet:

> 8 I saw by night, and behold, a man riding on a red horse, and it stood among the myrtle trees in the hollow; and behind him were horses: red, sorrel, and white.
> 9 Then I said, "My lord, what are these?" So the angel who talked with me said to me, "I will show you what they are."
> 10 And the man who stood among the myrtle trees answered and said, "These are the ones whom the Lord has sent to walk to and fro throughout the earth."
> 11 So they answered the Angel of the Lord, who stood among the myrtle trees, and said, "We have walked to and fro throughout the earth, and behold, all the earth is resting quietly."

Here, Zechariah presents an image of four horsemen similar (though, as in our analysis of the four living creatures, not precisely identical) to the four horsemen of Revelation chapter 6. Zechariah is told by the angel with whom he is conversing that these are beings sent by God to "walk to and fro throughout the earth" (verse 10). We find a similar account a few chapters later, in Zechariah 6:1-7:

> 1 Then I turned and raised my eyes and looked, and behold, four chariots were coming from between two mountains, and the mountains were mountains of bronze.
> 2 With the first chariot were red horses, with the second chariot black horses,
> 3 with the third chariot white horses, and with the fourth chariot dappled horses—strong steeds.
> 4 Then I answered and said to the angel who talked with me, "What are these, my lord?"
> 5 And the angel answered and said to me, "These are four spirits of heaven, who go out from their station before the Lord of all the earth.
> 6 "The one with the black horses is going to the north country, the white are going after them, and the dappled are going toward the south country."
> 7 Then the strong steeds went out, eager to go, that they might walk to and fro throughout the earth. And He said, "Go, walk to and fro throughout the earth." So they walked to and fro throughout the earth.

Here, slightly different imagery is used, but essentially the same thing is being depicted as in the prior passage: beings sent by God to fulfill some purpose on Earth. In this passage, Zechariah describes these as "four spirits of heaven, who go out from their station before the Lord of all the earth" (verse 5). Simply put, these are angelic beings who are given the task of patrolling—and, as we derive from John's description in Revelation, influencing—our world. The phrase "go out" is a present participle, indicating continuous action, which suggests that there have always been angels with this function. These beings continue to influence world events to this present day. Note that the "north country" and "south country" in this passage are symbolic of all governments throughout the Earth, so we are to understand that these angels influence not at the level of individuals or even individual nations, but political, social, and economic systems on a global scale. This, too, correlates well with John's depiction of these beings and offers us an important clue about just how they are working to maneuver this age toward its end, about the exact nature of their function.

Some may find it difficult to mentally separate these riders from the Tribulation period—after all, the very term "Four Horsemen of the Apocalypse" implies that they belong to the seven-year Great Tribulation. However, this term, like many other popular ones—as we've seen—does not actually appear in the Bible. This is a good example of how cautious we need to be with popular terminology. Catchy terms and phrases can quickly become part of generally accepted "Truth" regardless of whether the impressions they create are completely accurate or based in Scripture. These Four Horsemen are really not part of "the Apocalypse" (in its popular usage, referring to the Great Tribulation); they just prod mankind in its direction. Even Jesus, when telling His Disciples about the End Times, began by describing the conditions that would lead up to this period. Recall that He tells them there will be false prophets; that they would hear of "wars and rumors of wars"; that there would be famines, pestilences, and earthquakes; that lawlessness would abound and love would diminish. But, He told them, "all these things must come to pass, *but the end is not yet*" (Matthew 24:4-14). Jesus described conditions that are increasingly familiar to us all, and John in the Book of Revelation likewise describes cumulative conditions that will precede the seven years of the Great Tribulation, the end of this age.

Of course, these conditions will worsen as we draw nearer to the end, but John implies a particular aspect that is critical: they must become worldwide in scope. Again, the Four Horsemen influence war, famine, disease, and scarcity on Earth, conditions that have been around since the dawn of civilization. On some level, we might say that these, in fact, define civilization. Humans organize to compete for resources, which are limited, and this inevitably leads to imbalances in peoples' well-being, which in turn leads to conflict and war. Human beings have struggled in this pattern since Adam and Eve first left that perfect condition that was the Garden of Eden. But John intends to introduce us to a new twist on this old theme, and his wording in describing the influences of the Four Horsemen makes it clear. The Second Horseman, the one on the red horse, writes John, comes "to take peace from the earth" (Revelation 6:4). Similarly, the Fourth Horseman, on the pale horse, is given power over "a fourth of the earth" (verse 8). So, what John is describing is not to be understood in the context of a people, nation, or region, but the whole world. Perhaps surprisingly, these conditions—as history has already proven, as we're about to see—form the very prerequisites to the globalism that will facilitate the coming of the Antichrist. According to Daniel, Jesus, Paul, and John, the rise of this man who personifies rebellion against God is the hallmark of the period that we call the Great Tribulation, and the Antichrist cannot come until the world has evolved to accommodate the global control that will define his reign. It is the task of the Four Horsemen of Revelation 6 to push Planet Earth toward this "one world" scenario.

Let's consider this more closely. Almost since the time of Adam, humans have tended toward having a global mindset. Ironically, this nature was placed in us by God Himself. Before He even created us, He determined that we would be rulers over this world (Genesis 1:26):

> 26 Then God said, "Let Us make man in Our image, according to Our likeness; let them have dominion over the fish of the sea, over the birds of the air, and over the cattle, over all the

earth and over every creeping thing that creeps on the earth."

His intent, of course, was that we would rule the Earth and that He would rule us. But in a very poor exercise of our free will—also a trait intentionally placed in us by God—we chose a different path. Adam and Eve rebelled, and humankind began the process of dominating the world according to our own devices. Let's consider an early example of this. A dozen or so generations after Adam, and just five generations after God had destroyed most of the human race (save for Noah and his family) with the Flood, a sort of secular globalism—the height of rebellion against God—manifested its inevitable fruit in a place called Shinar (Genesis 11:1-9):

1. Now the whole earth had one language and one speech.
2. And it came to pass, as they journeyed from the east, that they found a plain in the land of Shinar, and they dwelt there.
3. Then they said to one another, "Come, let us make bricks and bake them thoroughly." They had brick for stone, and they had asphalt for mortar.
4. And they said, "Come, let us build ourselves a city, and a tower whose top is in the heavens; let us make a name for ourselves, lest we be scattered abroad over the face of the whole earth."
5. But the Lord came down to see the city and the tower which the sons of men had built.
6. And the Lord said, "Indeed the people are one and they all have one language, and this is what they begin to do; now nothing that they propose to do will be withheld from them.
7. "Come, let Us go down and there confuse their language, that they may not understand one another's speech."
8. So the Lord scattered them abroad from there over the face of all the earth, and they ceased building the city.
9. Therefore its name is called Babel, because there the Lord confused the language of all the earth; and from there the Lord scattered them abroad over the face of all the earth.

Was God really concerned about the ambitions of this people, however self-serving and egotistical? Many of us were taught as children in Sunday school that God was angered by those constructing the so-called Tower of Babel because they sought to invade Heaven. But this is not what the Bible tells us. No, their "sin" was much more formidable. We are introduced to it in verse 1: "Now the whole earth had one language and one speech." Those who endeavored to build the great city and its tower had a singular purpose: to exalt their own efforts and ensure their unity. God's judgment came swiftly, and the root of His concern was clear: "Indeed the people are one and they all have one language, and this is what they begin to do; now nothing that they propose to do will be withheld from them" (verse 6). So He confused their speech and scattered them "over the face of all the earth." This event, which occurred some five thousand years ago, provides us a very early example of a globalist worldview and God's response to it. Since that incident on the plain of Shinar man has been striving endlessly to reclaim that most powerful of human conditions: a world that embraces a sole language and culture, and a single political socioeconomic system. This is evidenced by the multiple attempts at global empire-building that have occurred continuously since Babel's fall. All have failed, but one day, when God says it's time, humankind will succeed. And this—the height of man's rebellion against God—will prompt Him to usher in the last of the Last Days.

Indeed, every aspect of civilization has been leading up to this pivotal moment in man's history. What God put asunder at Babel, man will soon finally accomplish in the form of a one-world system. And the Four Horsemen of Revelation are even now driving us toward this ultimate human endeavor. Let's consider this idea in the context of recent human history.

The breaking of the Scroll's First Seal introduces us to the rider on the white horse, who has "a bow" and "a crown" and who goes out "conquering and to conquer" (verse 2 of our Revelation passage). Again, the bow here indicates military might and the crown a form of authority or rule. But what specifically is this imagery meant to convey? It's useful to note here that the symbolism of a crown does not maintain a consistent theme throughout Revelation, so we're given some flexibility in interpreting the type of authority in question. You'll recall that the twenty-four elders introduced in Revelation chapter 4 wore crowns, that in two of the church letters of chapters 2 and 3 we are each promised a crown (assuming that we remain faithful to the end), and that later in Revelation Jesus Himself is depicted wearing a crown (or crowns) as He returns to Earth.[113] But as we proceed through John's text, we'll encounter locusts (which comprise one of the Tribulation plagues) wearing crowns,[114] and even the Antichrist is depicted as having "ten crowns,"[115] as we'll see. In each case, the crown symbolism indicates authority but with no assumption about its nature—it may be positive, negative, or neutral. Still, all authority derives from God, as Paul tells us in Romans 13:1:

> 1 Let every soul be subject to the governing authorities. For there is no authority except from God, and the authorities that exist are appointed by God.

Here, Paul is referring to the governments of this world, and, as it turns out, this is the form of authority meant to be conveyed by the crown worn by our First Horseman. In other words, the rider on the white horse does not actually do the "conquering" that is mentioned, but he influences the stronger nations of this world to subdue, by military means, the weaker ones; that is, to establish authority over them. Again, humans have been engaged in the sport of trying to take over and control one another since the dawn of civilization. Familiar historical examples of nations and individuals who have made policies of conquering via military force include Egypt, Assyria, Babylon, Medo-Persia, Greece, Rome, Alexander the Great, Hannibal, Genghis Khan, and Napoleon. But never in history—until very recently, that is—did conquest define a global culture, as our First Horseman depicts. The ambitions of nations and individuals may have had global ramifications, but the spirit of conquest, generally speaking, typically rested on only one entity at a time. That is, until the nineteenth century A.D.

---

[113] Revelation 19:12
[114] Revelation 9:7
[115] Revelation 13:1

In 1776, a Scottish economist named Adam Smith published what even today is considered the "bible" of capitalism, "An Inquiry into the Nature and Causes of the Wealth of Nations." It was no coincidence that the book's release occurred in the same year as the signing of the Declaration of Independence, the document that formed the foundation of what would be the United States of America. Indeed, Smith, watching from the British Isles, considered that grand experiment on the other side of the Atlantic to be the most viable environment in which his ideas might blossom and flourish. In his book, Smith presented the most rudimentary concepts of this economic theory that he didn't so much invent as articulate. But his ideas changed the world. In a famous passage in the book, Smith describes the manufacturing of a pin—first by an individual craftsman, the modus operandi of production for all prior history of mankind, and next in a factory-type setting, where multiple laborers would participate in the pin's creation by the performance of very simple individual tasks. The individual worker would no longer need to be skilled in the entire process of producing a pin, but would need only to be able to accomplish his or her specific step. Smith posited that by using this approach, pin production, thanks to the efficiency of what would later be called a production line, could be increased exponentially. Many more pins would be produced at a greatly reduced cost. This is the essence of capitalism, and—applied to all production, not just pins—could, and did, revolutionize the world.

Adam Smith guessed well that his ideas might take root in the budding United States, and it wasn't long before industrial capitalism spread throughout his native Europe as well. The so-called Scientific Revolution of the seventeenth century, which paved the way for the invention of all manner of machinery, combined with Smith's concepts of mass production, would in a matter of years usher in what has come to be known as the Industrial Revolution. At the same time that all of this was happening, another kind of revolution was emerging, a philosophical one known as the Enlightenment, whereby a multitude of great thinkers began to imagine that humankind was progressing toward a utopia of liberal thought and world peace. The Industrial Revolution and the Enlightenment were both borne of the same paradigm—known in social sciences as Modernization, a process that led the world from the Renaissance into the modern age—but, ironically, the fruits of industrialism would prove the philosophers shockingly mistaken.

The Industrial Revolution brought great efficiency, as had been hoped, but with this efficiency came a great surplus of goods that the poorly paid laborers simply could not afford to buy. Equally upsetting, greater production meant a greater need for resources (raw materials, workers, etc.), which all of the industrializing nations understood were in limited supply. But built into industrialization was the solution to its problems: if pins and shoes and textiles could be mass-produced, so could weapons of war. And a formidable military force would be the industrialized nation's ticket not just to the raw materials of the non-industrialized nations but also to the markets of the world. Goods could continue to be produced and buyers for those goods ensured, and the wealthy nations would continue to grow wealthier. This would be empire-building at its grandest. But there was one problem: competition. Remember that the First Horseman instigates conquest on a world scale. Indeed, the imperialism of the nineteenth century was global in nature. Some dozen countries from three continents went to work slicing up the world into colonies and protectorates. Every populated continent on Earth was impacted, and dozens of previously sovereign nations were gobbled up or otherwise exploited. As symbolized by our First Horseman's bow, militarism was the order of the day. Over the next hundred years, the imperialists of the world, which included ten European powers, Japan, and the United States, amassed great armed forces to help secure and maintain their colonies and to stave off their competitors. Which brings us to our Second Horseman of Revelation chapter 6, the rider on the red horse...

When Jesus opens the Second Seal on the Scroll in Revelation 6:3-4, John is introduced to another horse, "fiery red," whose rider's task is "to take peace from the earth, and that people should kill one another; and there was given to him a great sword." This horseman's purpose is not to influence killing on an individual level, but on a global scale: to usher in war—*world* war. And as this horseman follows the first, so too did this new kind of war inevitably follow the Age of Imperialism. As the industrial powers of the world continued to compete for resources and markets, and as they continued to build up their militaries to unprecedented levels of might, tensions mounted on a global scale. At a peace conference at The Hague in the Netherlands in 1899, Germany's Minister of Foreign Affairs, Baron von Holstein said, "For the state, there is no higher aim than the preservation of its own interests; among the Great Powers these will not necessarily coincide with the maintenance of peace, but rather with the hostile policy of enemies and rivals."[116] This sentiment had fully manifested some twenty years earlier with the formation by Germany of an alliance with Austria-Hungary and Italy called the Triple Alliance. The turn of the twentieth century found the competing powers feeling threatened enough by this "super power" that by 1907 Britain, France and Russia had established their own alliance, the Triple Entente.[117] And yet, in spite of these pockets of cooperation among nations, the world was clearly in a state of international anarchy. No sovereign industrial power recognized any authority over itself. The perception of a need for something entirely new—some form of *world government*—would begin to materialize when all of this global chaos came to a head on June 28, 1914. Archduke Francis Ferdinand, heir to the Austrian throne, and his wife were returning to Austria after a brief visit to Bosnia when they were assassinated in the streets of Sarajevo by Serbian nationalists seeking independence from the Austro-Hungarian Empire. This event sparked a chain reaction of international power-posturing that would rapidly lead to the world's first truly global war. The Austrians responded to the Serbs' despicable act with an ultimatum, and, in what in hindsight might be viewed as botched diplomacy, refused to negotiate terms. Instead, they mobilized their military forces as a show of force. Suddenly, it seemed, every nation in Europe had a reputation to defend. Germany, Russia, and France declared support for their respective sides in the conflict, and on August 1st Russia mobilized its troops. Germany quickly followed suit, as did France and then Britain. Eventually, Japan,

---

[116] *Sources of the Western Tradition: From the Renaissance to the Present*, Marvin Perry, Joseph R. Peden, Theodore Hermann Von Laue (2006; Houghton Mifflin)
[117] *A Brief History of the Western World*, Thomas H. Greer (1987; Harcourt Brace Jovanovich, Inc.)

Turkey, and the United States were drawn into the conflict, and it seemed that no country on Earth was untouched by it.[118]

At last, in November of 1918, the war came to an end with the signing in Paris of the Treaty of Versailles, which established the League of Nations, mankind's first attempt at true world government. But in yet another act of unskilled diplomacy, the document held Germany totally accountable for the war and heaped as much anguish and humiliation as possible upon the German people. Said Philippe Scheidemann, Prime Minister of the Weimar Republic, "This treaty shall not be our law manual for the future... Woe to them who have conjured up the war, but threefold woe to them who postpone real peace for a single day."[119] Indeed, the economic strain imposed by the Treaty of Versailles on Germany would be so intensified by the Great Depression, which followed just a decade later, as to pave the way for none other than Adolf Hitler. We have the luxury of questioning the sanity of a people that would welcome the ideas of such an evil man, but when it became cheaper for Germans to burn paper money than to buy fuel to keep their families alive, perhaps fascism simply became for them a desperate, last alternative for survival. The "peace" that followed World War I would be diminished to a mere ceasefire when the world's soldiers began preparing again for battle following Germany's annexation of Austria on March 13, 1938.[120] It would not be entirely incorrect to say that World War I and World War II were really two phases of a single global conflict. And this World War, ushered in by the rider on the fiery red horse, leads, as you might have guessed, to our Third Horseman of Revelation 6.

When Jesus breaks the Third Seal on the Scroll, the third rider, who sits on a black horse and has "a pair of scales in his hand," is unleashed upon the world (verse 5 of our Revelation passage). Elsewhere in the Word of God, scales are used to symbolize commerce. For example, the Prophet Amos was shown a vision in which dishonesty among merchants was portrayed (Amos 8:4-6):

---

[118] *Ibid.*
[119] *A Brief History of the Western World*, Thomas H. Greer (1987; Harcourt Brace Jovanovich, Inc.)
[120] *Ibid.*

4   Hear this, you who swallow up the needy, and make the poor of the land fail,
5   saying: "When will the New Moon be past, that we may sell grain? And the Sabbath, that we may trade wheat? Making the ephah small and the shekel large, falsifying the scales by deceit,
6   that we may buy the poor for silver, and the needy for a pair of sandals—even sell the bad wheat?"

Similarly, the rider on the black horse is meant to reveal something to John about the economy, but remember that in this case it will be on a global scale; it will derive from man's own actions (albeit influenced by this operative from God); and it will be an outcome of the Second Horseman's accomplishment, world war. The specific nature of this future economic condition is provided in verse 6 of our Revelation passage, where John hears, "A quart of wheat for a denarius, and three quarts of barley for a denarius; and do not harm the oil and the wine." In John's day, the average laborer earned one denarius for a day's work, which could buy him or her about eight times the amount of wheat or barley as is depicted here. So, the first part of this statement taken alone might suggest simply extreme inflation. However, the latter part, "and do not harm the oil and the wine," reveals much more. Oil and wine, here symbolizing luxury, are juxtaposed to wheat and barley, which in this context represent basic sustenance. We therefore are to understand this of the economic condition that is being described: the rich will get richer and the poor will get poorer. In other words, extreme economic disparity is predicted on a global scale. It might be tempting for the reader to say, "I can relate—a dollar just doesn't buy what it used to." Or we might bemoan the huge gap between, say, Bill Gates' bank account balance and our own. But Revelation is describing something much more extreme and far-reaching than this. Let's continue in our analysis of recent world history.

The conclusion of World War II brought with it an end to much of the empire-building that had preceded the period of global armed conflict. The old, Industrial Age style of imperialism was more or less dead, and, indeed, many of the countries that had been colonized during those days of international conquest regained varying degrees of autonomy and nationhood. The underdeveloped countries had their independence, or at least some semblance of their national identities, again. But much had changed over the prior two centuries. Previously self-sufficient domestic economies were now inextricably linked to the new *global* economy. As before, the industrial powers of the world simply could not maintain their wealth and power without the non-industrials. And now, non-industrialized countries had been so transformed to serve the production and market needs of the industrialized ones as to be irreversibly handicapped, unable to achieve any level of economic independence. While world war had removed many of the world's political and military yokes, the socioeconomic ones remained. A new kind of imperialism was in order, this time not based on military conquest—the First Horseman's job was long since done—but rather economic, even cultural, conquest. No nation on Earth realistically had the option of abandoning the old economic relationships. So the industrial powers continued to industrialize and build wealth, and the rest of the world progressed deeper and deeper into the role of consumer and raw material producer. Unfortunately, the global capitalism that has defined the world since the end of World War II has, in accordance with the task of our Third Horseman, resulted in the rich getting richer and the poor getting poorer, on a *global* scale. Indeed, between the years 1960 and 2000, the gap between the richest fifth of the world's population and the poorest fifth more than doubled. Today, about 90% of the world's wealth is in the hands of 20% of its population; the 20% of the people at the bottom lay claim to only 1%.[121] This is global economic disparity at its extreme, unprecedented in the history of mankind, and it is the direct result of the global economy that we were all warned to watch out for during those barn meetings back in the 1970s. In reality, the world system is here, and has been in the works since before our great-great-grandparents were born. It just hasn't yet fully matured...but it's getting there.

---

[121] *Societies, Networks, and Transitions: A Global History*, Craig Lockard (2014; Cengage Learning)

This all may seem a harsh criticism of capitalism, since it was the birth of this economic paradigm that set all of the forces depicted by our Four Horsemen in motion. Some clarification is in order here, as this is a key issue that will come up again when we consider the nature of the emerging world government that defines the reign of the Antichrist. Merriam-Webster's Collegiate Dictionary defines "capitalism" as "an economic system characterized by private or corporate ownership of capital goods, by investments that are determined by private decision, and by prices, production, and the distribution of goods that are determined mainly by competition in a free market."[122] Private ownership, private investment, a free market—all of these things no doubt sound more or less positive to most of us. Freedom has a nice ring to it, perhaps especially when it comes to matters of money and ownership. And, indeed, capitalism is arguably the "best" system of economy that man has come up with. Marxist socialism (or "communism")—which seeks to eradicate the problems of modern capitalism by shifting ownership of the means of production and the control of resources to a hopefully-benevolent state—has been the main competing system over the last century or so. But for the most part capitalism—which at least creates the appearance of hope for a better life for all of its participants—has won out. Without engaging in an in-depth comparison of capitalism and Marxist-socialism (or any other economic system that man has created), suffice it to say that capitalism has proven to be an extremely effective approach to economy, and its success seems inevitable. We even read in the Word about God's people accumulating wealth through trade and other free market mechanisms, and, indeed, we are told that God "has pleasure in the prosperity of His servant" (Psalms 35:27). I believe very strongly that God wants His people to prosper, not only spiritually but materially as well. There is much evidence in the Bible for this, but as believers we should hesitate to limit God to a single economic system in which His blessings for us may materialize. God can—and does—prosper His people within whatever economic environment we find ourselves, personal definitions of prosperity notwithstanding. If we can mentally separate God and capitalism and see capitalism for what it is—a morally neutral approach to

---

[122] *Merriam-Webster's Collegiate Dictionary* (2008; Merriam-Webster, Inc.)

material life—then it becomes easier to be objective about it, to admit that, like all human inventions, it can produce good and it can produce evil. Global capitalism may greatly enhance the quality and value of my Jeep Wrangler and my Nikes, but it has also found 1.5 billion people in the world trying to survive on incomes of less than a dollar a day. Should I feel guilty about this? Perhaps or perhaps not, but I nonetheless should be honest about the world in which I live. The ability to construct buildings is a neutral human invention that enabled those on the plain of Shinar to build the Tower of Babel. Capitalism, likewise, is just an economic system but one that happens to be leading us toward the world government of the Antichrist, as we'll discuss more in-depth later. In the meantime, back to our Four Horsemen.

In Revelation 6:7-8, Jesus breaks the Fourth Seal on the Scroll, and John sees the last of the Four Horsemen ride out. This rider sits on a pale horse, and is identified as an entity called "Death," who is accompanied here by "Hades." These two are depicted in this passage and in other places in the Bible as some sort of beings, but elsewhere they are presented, seemingly, as places. Recall, for example, Jesus' words in Revelation 1:18:

> 18 "I am He who lives, and was dead, and behold, I am alive forevermore. Amen. And I have the keys of Hades and of Death.

The word "keys" here suggests that Hades and Death are locations, not entities. Further along in Revelation, we'll read,[123] "...and Death and Hades delivered up the dead who were in them" (Revelation 20:13), which sounds as if these two are both beings and places *simultaneously*. Strange, but, again, we needn't struggle too hard to form concrete images of things that are presented in prophetic texts. Remember, this is a medium rich in metaphor. Like the other three horsemen, we should simply understand Death and Hades here to represent a divine force that is purposed to bring about a particular condition on Earth. And this, too, follows from the prior condition, and is global in scope and unprecedented in human history. Their specific task is detailed in

---

[123] In Part 4 of this book series

verse 8, where we are told, "And power was given to them over a fourth of the earth, to kill with sword, with hunger, with death, and by the beasts of the earth." In other words, we are to understand, arising from the conditions brought about by the prior three horsemen and the state of the world in general, that we can expect to see widespread death by war, famine, and disease. This correlates well with Jesus' words about what to expect in the years leading up to the Great Tribulation. Recall Matthew 24:6-8:

> 6 "And you will hear of wars and rumors of wars. See that you are not troubled; for all these things must come to pass, but the end is not yet.
> 7 "For nation will rise against nation, and kingdom against kingdom. And there will be famines, pestilences, and earthquakes in various places.
> 8 "All these are the beginning of sorrows."

The phrase "over a fourth of the earth" in our Revelation passage indicates that these phenomena are indeed global in scope, but nonetheless limited. They directly affect many, but not all, of our world's population. Indeed, life has seemed fairly comfortable for me, someone who grew up in late twentieth-century American suburbia, but the century into which I was born was fraught with more suffering and death than in all of prior human history. Let's consider the numbers.

The first modus operandi of death associated with our Fourth Horseman is "to kill with sword." This indicates war and violent oppression. In the centuries leading up to the 1800s, death by war on average was about half a percent or less worldwide. But in the nineteenth century, thanks to advances in technology and other factors related to the Industrial Revolution and imperialism characterized by our First Horseman, the percentage had at least doubled to 1%. And in the twentieth century, the percentage leaped to a staggering 4 to 5%. Perhaps as many as a quarter of a billion people died during the last hundred years thanks to man's increasingly efficient ability to destroy himself. Death by war has indeed reached global, epidemic proportions, as predicted in Revelation. Admittedly, the numbers have begun to improve—albeit, only slightly—in recent decades. But it's important for us to remember that we must analyze prophecy from a broad historical perspective. Looking at the entire range of human history, we see that death by war has dramatically surged in our time. And even as I write this book, the world seems again on track toward a major conflict of global proportions, only this time it will not be over territory or resources or even ideology. What seems to be on our horizon is nothing less than a clash of civilizations. And make no mistake: another worldwide conflagration, with the weapons and technology of today, could conceivably double the mortality achieved in all of the last century of warfare.

The second way that our Fourth Horseman is said to bring about widespread death on Earth is "with hunger." Famine has been a fact of human existence virtually from the beginning. The studied Christian will recall that the Israelites many thousands of years ago came to live in Egypt—where they spent the next four hundred years in slavery—because of a great famine in that region of the world.[124] Similar episodes of mass starvation have occurred throughout history, right up to Ireland's infamous potato blight of the nineteenth century. But they have always been limited in scope and duration...until the twentieth century, that is. Never in the history of mankind has hunger been so widespread and so chronic as in the last hundred years. The imperialism, world war, and economic disparity of our first three horsemen, plus a population explosion and unprecedented environmental disasters—also, some would argue, the result of man's failed efforts to manage his world—have spawned famine on a scale of epidemic proportions. Let's consider how these factors combine to create a crisis of the magnitude implied in Revelation. In John's day, the world's population was holding steady at about 100 million people, but by the time of the American Revolution, thanks to the advances in science and technology of the preceding centuries, the population had soared to 1 billion. By the start of World War II, this had doubled to 2 billion, and today—just a half century or so later—the Earth plays host to some 6.2 billion people. At the current rate of growth, the population could reach 10.9 billion by 2050. One would presume that in the past hundred years the Earth's resources have come under severe stress, and one would be right. Today,

---

[124] Genesis chapters 41 through 46

more than 415 million people live in countries without sufficient agricultural capabilities; with desertification occurring at a rate of 25 billion tons of soil per year, this number will increase to 1.4 billion by 2025.[125] Most of the world's fisheries are likewise maxed out or in decline. The result is that today, according to estimates by the World Health Organization, as much as one-third of the world's population is undernourished and another one-sixth is starving to death. Indeed, each year some 15 million children die of starvation; one hundred will have died in the time it takes you to finish reading this paragraph. And sustained changes in the climate, caused at least in part by all of the pollution that we're dumping into the air, will bring more tropical storms, heat waves, droughts, and floods, resulting in continuing damage to crops and fisheries and ensuring that worldwide famine will remain on the rise. Some argue that reducing economic disparity in the world, characterized by our Third Horseman, will alleviate this problem. But try convincing your average American to move into a smaller house or give up his smartphone or trade his car in for a bicycle so that everyone in the world gets to eat. This just isn't part of most humans' nature.

The final method of killing attributed to our Fourth Horseman is "by the beasts of the earth." We've uncovered much evidence that the Four Horsemen of Revelation chapter 6 point to the last two centuries of human history—indeed, most Evangelical Christians believe that we are the generation that will see the last of the Last Days.[126] And, as we've discussed, the Fourth Horseman depicts the late twentieth and early twenty-first centuries. It is therefore problematic to assume too literal an interpretation for this horseman's final method of death. We could point to the rising number of shark attacks around the world or something, but remember that we're looking for a phenomenon of global proportion resulting in deaths on a mass scale. No such phenomenon is occurring related to the animal kingdom...unless, of course, we consider its tiniest members. John uses fairly poetic speech to describe the Four Horsemen and their respective tasks. It

---

[125] *The Population Bomb*, Paul R. Ehrlich (1995; Buccaneer Books)
[126] Evangelical Beliefs and Practices (2011; Pew Research Center's Religion & Public Life Project)

therefore seems reasonable to assume that, in harmony with this approach, John writes "by the beasts of the earth" to describe death by disease. In a literary context, viruses and bacteria can be called "beasts" as legitimately as a pack of ferocious wolves or herd of angry elephants, and this interpretation keeps us grounded in reality—science fiction and fantasy make for fun reading, but they can be dangerous distractions when attempting to understand prophecy. Another clue that John is referring here to disease is that this follows the pattern of the Four Horsemen. The effects of each logically leads to the effects of the next. It would be difficult to blame a scuba diver's unfortunate encounter with a great white shark on economic disparity. But as mass death by conflict and hunger is an expected outcome of two centuries of industrialization, imperialism, and world war, so too is the worldwide proliferation of disease. The world's poor not only lack food, but 2.3 billion suffer from sickness attributed to poor drinking water; 12 million of these die each year. 2.4 billion people lack adequate sanitation, and more than a billion breathe air that doesn't meet minimum World Health Organization standards. Communicable diseases are also killing at epidemic levels. Malaria, tuberculosis, and AIDS alone accounted for 5.7 million deaths in 2001, one-tenth of the world total. And new diseases and strains are appearing on a regular basis.[127] For all our intelligence and technology, the bugs continue to stay one step in front of us.

If all of this seems terribly negative, it should. The world imagines that man can solve his problems through ingenuity—that a Star Trek–like utopia where mankind has achieved an ideal existence through technology and human wisdom is feasible. But it's our cleverness that has gotten us into all of this trouble. We are wonderfully made and capable of so much, but apart from God our creativity can ultimately have only dire consequences. This is the future that the Bible predicts, the point on the prophetic timeline where we—if our analysis of the Four Horsemen is correct—now find ourselves. Though humankind fell into sin, God did not remove our dominion over this planet, and He's going to leave us in charge…right up until we prove, through a horrific act, that our

---

[127] *Beyond Borders: Thinking Critically About Global Issues*, Paula S. Rothenberg (2005; Worth Publishers)

way is the way of destruction. But before that moment, the Fifth Seal must be broken.

Revelation 6:9-6:11 ~ The Cries of the Martyrs

> 9 When He opened the fifth seal, I saw under the altar the souls of those who had been slain for the word of God and for the testimony which they held.
> 10 And they cried with a loud voice, saying, "How long, O Lord, holy and true, until You judge and avenge our blood on those who dwell on the earth?"
> 11 Then a white robe was given to each of them; and it was said to them that they should rest a little while longer, until both the number of their fellow servants and their brethren, who would be killed as they were, was completed.

Merriam-Webster's Collegiate Dictionary defines the word "martyr" as "a person who voluntarily suffers death as the penalty of witnessing to and refusing to renounce a religion."[128] This is a brief description, but there's a lot going on here. A martyr, according to this definition, is not simply a Christian who is targeted and killed because of his faith. The term "martyr" assumes that death is *voluntary*, that the individual knows that his life is in imminent danger because he is a Christian but refuses to surrender his faith. As I am writing this, hundreds—thousands—of Christians in the Middle East are being slaughtered by Muslim extremists who are intent on purging their region of all non-Muslims. Our tendency, of course, is to label those unfortunate believers as martyrs, and for many this may indeed be the case according to the strictest meaning of the word. Reportedly, in many cases, the Islamist executioners give their victims the choice to renounce their faith and convert to Islam or face death. Those who willingly die in such cases would accurately be called martyrs. It may seem that we're being nitpicky about the definition of martyrdom, but a proper grasp of this term is, in fact, critical to our understanding of one facet of the Great Tribulation that we'll encounter in a later chapter.

---

[128] *Merriam-Webster's Collegiate Dictionary* (2008; Merriam-Webster, Inc.)

In the meantime, the reader may notice that the word "martyr" doesn't actually appear in this passage in Revelation. Actually, this term is used only three times in the Bible—once in Acts in referring to the Apostle Stephen[129] and twice in Revelation.[130] But it is clear that it is martyrs who are being described here: "those who had been slain for the word of God and for the testimony which they held" (verse 9). Martyrdom is, in fact, a consistent theme throughout the New Testament. All of Jesus' twelve Disciples except Judas and John were martyred, as were the Apostle Paul and many other early Christians. Jesus Himself might be considered the first Christian martyr, though this distinction is typically given to Stephen, whose martyrdom is described for us in Acts 7:54-60 (bracketed comment mine):

> 54 When they heard these things they were cut to the heart, and they gnashed at him [Stephen] with their teeth.
> 55 But he, being full of the Holy Spirit, gazed into heaven and saw the glory of God, and Jesus standing at the right hand of God,
> 56 and said, "Look! I see the heavens opened and the Son of Man standing at the right hand of God!"
> 57 Then they cried out with a loud voice, stopped their ears, and ran at him with one accord;
> 58 and they cast him out of the city and stoned him. And the witnesses laid down their clothes at the feet of a young man named Saul.
> 59 And they stoned Stephen as he was calling on God and saying, "Lord Jesus, receive my spirit."
> 60 Then he knelt down and cried out with a loud voice, "Lord, do not charge them with this sin." And when he had said this, he fell asleep.

Here is a picture of the height of grace when confronted with the most severe form of persecution. Stephen is about to die, but instead of sobbing and begging for his life he focuses his attention away from his murderers and on Jesus. And like his Lord on the Cross, Stephen's last request is that God forgive his tormentors for

---

[129] Acts 22:20
[130] Revelation 2:13 and Revelation 17:6

their act. But the most striking thing in this passage is not Stephen's disposition, but Jesus'. Verses 55 and 56 tell us that Jesus, who we know from elsewhere in Scripture is *seated* at the right hand of God, is here standing up. Why? It is to honor Stephen for his willingness to sacrifice his life for Jesus just as Jesus sacrificed His for us, and to receive this courageous soul into Heaven. Our generation of believers sometimes is so focused on the blessings of Christianity that we forget (or deny) that there are costs associated with this walk as well. But our passage in Revelation chapter 6 tells us that there are more martyrs to come. And although this Revelation scene of the martyrs "under the altar" (an Old Testament image symbolizing the shedding of innocent blood) depicts believers who have surrendered their lives for the sake of Christ throughout the ages, John makes it clear that there will be more added to their number in this age, and in the time that is coming (verse 11 of our Revelation passage).

Indeed, some—perhaps many—Christians will be given the opportunity to "voluntarily" surrender their lives in defense of their faith during the Great Tribulation. Few scholars deny this aspect of End Times prophecy, but since martyrdom is rather unpalatable (at least to our flesh) and, more importantly, since this further suggests that Christians will in fact be present during the Great Tribulation—providing yet more evidence for a Post-Tribulation Rapture—various explanations have been formulated to shift the martyrs' identities away from us and onto others. The simplest and most popular is this: there will indeed be Christians martyred during the Great Tribulation; this cannot be denied; but these must be people who "get saved"—who become Christians—*after* the Rapture, and who subsequently march to their deaths at the hands of the Antichrist and his minions. So convinced of this scenario are those at the forefront of mainstream Christianity that several years ago several prominent teachers—whom, I want to emphasize, I have great respect for—collaborated on a video message to those who are "left behind" after the Rapture.[131] In it, hope and encouragement are conveyed to the no-doubt-bewildered unsaved loved ones of now-disappeared Christians and others who only then may be ready to listen to the message of the Gospel. They

---

[131] *Vanished* (DVD), John Hagee (2008; Cloud Ten Pictures)

are told that some of their number will face execution for their newly embraced beliefs but to stand firm. This video message is an admirable gesture, but any salvations that occur during the Great Tribulation will not be with the rest of the Body of Christ in absentia. The Bible (and other sources) makes it clear that there will be new believers added to our number during the Tribulation period. But people won't be leading themselves to Christ. As always, it will be the task of existing Christians to fulfill the Great Commission, to preach salvation to the lost. Alas, this is not going to be accomplished via DVD.

While the martyrs promised by the Fifth Seal may indeed include a few Tribulation-period converts, we can be sure that many—most—will be more seasoned believers, those of us mature enough in our faith to boldly face this task. Admittedly, although we as believers know that we have eternal life to look forward to, death at the hands of a tyrannical Antichrist and his army is nonetheless to our flesh an unsettling proposition. But martyrdom is only one of many things that we as the End Times Church must prepare ourselves to face. Another of these things—a truly unthinkable horror—is destined to take place just before the Great Tribulation begins. It is, in fact, what prompts God finally to usher in the Tribulation period. Man's attempt to govern himself throughout the millennia is about to come to fruition.

Revelation 6:12-6:17 ~ A Coming Nuclear Holocaust

12 I looked when He opened the sixth seal, and behold, there was a great earthquake; and the sun became black as sackcloth of hair, and the moon became like blood.
13 And the stars of heaven fell to the earth, as a fig tree drops its late figs when it is shaken by a mighty wind.
14 Then the sky receded as a scroll when it is rolled up, and every mountain and island was moved out of its place.
15 And the kings of the earth, the great men, the rich men, the commanders, the mighty men, every slave and every free man, hid themselves in the caves and in the rocks of the mountains,

16 and said to the mountains and rocks, "Fall on us and hide us from the face of Him who sits on the throne and from the wrath of the Lamb!
17 "For the great day of His wrath has come, and who is able to stand?"

Here, we encounter imagery that practically defines the Apocalypse genre: great earthquake, blackened sun, moon turned to blood, stars falling from heaven, etc. It's easy to feel a bit overwhelmed by all of this, but let's remember that John wrote Revelation in poetic form, and if we approach it soberly it is possible to gain some understanding. First, let's recall that the Book of Revelation describes real events, but using highly symbolic language. It is often possible to decipher these symbols by locating other passages in the Bible from which they're derived. This would seem—at least at first glance—to be the case here. Let's take a look at a bit of the Old Testament prophet Joel's description of the end of the age (Joel 2:30-32):

30 "And I will show wonders in the heavens and in the earth: blood and fire and pillars of smoke.
31 The sun shall be turned into darkness, and the moon into blood, before the coming of the great and awesome day of the Lord.
32 And it shall come to pass that whoever calls on the name of the Lord shall be saved. For in Mount Zion and in Jerusalem there shall be deliverance, as the Lord has said, among the remnant whom the Lord calls.

We'll study the Book of Joel in more depth later, but for now let's note the common imagery between this scripture and our Revelation passage. In both cases, a tremendous event is described that includes the sun turning to darkness and the moon becoming like blood. Since both passages pertain to the End Times and since they invoke common imagery, it's tempting to assume that they're describing the same thing. But we should not automatically conclude this. A critical point to remember when interpreting Scripture (prophetic or otherwise) by cross-referencing other Scripture is that imagery, however extraordinary, might be applied to more than one thing or event. Fire and smoke and the darkening of the sun and moon can be caused by more than one kind of phenomenon. And, as it turns out, these conditions do occur, by different means, more than once in the final years of human history.

So, let's see whether we can come up with a good guess about the specific kind of event that John is describing in our current passage, then we'll get back to Joel later in our study. Again, John writes regarding the Sixth Seal that "the sun became black as sackcloth of hair, and the moon became like blood" (verse 12 of our Revelation passage). Notice that he's using simile here: the sun did not literally become sackcloth and the moon did not literally turn into blood, but the sun became black *as* sackcloth and the moon became *like* blood. John is merely describing their appearance. I teach a Bible study at my church every week, and (you may not be surprised to learn) the topic of the End Times is the main theme. One particularly enthusiastic attendee keeps an eye on current events and often calls me with the announcement, "The end is beginning!" (I always try to talk him down, of course—it's easy to see in everyday occurrences extraordinary things for which we're searching too fervently.) Not long ago, this friend phoned to alert me to the appearance of the sun and moon in the daytime sky. The sun looked a bit darkened and the moon was a reddish hue. At first glance this seemed an exciting development, but, alas, the cause was quickly traced to a large forest fire in a neighboring state. Winds were pushing the smoke in our direction and this caused the sun and moon to appear—at least to some degree—as described in Joel, in Revelation, and in other passages throughout the Bible. Of course, in this case, this was not a portent of the end. But it did, in fact, demonstrate what might cause the sun and moon to appear as described—heavy particulates in the air, including smoke and ash.

Again, many phenomena can produce this effect, some natural, some manmade. But if we concede that such things as the darkening of the sun and moon (not to mention earthquakes, lightning, thunder, hail, etc.) can have more than a single cause and may occur on more than one occasion during the last of the Last Days, how can we hope to understand what the Sixth Seal actually represents? Perhaps the best approach is to consider its *context*. Recall that the first Four Seals (the Four Horsemen), though influenced by God, nonetheless represent *manmade* phenomena. Even the Fifth Seal, though seen not on Earth but in Heaven, could be said to result from human action—the martyrs John glimpses under the altar are there because men killed them, and because the martyrs, themselves, accepted martyrdom. Could it be that the Sixth Seal describes an event that is likewise brought about by man? Perhaps the greatest evidence that this is indeed the case is what will follow the Sixth Seal. As we'll discover in the next section[132], just before God unleashes the plagues that comprise the start of the Great Tribulation—natural phenomena that will be sent by God Himself to begin this period of final judgment against man's world system—He will send an angel around the world to seal His people for protection against His plagues. If the Sixth Seal depicted something not caused by man but sent by God—if it was likewise an act of His judgment—wouldn't we expect Him to seal us for protection *before* the Sixth Seal, rather than after? The explanation is simple. The Sixth Seal, like the others, is not a natural event but a manmade one that along with the others constitutes the prelude to the Great Tribulation. As stated earlier, the Tribulation period will begin when God decides that it is time, and it will be by His own hand and using His own devices: which is to say, natural phenomena. And God will decide that the time has come when man has proven once and for all that he is, apart from God, ultimately capable only of self-destruction. This is what the Sixth Seal depicts: a final destructive act of humankind that will compel God to at last begin the process of bringing to an end our tainted governance of this planet.

Let's consider this notion in the context of our time. Doing so assumes that we are, in fact, very near to the last of the Last Days. And, indeed, there is ample reason to believe this, as we will see more and more as our study progresses. So, we'll examine the Sixth Seal in light of man's current capabilities in order to consider whether this generation is indeed capable of producing a scenario like the one that is depicted. In presenting the events that follow from the breaking of the Sixth Seal, John describes a great earthquake, the darkening of the sky, the "stars of heaven" falling

---

[132] Section "Revelation 7:1-7:8 ~ We Are Not Appointed to Wrath"

to the Earth, the sky receding "as a scroll," and the displacement of "every mountain and island." We understand that John wrote Revelation in poetic form, and, indeed, we wouldn't want to try to interpret his words here as precisely literal. For example, it's not possible for stars to fall to Earth. Sometimes we see what we call "falling stars" in the night sky, but these are actually just tiny grains of rocky or metallic material. If a real star, like the sun, came anywhere near the Earth, our entire planet would be incinerated. So, John is simply describing something that *looks* like stars falling to the Earth. Likewise, any force that would cause literally "every mountain and island" to move from its place would probably annihilate every higher form of life on Earth, thus rendering moot the remainder of the Book of Revelation. Nevertheless, it's clear that John is describing some monumental event that has a profound impact on the whole world. Does man have any devices at his disposal that could produce an effect like the one represented by the Sixth Seal? Of course, and this, like the effects of the Four Horsemen of the first four seals, derives from the last two centuries of industrialization, modernization, and conflict. If our analysis is correct, the next event to watch for on the prophetic timeline is nuclear war.

Let's attempt to apply this hypothesis—and we must concede that all attempts to interpret prophetic details before they happen are ultimately that—to John's description of the Sixth Seal. If what John was shown after observing the martyrs in Heaven (the Fifth Seal) was a nuclear war on Earth, he might well describe the vision of the delivery devices descending on their targets as "stars" falling from heaven to the Earth. These might include devices such as InterContinental Ballistic Missiles (ICBMs), Submarine-Launched Ballistic Missiles (SLBMs), and Multiple Independently-targetable Reentry Vehicles (MIRVs).[133] In other words—if we're analyzing this particular detail correctly—John did not see the detonation of "dirty bombs" or "suitcase nukes," weapons typically associated with terrorism, but perhaps high-tech (and expensive) missiles. This implies that such a war will happen among *nations*. But whether or not this is the case, and however large or small the altercation, and

---

[133] *Encyclopedia of United States National Security*, Richard J. Samuels (2005; SAGE Publications)

whoever the belligerents are, this interpretation—that a nuclear conflict is what John is describing—correlates well with our first five Seals. Like the first five, the Sixth Seal will be by the hand of man, possible only in (in fact, attributable to) the modern age, and will be *global* in scope, or, at least, in consequence.

When the missiles reach their targets and their payloads are detonated, John writes, "Then the sky receded as a scroll when it is rolled up, and every mountain and island was moved out of its place" (verse 14). Back in school, many of us were shown films of atomic bombs being tested in the Nevada desert. Today, we can see them on history shows on TV, or on the Internet. When such a bomb is exploded, indeed, the sky appears to recede like a scroll being rolled up, and it seems that everything in the blast range, no matter how immovable, is displaced. The ground trembles like a great earthquake. And indeed, the resulting plume of smoke and dust can block out the sun and moon for weeks, even months.[134] And those films depict bombs that are mere firecrackers compared to today's nuclear warheads. If just one strategic nuclear weapon were used today, the effects would be a thousand times more severe than those suffered in Hiroshima and Nagasaki and would last for years. But John may not be describing just one of these, but perhaps many—an unprecedented altercation. Whatever the case, everyone on Earth, he tells us—"the kings of the earth, the great men, the rich men, the commanders, the mighty men, every slave and every free man" (verse 15)—will be affected. Many will perceive this event as "the wrath of God," or some variation on this theme, and a widespread sense of doom will ensue.

Again, this interpretation of the Sixth Seal, while speculative, seems to be very much in harmony with the context in which it appears and with our assumption about where we are on the prophetic timeline. But, one might ask, how likely is it—really—that some sort of nuclear conflict is imminent? Some scholars of international relations would answer, very. After all, when has man ever invented a weapon whose purpose was *not* to be used? During the Cold War, the opposite perception—that nuclear weapons were more for

---

[134] *Nuclear Winter: Implications for U.S. and Soviet Nuclear Strategy*, Philip J. Romero (1984; Rand Corporation)

show than for actual use—may have seemed reasonable. But the days of détente and MAD ("Mutual Assured Destruction," a concept that supposedly rendered a first strike between the world's two superpowers unthinkable) are over. No longer is the world essentially divided into two camps dominated by the United States and the Soviet Union. Instead, today's world tends more toward a sort of international anarchy. One might presume that the United States will continue to use temperance where its nuclear arsenal is concerned. But can we safely assume the same about Russia, who seems still to be struggling to define its role in the post–Cold War world; who increasingly shows signs of longing for its old superpower days; whose political, social, and economic turmoil (both internal and vis-à-vis its former-Soviet Bloc neighbors) seems only to be growing worse; and who continues actively to take a counter-America (and counter-Israel) stance in the Middle East? Even if Russia can be trusted not to use its nukes, how confident can we be that Moscow won't transfer its technology, or even an actual weapon, to a less-responsible power?[135] Of much greater concern is the newest member of the nuclear club, North Korea, who successfully tested a weapon on October 9, 2006, and who is a renegade state—in political science vernacular, a pariah—that seems bent on destabilizing the current world order.[136] Other nuclear powers include Great Britain, France, China, India, and Pakistan. And Israel, too, is widely believed to have nuclear weapons.[137]

But more troubling than any existing nuclear power is a state that is at this very moment working feverishly, against all international objections, to obtain nuclear weapons capabilities: Iran. When North Korea—who, again, seems determined to upset the current world order—detonated its first nuclear device in 2006, Iranian scientists were present, and the Iranians were there again when the North Koreans conducted even more successful tests in 2009 and

---

[135] *Nuclear Weapons and Nonproliferation: A Reference Handbook (Contemporary World Issues)*, Sarah J. Diehl and James Clay Moltz (2007; ABC-CLIO)
[136] North Korean Nuclear Operationality: Regional Security and Nonproliferation, Gregory J. Moore (2013; Johns Hopkins University Press)
[137] *The Worst-Kept Secret: Israel's Bargain with the Bomb*, Avner Cohen (2010; Columbia University Press)

2013.[138] It seems clear: Pyongyang is sharing its nuclear weapons technology with Tehran. Most analysts agree that Iran is mere months away from achieving its goal. Some believe that the Islamist regime already possesses the ability to deliver and detonate a low-yield nuke.[139] Whatever the case—however soon in our future Iran obtains a nuclear weapon—Iran's leadership is not remaining silent about its intended use. In December 2000, in a televised speech, former president (and advisor to Iran's Supreme Leader, Ali Hosseini Khamenei), Akbar Hashemi Rafsanjani, proclaimed:

"If one day, a very important day, of course, the Islamic World will also be equipped with the weapons available to Israel now, the imperialist strategy will reach an impasse, because the employment of even one atomic bomb inside Israel will wipe it off the face of the Earth."[140]

Rafsanjani's successor, Mahmoud Ahmadinejad, regularly made similar statements. On April 14, 2006, just three days after announcing that Iran had successfully achieved uranium enrichment[141]—a critical step in developing a weapon—President Ahmadinejad said at a pro-Palestinian conference:

"Like it or not, the Zionist regime is heading toward annihilation… The Zionist regime is a rotten, dried tree that will be eliminated by one storm."[142]

As disconcerting is the idea that a nation like Iran—who is openly bent on the destruction of the nation of Israel—may soon have (or perhaps already has) nuclear weapons capabilities, perhaps equally troubling is the prospect that a non-state actor—a terrorist

---

[138] North Korean Nuclear Operationality: Regional Security and Nonproliferation, Gregory J. Moore (2013; Johns Hopkins University Press)
[139] "Iran can now build and deliver nukes, US intel reports," Marissa Newman (*The Times of Israel*; January 29, 2014)
[140] "Iran and Syria as Strategic Support for Palestinian Terrorism" (Israel Ministry of Foreign Affairs; September 30, 2002)
[141] "Iran and the UN: 2006 at a Glance" (Britain Israel Communications and Research Centre; December 23, 2006)
[142] "Iran President: Israel Will Be Annihilated" (Associated Press; April 14, 2006)

organization like al-Qaeda or the newly emerging Islamic State (ISIS)—will one day soon get their hands on a nuclear device. Every radical Islamist group's stated aim is precisely the same as Iran's: to destroy the nation of Israel. But, unlike Iran, these groups don't suffer from the messy liability of having their own nation to protect. Israel could counter an Iranian attack with a strike on Tehran, which would, for all intents and purposes, destroy the Iranian regime. Terrorist organizations, on the other hand, are typically comprised of cells that are scattered throughout multiple countries, even multiple continents. How could Israel successfully counter a nuclear attack by one of these groups? Our analysis earlier speculated that Revelation's Sixth Seal depicts a large-scale exchange of nuclear missiles among nation-states, but we should note that even a single, low-yield nuclear device detonated by terrorists in downtown Tel Aviv (in which case the "stars of heaven [falling] to the earth" described by John in verse 13 of our current passage would instead depict an exchange of conventional rockets that precedes the use of a single nuclear weapon) would upset today's world order more than almost any other event imaginable.

On December 26, 1991, the Soviet Union was officially dissolved. In the decade that followed, we all wondered what shape the post–Cold War world would eventually take. Would a sort of global democracy emerge, an international utopia benevolently headed by the sole surviving superpower, the United States? Would a new superpower—perhaps China—rise to dominance and challenge America's position as hegemon? Or perhaps there would be no strong global leadership at all, and the world would decay into a chaotic conglomerate of staunchly independent states vying for position and resources. Any of these seemed viable possibilities, and very few of us could have imagined the scenario that would actually come to pass. We got our first glimpse of the new world order—the one that, arguably, is going to define the final years leading up to the Great Tribulation—on September 11, 2001, when Islamist terrorists hijacked four passenger planes and used them to strike the symbol of America's military might, the Pentagon; and to reduce to rubble the symbol of America's economic might, New

York City's World Trade Center.[143] But to truly understand that event—and how it has shaped the world that we live in today, one defined by rising Islamist extremism in the Middle East and throughout the world—we must first understand the true motives behind the attack of 9/11. Just one month after that day—which saw some 3,000 people killed in the single worst terrorist strike against the U.S. in history—Osama bin Laden, the leader of the group that carried out the attack, made this statement in an interview given to the *Al Jazeera* television network:

"We swore that America wouldn't live in security until we live it truly in Palestine. This showed the reality of America, which puts Israel's interest above its own people's interest. America won't get out of this crisis until it gets out of the Arabian Peninsula, and until it stops its support of Israel."[144]

Indeed, the growing strife that these days seems to permeate the entire world is focused on the tiny nation of Israel. The global paradigm in which we find ourselves today is defined to a large extent by an unprecedented spite for Israel, a hatred that is bent on the Jewish state's destruction and that seems to be growing more widespread with each passing moment. As our study progresses, we will see more and more that Israel—and more specifically, Jerusalem, and most specifically of all, the Temple Mount—truly is at the epicenter of the End Times story. If Revelation's Sixth Seal is, in fact, describing some sort of nuclear altercation, it seems a good guess that Israel will be at the center of it.

We can only speculate how widespread the nuclear conflict described by John's Sixth Seal might be, but there is no doubt that the whole world will be affected. There will be widespread horror, but not utter destruction. Israel and the U.S. will survive, as will the world's governing body, the United Nations (or its successor). Commerce will continue and life will go on. But the challenge to human resilience will have only just begun. The Sixth Seal—the full

---

[143] *The Looming Tower: Al-Qaeda and the Road to 9/11*, Lawrence Wright (2006; Knopf)
[144] "Transcript of Bin Laden's October interview" (CNN.com; February 5, 2002)

fruition of man's failed attempt to govern himself and this world—is, for God, the last straw. Once this seal on the Scroll—the Scroll being God's decree of judgment that will comprise what we know as the Great Tribulation—is broken, God begins to set the stage for the final act of the great drama of human history.

Revelation 7:1-7:8 ~ We Are Not Appointed to Wrath

It's no surprise that the average Christian does not want to go through the Great Tribulation. Most of us understand that this is going to be an unprecedented time of trouble on Earth. As Jesus Himself put it in His great End Times dissertation, "For then there will be great tribulation, such as has not been since the beginning of the world until this time, no, nor ever shall be."[145] It's easy to understand, then, the enormous popularity of the Pre-Tribulation Rapture doctrine, however unscriptural this viewpoint happens to be. Instead of preparing for the trials associated with the Tribulation period, most contemporary mainstream Christians—including many of the most popular teachers of our day—have embraced the notion that if one is saved, one has a Golden Ticket out of here before things start to go truly bad. Instead of endeavoring to equip ourselves to endure the times that are coming, many promote a doctrine of escapism and present the false hope that steps can be taken now to avoid tribulation later. We choose to fear the Great Tribulation rather than to face it in faith. One scripture that is often pointed to as evidence that God intends to deliver Christians out of this world before the Great Tribulation begins is 1 Thessalonians 5:9:

> 9 For God did not appoint us to wrath, but to obtain salvation through our Lord Jesus Christ...

But as we discussed at length in Chapter 5 of this book, in the section "We Are Not Appointed to Wrath," there is a difference between wrath and tribulation. And it is possible to be subject to one without being subject to the other. As we acknowledged in that section, the Great Tribulation is indeed a time in which God will unleash His wrath and judgment upon this world—in fact, it is an

---

[145] Matthew 24:21

almost unprecedented cataclysmic act by God Himself that ushers in this period, as we'll see later in our study—but this does not mean that He intends to make us, His people, the target of it. On the contrary, God goes to great lengths to shield us from His contribution to the Tribulation just before He initiates this period, as we find in our current Revelation passage (Revelation 7:1-8):

1 After these things I saw four angels standing at the four corners of the earth, holding the four winds of the earth, that the wind should not blow on the earth, on the sea, or on any tree.
2 Then I saw another angel ascending from the east, having the seal of the living God. And he cried with a loud voice to the four angels to whom it was granted to harm the earth and the sea,
3 saying, "Do not harm the earth, the sea, or the trees till we have sealed the servants of our God on their foreheads."
4 And I heard the number of those who were sealed. One hundred and forty-four thousand of all the tribes of the children of Israel were sealed:
5 of the tribe of Judah twelve thousand were sealed; of the tribe of Reuben twelve thousand were sealed; of the tribe of Gad twelve thousand were sealed;
6 of the tribe of Asher twelve thousand were sealed; of the tribe of Naphtali twelve thousand were sealed; of the tribe of Manasseh twelve thousand were sealed;
7 of the tribe of Simeon twelve thousand were sealed; of the tribe of Levi twelve thousand were sealed; of the tribe of Issachar twelve thousand were sealed;
8 of the tribe of Zebulun twelve thousand were sealed; of the tribe of Joseph twelve thousand were sealed; of the tribe of Benjamin twelve thousand were sealed.

In this passage, we find an angelic host whose task it is "to harm the earth and the sea." But they are restrained. Although they are in position to release the forces that will wreak havoc on the Earth—demonstrating that God, in response to the deeds of man represented by the First, Second, Third, Fourth, Fifth, and especially Sixth Seals, is at last ready to begin the Great Tribulation—the angels will not proceed until one last thing is done. Namely, God's people must first be sealed for protection against whatever it is that God is about to bring on the Earth. Here, we also get our first clue about what form God's wrath will take. Notice the terminology used. The angels are "holding the four winds of the earth" to prevent them from blowing on the Earth, the sea, and the trees. The image here is of *natural* phenomena, in contrast to the *manmade* events and conditions that comprise the seals that precede this passage. Why would we imagine that God would use anything other than His existing creation—nature—to accomplish His judgment on Earth? This is the form that God's wrath has always taken, as in the flood of Noah's day,[146] the meteorite storm that destroyed Sodom and Gomorrah,[147] and the un-parting of the Red Sea upon Pharaoh's armies.[148]

We'll get a close look at the events that comprise the start of the Great Tribulation shortly. But first, let's consider who it is that God intends to seal for protection against these things. Who are the 144,000? In verse 4 of our passage, John tells us that this group is composed "of all the tribes of the children of Israel." As we discussed earlier in this book, many scholars mistakenly believe that the number 144,000 is to be taken literally.[149] Likewise, the identity of those who comprise this group is also commonly misconstrued. Some groups—such as the Jehovah's Witnesses[150]—claim that *they* are Revelation's 144,000. But the most common misconception—a view held by many proponents of the Pre-Tribulation Rapture—is that the 144,000 is made up strictly of Jews. Admittedly, we can see the basis of this argument in our passage: John explicitly refers to the tribes of Israel and then enumerates those twelve tribes.

However, just as the number 144,000 is not literal but symbolic—meant to convey a certain meaning—so, too, is John's depiction of this group's members. Let's review our analysis of the number 144,000. You'll recall from our earlier discussion, on the duality of

---

[146] Genesis 7:1-24
[147] Genesis 19:12-29
[148] Exodus 14:1-31
[149] Discussed in Chapter 5 "The Pre-Tribulation Rapture," in the section "Church Not Mentioned During Depiction of Tribulation in Book of Revelation"
[150] *From Paradise Lost to Paradise Regained*, Watchtower Society (1958; Watchtower Society)

the Old and New Israel in the Book of Revelation,[151] that this number is meant to symbolize the entirety of God's people, spanning all of history, throughout the Old and New Testaments, in perfection. This perfection is evoked by multiplying the number 12 representing the 12 tribes of the nation of Israel, by the number 12 representing the 12 Disciples of Christ, by the number 1,000 which conveys perfection, as symbolized in ancient times by the perfect numerical cube, 10 x 10 x 10. But now that we've arrived at our current Revelation passage, wherein the 144,000 are described, how do we reconcile John's depiction of this group—again, he not only refers to "the tribes of the children of Israel" (verse 4), but actually names each of the twelve tribes—with our conclusion that the 144,000 includes not only Jews but Christians as well?

One clue reveals itself upon closer examination of John's list of tribes. First, notice the names of the tribes as presented: Judah, Reuben, Gad, Asher, Naphtali, Manasseh, Simeon, Levi, Issachar, Zebulun, Joseph, and Benjamin. At first glance, this seems fairly straightforward, but a simple comparison of this list to the actual sons of Jacob for whom the tribes were named[152] reveals some surprises. The most obvious is that Dan—one of Jacob's sons by Rachel's maidservant Bilhah—is missing. Dan's full brother Naphtali (who is also Bilhah's son) is present, but Dan has been replaced by Manasseh. Manasseh, however, is not one of Jacob's sons but rather his *grandson*—he is the son of Jacob's son Joseph. Joseph is also in John's list, which seems particularly strange. Technically, the tribe of Joseph is considered to have been split into two tribes, named for his sons, Manasseh and Ephraim. We might expect, then, Manasseh and Ephraim to be listed together in this case, and for Joseph to be excluded, but instead we find Manasseh and Joseph listed together. It seems clear: John's list is not meant to be a literal presentation of the "physical" Israel. He does not mean to indicate literal Jews, but is attempting to convey something else entirely.

---

[151] Chapter 5 "The Pre-Tribulation Rapture"; section "Church Not Mentioned During Depiction of Tribulation in Book of Revelation"
[152] See Genesis 35:23-26

THE SCROLL WITH THE SEVEN SEALS: PRELUDE TO THE GREAT TRIBULATION

To determine what John is trying to tell us, we should begin by asking why Dan and Ephraim have been excluded from his list. Chapter 18 of the Book of Judges presents an account of the worship of false gods that had crept into the tribe of Ephraim, and the Danites' subsequent adoption of this practice. Both tribes—Ephraim in particular—were chastised throughout the Old Testament for their idolatry. It seems reasonable to conclude, then, that John's exclusion of Dan and Ephraim from his list is because Revelation's 144,000 are meant to represent not the physical Israel, but the *spiritual* Israel.

But before we consider the concept of a "spiritual Israel," let's ask one more question: why does John bother to include Joseph in his list of tribes? After all, if it isn't really logical to list Joseph and Manasseh together (remember, the tribe of Manasseh essentially constitutes half of the tribe of Joseph), why not just leave Joseph's name out along with Dan's and Ephraim's? The answer is simple: the physical Israel includes twelve tribes, so the spiritual one must as well. In Western Christian culture, we tend to shy away from "numerology"—indeed, many relegate this concept to the realm of the occult—but numbers in the Bible can be extremely meaningful, not only in the Book of Revelation but throughout God's Word. Generally speaking, the number twelve in Biblical terms represents completeness, or—more telling—a perfect theocratic government.[153] So, the number twelve in representing Israel's composition is meant to convey God's intention for His people: that they rely upon Him, not an earthly form of government, for their total guidance and direction. And it also looks forward to our role in God's coming government on Earth, the Millennial Reign of Christ that will follow the seven-year Great Tribulation.[154] The importance of maintaining consistency in regard to the number twelve is demonstrated with the New Covenant Church as well. Recall that the number of Jesus' Disciples was reduced from twelve to eleven when Judas Iscariot hung himself after betraying Jesus.[155] This—a change in the number of primary Disciples—might not seem like an important matter, but

---

[153] *Number in Scripture*, E.W. Bullinger (1985; Kregel Publications)
[154] Revelation 20:4-6
[155] Matthew 27:3-10

look what took place shortly after Jesus' resurrection and ascension (Acts 1:15-26):

> 15 And in those days Peter stood up in the midst of the disciples (altogether the number of names was about a hundred and twenty), and said,
> 16 "Men and brethren, this Scripture had to be fulfilled, which the Holy Spirit spoke before by the mouth of David concerning Judas, who became a guide to those who arrested Jesus;
> 17 "for he was numbered with us and obtained a part in this ministry."
> 18 (Now this man purchased a field with the wages of iniquity; and falling headlong, he burst open in the middle and all his entrails gushed out.
> 19 And it became known to all those dwelling in Jerusalem; so that field is called in their own language, Akel Dama, that is, Field of Blood.)
> 20 "For it is written in the Book of Psalms: 'Let his dwelling place be desolate, and let no one live in it'; and, 'Let another take his office.'
> 21 "Therefore, of these men who have accompanied us all the time that the Lord Jesus went in and out among us,
> 22 "beginning from the baptism of John to that day when He was taken up from us, one of these must become a witness with us of His resurrection."
> 23 And they proposed two: Joseph called Barsabas, who was surnamed Justus, and Matthias.
> 24 And they prayed and said, "You, O Lord, who know the hearts of all, show which of these two You have chosen
> 25 "to take part in this ministry and apostleship from which Judas by transgression fell, that he might go to his own place."
> 26 And they cast their lots, and the lot fell on Matthias. And he was numbered with the eleven apostles.

So, we see that even after Jesus' earthly ministry was concluded, it was important that the number of His Disciples remain at twelve—not eleven, as they had been reduced to; and likewise, not at thirteen, which could have been more easily accomplished by allowing both Barsabas and Matthias to be counted among them. Again, the key number representing both the Old Covenant people and New is twelve, and John's list—which depicts a spiritual Israel that is comprised of both of these groups—simply reflects this.

One final clue that John's enumeration of the twelve tribes is meant to convey not the physical Israel but a spiritual one is the real-world impracticality of a literal interpretation. In order for John's 144,000 to be composed of members of each of the distinct tribes he names, it would be necessary for modern-day representatives of each of these tribes to step forward and claim tribal affiliation. Generally speaking, this is not a problem where two of the tribes—Judah and Levi—are concerned. But for the other ten, this has not been feasible since some half a dozen centuries before John even penned the Book of Revelation. The story of Israel's so-called Ten Lost Tribes is told in the Second Book of the Kings, where we read (2 Kings 17:6-8):

> 6   In the ninth year of Hoshea, the king of Assyria took Samaria and carried Israel away to Assyria, and placed them in Halah and by the Habor, the River of Gozan, and in the cities of the Medes.
> 7   For so it was that the children of Israel had sinned against the Lord their God, who had brought them up out of the land of Egypt, from under the hand of Pharaoh king of Egypt; and they had feared other gods,
> 8   and had walked in the statutes of the nations whom the Lord had cast out from before the children of Israel, and of the kings of Israel, which they had made.

This passage recounts an event that took place in 722 B.C., when all of the tribes of the northern kingdom of Israel were exiled to upper Mesopotamia and Medes by the Assyrian monarch Shalmaneser V. These included Reuben, Simeon, Issachar, Zebulun, Dan, Naphtali, Gad, Asher, Ephraim, and Manasseh (again, these latter two were the sons of Joseph, whose tribe was split for the purpose of land allocation; the tribe of Levi was, generally speaking, not given land, as the Levites' inheritance was the priesthood). All of the members of these "lost tribes" were forcibly intermingled with other minority groups in order to promote intermarriage with non-Jews, thereby decreasing the likelihood of resistance to the resettling over the long term. By John's day, it is not likely that a single person descended from the Ten Lost Tribes had pure tribal blood running through his veins—the blood of Reuben, Simeon, Issachar, Zebulun, and the rest had become mixed, not only with each other (most likely) but with the blood of foreigners as well. The southern kingdom of Judah—which included the tribes of Judah, Benjamin, and Levi (who, as priests, were fortunate enough to be living in Jerusalem in order to administer the Temple)—escaped invasion. Some 150 years later, during the Babylonian captivity of the sixth century B.C., the Benjamites were absorbed into the tribe of Judah. And so, today, every Jew on Earth can trace his lineage to one of only two tribes: either Judah or Levi.

Although it's clear, then, that John's list of "all the tribes of the children of Israel" is not describing the literal, physical nation of Israel but rather a conceptual, spiritual one, the idea that he means to include Christians in this may nonetheless seem awkward. After all, I am a Christian, not a Jew. I am a member of the Body of Christ, not a citizen of Israel. However, the Apostle Paul tells us that as Christians we *are* Jews, and we are Israel. In Romans 2:28-29, Paul writes:

> 28 For he is not a Jew who is one outwardly, nor is circumcision that which is outward in the flesh;
> 29 but he is a Jew who is one inwardly; and circumcision is that of the heart, in the Spirit, not in the letter; whose praise is not from men but from God.

And in Galatians 6:15-16, Paul tells us (emphasis mine):

> 15 For in Christ Jesus neither circumcision nor uncircumcision avails anything, but a new creation.
> 16 And as many as walk according to this rule, peace and mercy be upon them, and upon the *Israel* of God.

Admittedly, by assigning Christians, as "spiritual Jews," to actual tribes—as he seems to do in our Revelation passage—John is taking this concept a step further than Paul. But in a text as highly poetic and as richly symbolic as the Book of Revelation, this should not be completely surprising. And when we encounter the 144,000 again later, in Revelation chapter 14, John's expanded description there will make it abundantly clear that he does indeed mean to include Christians in this group, as we'll see.

Let's wrap up our look at our current passage by considering what John means by "sealed...on their foreheads" (verse 3). As you might have guessed, John is most likely not referring to a literal "sealing"—that is, a physical mark—here. Instead, this is an invisible—a spiritual—means of differentiating the true servants of God so that they will be spared when God's judgment comes down upon the rest of the world. This may seem a bit strange. After all, aren't we as believers already "sealed" in a sense? Paul tells us so in Ephesians 1:13-14 (emphasis mine):

> 13 In Him you also trusted, after you heard the word of truth, the gospel of your salvation; in whom also, having believed, you were *sealed* with the Holy Spirit of promise,
> 14 who is the guarantee of our inheritance until the redemption of the purchased possession, to the praise of His glory.

Here, we are to understand that, as believers, we have been sealed—authenticated and confirmed—by the Holy Spirit, who functions as the guarantor of our salvation until our ultimate redemption at Christ's return. So, why must we be sealed again, as Revelation chapter 7 depicts? This idea—that we as God's people need extra protection, some sort of special seal to set us apart, prior to a period of God's manifest judgment on earth—may seem strange, but it is not without scriptural precedent. The Prophet Ezekiel records one such incident. In Ezekiel 8:17-9:7, he describes God's judgment against a depraved Jerusalem (emphasis mine):

> 17 And He said to me, "Have you seen this, O son of man? Is it a trivial thing to the house of Judah to commit the abominations which they commit here? For they have filled the land with violence; then they have returned to provoke Me to anger. Indeed they put the branch to their nose.

18 "Therefore I also will act in fury. My eye will not spare nor will I have pity; and though they cry in My ears with a loud voice, I will not hear them."
1 Then He called out in my hearing with a loud voice, saying, "Let those who have charge over the city draw near, each with a deadly weapon in his hand."
2 And suddenly six men came from the direction of the upper gate, which faces north, each with his battle-ax in his hand. One man among them was clothed with linen and had a writer's inkhorn at his side. They went in and stood beside the bronze altar.
3 Now the glory of the God of Israel had gone up from the cherub, where it had been, to the threshold of the temple. And He called to the man clothed with linen, who had the writer's inkhorn at his side;
4 and the Lord said to him, "Go through the midst of the city, through the midst of Jerusalem, and *put a mark on the foreheads* of the men who sigh and cry over all the abominations that are done within it."
5 To the others He said in my hearing, "Go after him through the city and kill; do not let your eye spare, nor have any pity.
6 "Utterly slay old and young men, maidens and little children and women; but do not come near anyone on whom is the mark; and begin at My sanctuary." So they began with the elders who were before the temple.
7 Then He said to them, "Defile the temple, and fill the courts with the slain. Go out!" And they went out and killed in the city.

Here we are presented an image of God's judgment against Israel for its sins against Him. However, this is not an actual event but rather a vision given to Ezekiel to symbolize the ravaging of Jerusalem by the armies of Babylon some five years later.[156] The "six men" introduced in verse 2 depict angel-warriors who carry out God's judgment, but the real-world agents of God's wrath would be a people who didn't even know Him, the Chaldeans. This is a good example of the degree to which God influences events and nations—even ungodly nations—to carry out His will, as we saw

---

[156] 2 Kings 25:1-21

with our Four Horsemen. It is also a good example of how highly symbolic prophecy can be. The remnant in Israel did not receive a literal, physical mark on their foreheads prior to the Babylonian invasion, and neither will we before the Great Tribulation. But rest assured that—thanks to the invisible, spiritual seal that we receive—we will be exempt from the wrath of God that will define that period.

Though the mark of God in Ezekiel and Revelation is symbolic—that is, not literal, not physical—it's worthwhile here to consider the ultimate type and shadow of this concept. Perhaps the most important parallel of God's people enduring—and making it to the other side of—the Great Tribulation is the story of the deliverance of the Israelites from Egypt. As pointed out in our earlier chapter on the Pre-Tribulation Rapture,[157] God did not deliver His people out of Egypt prior to the Ten Plagues—which are a foreshadow the Seven Trumpets and Seven Bowls of the Great Tribulation, as we'll see—but He did miraculously protect them through this time of judgment. The most dramatic of these plagues, the tenth, gives us the ultimate archetype of the sealing of God's people in our Revelation passage (Exodus 12:1-13):

1 Now the Lord spoke to Moses and Aaron in the land of Egypt, saying,
2 "This month shall be your beginning of months; it shall be the first month of the year to you.
3 "Speak to all the congregation of Israel, saying: 'On the tenth of this month every man shall take for himself a lamb, according to the house of his father, a lamb for a household.
4 'And if the household is too small for the lamb, let him and his neighbor next to his house take it according to the number of the persons; according to each man's need you shall make your count for the lamb.
5 'Your lamb shall be without blemish, a male of the first year. You may take it from the sheep or from the goats.

---

[157] Chapter 5 "The Pre-Tribulation Rapture"; section "The 'Loving Father' Argument"

6   'Now you shall keep it until the fourteenth day of the same month. Then the whole assembly of the congregation of Israel shall kill it at twilight.
7   'And they shall take some of the blood and put it on the two doorposts and on the lintel of the houses where they eat it.
8   'Then they shall eat the flesh on that night; roasted in fire, with unleavened bread and with bitter herbs they shall eat it.
9   "Do not eat it raw, nor boiled at all with water, but roasted in fire—its head with its legs and its entrails.
10 'You shall let none of it remain until morning, and what remains of it until morning you shall burn with fire.
11 'And thus you shall eat it: with a belt on your waist, your sandals on your feet, and your staff in your hand. So you shall eat it in haste. It is the Lord's Passover.
12 'For I will pass through the land of Egypt on that night, and will strike all the firstborn in the land of Egypt, both man and beast; and against all the gods of Egypt I will execute judgment: I am the Lord.
13 'Now the blood shall be a sign for you on the houses where you are. And when I see the blood, I will pass over you; and the plague shall not be on you to destroy you when I strike the land of Egypt.'"

The reader may already be aware that this, the Lord's Passover, is the principal type and shadow of the sacrifice of the ultimate "lamb without blemish,"[158] Jesus Christ. This is reflected in the practice that most of us know today as Communion, instituted by Jesus as He celebrated the time of Passover with His Disciples at the so-called Last Supper (Luke 22:14-20):

14 When the hour had come, He sat down, and the twelve apostles with Him.
15 Then He said to them, "With fervent desire I have desired to eat this Passover with you before I suffer;
16 "for I say to you, I will no longer eat of it until it is fulfilled in the kingdom of God."

---

[158] John 1:29

17 Then He took the cup, and gave thanks, and said, "Take this and divide it among yourselves;
18 "for I say to you, I will not drink of the fruit of the vine until the kingdom of God comes."
19 And He took bread, gave thanks and broke it, and gave it to them, saying, "This is My body which is given for you; do this in remembrance of Me."
20 Likewise He also took the cup after supper, saying, "This cup is the new covenant in My blood, which is shed for you."

So, in Jesus we enjoy a new sort of "Passover." In that we "eat of His body" (that is, internalize His Word) and "drink of His blood" (receive the forgiveness for our sins, achieved by His sacrifice), we are saved—and we are protected from God's wrath, in this time and in the time to come. The sealing of the 144,000 just prior to the events that will define the last seven years of this age reminds us of this reassuring truth.

And so, contrary to one of the principal concerns of Pre-Tribulation Rapture proponents, our presence here on Earth during the Great Tribulation by no means mandates that we as Christians be subject to the acts of God that will help to define this period. In facing the last of the Last Days, our faith can—*must*— supersede our fears. In good times and in bad, we as believers are to trust God wholly and unswervingly, and He *will* guard and protect us, as the psalmist proclaims (Psalm 46:1-3):

1 God is our refuge and strength, a very present help in trouble.
2 Therefore we will not fear, even though the earth be removed, and though the mountains be carried into the midst of the sea;
3 though its waters roar and be troubled, though the mountains shake with its swelling.

Revelation 7:9-7:17 ~ On the Other Hand...

We saw in the previous section that God intends to protect His people from His contribution to the Great Tribulation. Since we now understand that we as Christians are destined to endure that time, this is good news. But there's some not-so-good news: God is not the only one who contributes to the Tribulation period. The Tribulation story is ultimately about man's attempt to be his own god—the "original sin" that got Adam and Eve evicted from the Garden—and his final showdown with the one true God, who ultimately has the victory. We would therefore expect humankind—influenced by Satan, of course, just as in the Garden—to have its own role to play in this period, and it does. The Antichrist, the so-called One World government, and the "Mark of the Beast" are all products of man's ultimate expression of self-rule. And the enemy to this endeavor is known: it is God and all manifestations of God on Earth, including, of course, we Christians. Because of this, we will be targeted, as we'll see. It is hard for many modern Christians—especially those who enjoy life in relative affluence, such as those of us in western nations like the United States—to imagine that God would permit us to face persecution on a mass scale, but recall Jesus' words about the Last Days in Matthew 24:9:

> 9 "Then they will deliver you up to tribulation and kill you, and you will be hated by all nations for My name's sake."

It is clear. As John told us in his presentation of the Fifth Seal (Revelation 6:9-11), some Christians will be martyred during the Great Tribulation. As we'll see, God intends to provide His people some protection *en masse* against the tyranny of the Antichrist and his regime. But just like Stephen[159] (and, indeed, most of Jesus' Disciples), and scores of early Christians,[160] and even many of our contemporary brothers and sisters around the world, some of us are simply destined to give our lives for the faith during the Tribulation. This is what our Revelation passage reveals (Revelation 7:9-17):

> 9 After these things I looked, and behold, a great multitude which no one could number, of all nations, tribes, peoples,

---

[159] Acts 7:54-60
[160] Foxe's Book of Martyrs, John Foxe (2010; Lighthouse Trails Publishing, LLC)

and tongues, standing before the throne and before the Lamb, clothed with white robes, with palm branches in their hands,

10 and crying out with a loud voice, saying, "Salvation belongs to our God who sits on the throne, and to the Lamb!"

11 All the angels stood around the throne and the elders and the four living creatures, and fell on their faces before the throne and worshiped God,

12 saying: "Amen! Blessing and glory and wisdom, thanksgiving and honor and power and might, be to our God forever and ever. Amen."

13 Then one of the elders answered, saying to me, "Who are these arrayed in white robes, and where did they come from?"

14 And I said to him, "Sir, you know." So he said to me, "These are the ones who come out of the great tribulation, and washed their robes and made them white in the blood of the Lamb.

15 "Therefore they are before the throne of God, and serve Him day and night in His temple. And He who sits on the throne will dwell among them.

16 "They shall neither hunger anymore nor thirst anymore; the sun shall not strike them, nor any heat;

17 "for the Lamb who is in the midst of the throne will shepherd them and lead them to living fountains of waters. And God will wipe away every tear from their eyes."

Here, we are presented a picture of the souls of a countless number of Christians standing in the throne room of God, as described in Revelation chapter 4. We are told that they are representative of *all* nations of the Earth, something that could not have been so only a century or so ago when many nations had not yet heard the Gospel. For all of man's atrocities in the twentieth century, the remnant of God's people among them did make great progress toward the Great Commission, the directive given by Jesus in the last three verses of the Book of Matthew (Matthew 28:18-20):

18 And Jesus came and spoke to them, saying, "All authority has been given to Me in heaven and on earth.

19 "Go therefore and make disciples of all the nations, baptizing them in the name of the Father and of the Son and of the Holy Spirit,

20 "teaching them to observe all things that I have commanded you; and lo, I am with you always, even to the end of the age." Amen.

Technology—man's creativity—has produced many things both good and bad. But most importantly it has allowed the Gospel of Christ truly to be preached throughout the world, in every language (or virtually so). In particular, advances in transportation and communications over the last hundred years has permitted the picture John presents to us in verse 9 of our Revelation passage to be feasible in our time, for the first time in human history. John, or rather God through John, may also here be hinting to us that the end will come only when the Great Commission has been fulfilled. This adds to our incentive to continue the thrust of global evangelism.

But John is not here lauding the accomplishment of our primary task as believers—to bring as many souls from around the world as possible into the Kingdom of God—but rather is emphasizing the fact that a "great multitude" of us (verse 9) are going to lose our lives during "the great tribulation" (verse 14). We might presume that not all Christians who die during the Tribulation period will do so at the hands of the Antichrist and his minions—perhaps many will die by natural means during this time—but the emphasis in our Revelation passage seems to be on martyrdom. Whatever the case, we can take some solace in the fact that whoever surrenders his earthly life in defense of his faith will be granted special status in Heaven (not to mention the Millennial Reign of Christ that follows the Tribulation[161]). Just as Jesus honored Stephen for his martyrdom by standing up from His throne in Heaven during Stephen's stoning, those of the Tribulation generation who make the ultimate physical sacrifice will be honored with a place "before the throne of God" (verse 15). John also assures us that these saints will "neither hunger anymore nor thirst anymore," nor suffer in any way, but will enjoy "living fountains of waters," eternal peace and

---

[161] Revelation 20:4-6

joy (verses 16-17). In our last passage (Revelation 7:1-8), we saw God's people prepared to go through the Great Tribulation by being given a seal of protection against God's wrath during this period. Here, we are prepared further with comforting words for those of us who may nevertheless lose our lives during this period.

John's text makes it clear. The Tribulation period is about to begin. And our current passage provides further confirmation of our thesis: that Christians are going to go through the Great Tribulation. This seems undeniable. John presents a picture of an innumerable mass of Christians (whose "robes" were made "white in the blood of the Lamb"), and is told that "these are the ones who come out of the great tribulation" (verse 14). We should note that although we've seen the term "great tribulation" twice before in Scripture (first in Jesus' dissertation on the End Times in Matthew chapter 24, and again in the letter to the church in Thyatira in Revelation chapter 2), this later passage is the only place in the Bible where we encounter the phrase "*the* great tribulation." Here, John is clearly describing a particular period, namely the last seven years of human history, Daniel's seventieth week.[162] And the masses of Christians that John sees are those who "come out of" the Great Tribulation. Notice that John does not write that they ascend to Heaven *before* the Tribulation—suggesting a Pre-Tribulation Rapture—but instead, they *come out of* this period. Does this then indicate a Mid-Tribulation Rapture; that is, a Rapture that occurs *during* the Great Tribulation, as some scholars have suggested? For this to be the case, there would have to be evidence that the masses that John is describing come out of the Tribulation as a group. But the contrary is true. In the original Greek, the term used here for "come out of" is a present participle, which indicates not a singular event, but a continual, ongoing process. So, here we see not a picture of the Rapture—multitudes of saints ascending to Heaven all at once—but instead a vision of Christians losing their lives, one at a time, throughout the Tribulation period.

And so, as has been demonstrated so much already, we see again that Christians will not be absent from this world during the Great

---

[162] Daniel 9:27

Tribulation. Whether the individual Christian happens to survive this period or not—some will and some won't, as we'll see even more plainly as our study progresses—it is becoming increasingly clear that the Church will be on Earth during this time. And those of us whose lives are destined to coincide with this final episode of human history are about to witness some remarkable things.

Revelation 8:1-8:6 ~ It Begins

The stage has at last been set for the Great Tribulation to begin. The Church has been admonished to become the pure and spotless bride for whom Christ will return. Through military and political conquest, world war, and greed on a global scale, man has proven that his way leads only to famine, disease, and destruction. And our attempt at self-rule has culminated in a horrific precipitating event, perhaps a nuclear war—a sort of "last straw," as far as God is concerned. Our Father is now ready to act. He's influenced the march of mankind since our species first rebelled against Him in the Garden of Eden, and He is now prepared to usher in the final seven years of human history, as our passage reveals (Revelation 8:1-6):

1. When He opened the seventh seal, there was silence in heaven for about half an hour.
2. And I saw the seven angels who stand before God, and to them were given seven trumpets.
3. Then another angel, having a golden censer, came and stood at the altar. He was given much incense, that he should offer it with the prayers of all the saints upon the golden altar which was before the throne.
4. And the smoke of the incense, with the prayers of the saints, ascended before God from the angel's hand.
5. Then the angel took the censer, filled it with fire from the altar, and threw it to the earth. And there were noises, thunderings, lightnings, and an earthquake.
6. So the seven angels who had the seven trumpets prepared themselves to sound.

Here, we are presented an image of what may be the most intense moment of anticipation in the history of humankind. The End is about to begin. Jesus breaks the seventh and final seal of the Scroll (as we now understand to be representative of the final centuries of human history) that only He is worthy to open (symbolic of God's influence over that history). After a brief dramatic pause, we find seven angels "who stand before God" (verse 2). In the first chapter of Revelation, we were introduced to a similar group of seven angels, symbolized there by seven stars in Jesus' right hand. Jesus explains in Revelation 1:20:

> 20 "The mystery of the seven stars which you saw in My right hand, and the seven golden lampstands: The seven stars are the angels of the seven churches, and the seven lampstands which you saw are the seven churches."

These seven angels, you might recall, subsequently become the addressees of the seven letters that Jesus dictates to John for the Seven Churches. These seven churches, we decided, are actually representative of the Church as a whole. So, ultimately, we can say that this particular group of seven angels—the ones assigned to the Seven Churches—are symbolic of some angelic force whose job it is to watch over God's people. In this sense, this body of angels need not be understood as a literal group of seven, but instead may simply be representative of God's divine covering over the Body of Christ, carried out by His spiritual forces in general.

Conversely, John may intend for us to interpret this new group more literally. These may actually be seven angels, equipped, in the form of seven trumpets, to unleash God's judgment on the Earth. But regardless of their actual composition—whether these are literally seven angels or, more broadly, God's angelic forces in general—what's most important is that we understand *how* these are empowered to carry out their task. Recall from our earlier discussion of Jesus' unique worthiness to open the Scroll—God's decree of judgment against this world system—that Jesus earned this right by coming to Earth in the form of a man and living without sin. A key element here obviously is that Jesus was sinless, but equally critical is the fact that He lived as a human being. In the Garden of Eden, God gave all authority over the Earth to man, so the authority to do anything on the Earth must, either directly or indirectly, come through man. This is why Satan works so hard to influence us to carry out his will, and why God continuously implores us to do His instead. Even here, although it is God who determines when and by what means the Great Tribulation begins, the mechanism that He uses for this purpose must be combined with "the prayers of all the saints" (verse 3). In John's vision, these prayers are offered with "much incense" (verse 3), which, in turn—and perhaps a bit redundantly—symbolizes the prayers of God's people. David suggests as much in Psalm 141:2a:

> 2   Let my prayer be set before You as incense...

Does this—the fact that it is our prayers that seem to prompt God to start this period—mean that we as Christians should be praying for the Great Tribulation to begin? This may seem a strange notion. But this is precisely what we're doing every time we pray according to Jesus' instructions. In Matthew 6:9-10, Jesus tells His Disciples, and, by extension, us:

> 9   "In this manner, therefore, pray: 'Our Father in heaven, hallowed be Your name.
> 10 'Your kingdom come. Your will be done on earth as it is in heaven...'"

When we pray this—the beginning of what has come to be known as "the Lord's Prayer"—we are praying for none other than the full manifestation of God's Kingdom here on Earth, which will begin upon Christ's physical return to our planet and the ushering in of His thousand-year reign.[163] While it is unlikely that any of us is explicitly praying for the Tribulation period to begin—who really wants that?—we should understand that the Great Tribulation is a necessary step on the path to the ultimate establishment of God's Kingdom here; to God's will being done on Earth in the same manner and to the same extent that it is done in Heaven. There are some hard years ahead, but Satan is not going to easily surrender the authority that Adam handed off to him so many millennia ago. An epic fight is coming, and it must come in order for Satan to be

---

[163] Revelation 20:4-6

"legally" stripped of his rights—here, and in the spiritual realm—once and for all.[164]

So, our prayers—the righteous petitions of God's people, who, as members of the human race, have dominion and authority over this world[165]—in effect "authorize" the event symbolized by the seventh and last seal on the Scroll. The imagery that John uses to depict this—the censer, the incense, the altar, and the fire—is derived from the Old Testament ritual of the Day of Atonement, as described (in part) in Leviticus 16:12-13 (bracketed comments mine):

> 12 "Then [the High Priest] shall take a censer full of burning coals of fire from the altar before the Lord, with his hands full of sweet incense beaten fine, and bring it inside the veil.
> 13 "And he shall put the incense on the fire before the Lord, that the cloud of incense may cover the mercy seat that is on the Testimony [the Ark of the Covenant], lest he die.

We should understand first and foremost that the fire of the altar—from where the coals upon which the incense is placed are taken—represents God's judgment. Incense is offered on this fire to symbolize repentance, to communicate to God our desire to be forgiven of our sins and reconciled to Him. Each year, Israel's High Priest would begin *Yom Kippur*—the day when all of the Jews' sins of the previous year would be atoned for—with this ritual. But this ritual's efficacy is most dramatically demonstrated by an event that took place not on the prescribed day, the Day of Atonement, but following an act of rebellion by the Israelites during their wilderness experience (Numbers 16:41-48):

> 41 On the next day all the congregation of the children of Israel complained against Moses and Aaron, saying, "You have killed the people of the Lord."
> 42 Now it happened, when the congregation had gathered against Moses and Aaron, that they turned toward the

---

[164] See Revelation chapter 12; we will discuss this in detail later.
[165] Genesis 1:26-28

tabernacle of meeting; and suddenly the cloud covered it, and the glory of the Lord appeared.

43 Then Moses and Aaron came before the tabernacle of meeting.

44 And the Lord spoke to Moses, saying,

45 "Get away from among this congregation, that I may consume them in a moment." And they fell on their faces.

46 So Moses said to Aaron, "Take a censer and put fire in it from the altar, put incense on it, and take it quickly to the congregation and make atonement for them; for wrath has gone out from the Lord. The plague has begun."

47 Then Aaron took it as Moses commanded, and ran into the midst of the assembly; and already the plague had begun among the people. So he put in the incense and made atonement for the people.

48 And he stood between the dead and the living; so the plague was stopped.

Here, we see the intercessory power of the incense offering. The High Priest, Aaron, puts incense on the altar fire, and he stands in the gap for the Israelites, and God's judgment against the people is abated. This system remained in effect throughout the time of the Tabernacle and the First and Second Temples: incense was placed on the fire, atonement was made for sin, and everyone was happy. But in verse 5 of our Revelation passage, instead of the sweet aroma of incense—our prayers—squelching the fire of God's wrath, something extraordinary happens. Millennia of God's grace and patience with this world and its allegiance to Satan come to an end. Fire is taken from the altar in Heaven and it is thrust at the Earth. God's judgment, no longer contained, is unleashed on an unprecedented scale.

The Great Tribulation begins…

Conclusion

We humans have made a real mess of things.

Some six thousand years ago in the Garden of Eden, Satan, in the guise of a serpent, promised Eve that if she committed just one simple act of rebellion against God, she could be like God, "knowing good and evil."[166] In other words, Eve and her husband Adam—both of whom took Satan's bait—would become their own gods, judging right from wrong according to their own reasoning. But committing this act of treason against God did not void the mandate that He'd placed inside of them: to "have dominion over the fish of the sea, over the birds of the air, and over the cattle, over all the earth and over every creeping thing that creeps on the earth" and to "fill the earth and subdue it."[167] Humankind's destiny was to rule and reign over the whole world, and Adam and Eve's descendants wasted little time in engaging in this endeavor, first fully manifested in the building of the Tower of Babel[168]—a monument to man's independence from God—by a blasphemous

---

[166] Genesis 3:5
[167] Genesis 1:26-28
[168] Genesis 11:1-9

king named Nimrod.[169] Since that time—since just a few generations after Noah—man has been striving to expand his self-rule beyond that first attempt in the land of Shinar to truly encompass the entire globe. And, as we saw in our analysis of the Four Horsemen,[170] we have finally achieved this worldwide self-governance in just the last two-and-a-half centuries of our history. The stage is at last set for Satan to show his hand, to reveal his true motive for enticing Adam and Eve to rebel against God so many millennia ago. He intends to commit the ultimate coup d'état—to claim this world for himself. The Antichrist is coming.

There are some trying times ahead of us—more trying than in all of human history. And, contrary to decades of popular Christian belief, the Bible plainly teaches that the Body of Christ is destined to remain on Earth to witness it all. No doubt, this is a surprising revelation to many in this generation. I, too, was raised on the Pre-Tribulation Rapture doctrine, and I remember the very moment—late one evening, in September of 1999—when I began to see what the Word of God really says about the Rapture. For me, it was nothing less than startling, and it was the very next day that I began writing this book series.

Does It Matter What We Believe?

In 1969—when my twin brother, Erin, and I were about two years old—my parents held a weekly Bible study at our family home in the little mountain town of Crestline, tucked away up in the pine trees of Southern California's San Bernardino Mountains. About twenty minutes down the twisty-turny Rim of the World Highway, in the tiny resort community of Arrowhead Springs, a young man named Hal Lindsey was helping out at the headquarters of Campus Crusade for Christ. He was also working on his first book. On several occasions, Hal made the nerve-wracking drive up the mountain to teach at my parents' Bible study; and to this day my father remembers standing around the kitchen with him after the meetings, drinking coffee, and enjoying listening to Hal talk about

---

[169] *The Antiquities of the Jews*, Josephus Flavius (2009; Wilder Publications)
[170] Discussed in Chapter 10 "The Scroll with the Seven Seals: Prelude to the Great Tribulation," in the section "Revelation 6:1–6:8 ~ The Four Horsemen"

the end of the world. The Jews had recaptured the Temple Mount in Jerusalem only two years earlier, in 1967, and my father recalls that this event more than any other seemed to stoke Hal's excitement. One year later, Hal Lindsey's book, *The Late Great Planet Earth*,[171] was published, and the modern-day Bible prophecy movement was born.

Before Hal Lindsey's groundbreaking work, Christian eschatology was a bit of a fringe topic—studied and taught over the centuries, but not an area of central interest for most Christians. But Lindsey changed all of that. After his book was published, the Christian End Times genre became an industry unto itself—a true phenomenon. *The Late Great Planet Earth* is one of the best-selling books of all time.[172] *The New York Times* credits Lindsey with being the best-selling non-fiction author of the 1970s.[173] Hal Lindsey accomplished something exceedingly important. The event that perhaps inspired him most of all to write his book—the reclaiming of the Temple Mount by the Jews in 1967—indeed began the countdown to the last of the Last Days. We are almost certainly the generation that will witness all of the things discussed in Lindsey's book (and in this book series). And, as such, this is the generation that needs to study, contemplate, teach, and discuss eschatology like no generation before us. The End Times should be a main focus for all modern believers, and Lindsey helped to bring this topic into the foreground. For this, Lindsey must be commended. This, however, was not the only result that his work accomplished.

The Late Great Planet Earth presented many concepts that were new to much of the Body of Christ at the time. Principal among these was the Pre-Tribulation Rapture doctrine, the belief that prior to the seven-year Great Tribulation all Christians will be whisked away to Heaven for safekeeping while the rest of mankind

---

[171] *The Late Great Planet Earth*, Hal Lindsey & Carole C. Carlson (1970; Zondervan)
[172] *The Norton Anthology of English Literature (Ninth Edition)* (2012; W. W. Norton & Company)
[173] *The End of the World As We Know It: Faith, Fatalism, and Apocalypse in America*, Daniel N. Wojcik (1999; NYU Press)

suffers unimaginable horrors here on Earth.[174] As we discussed in this book,[175] prior to the early nineteenth century—when an Irish Protestant clergyman named John Nelson Darby published a paper proposing a "secret Second Coming" for Christians[176]—the belief in a Pre-Tribulation Rapture simply did not exist. For the first 1,800 years of Christianity, it was universally understood among believers that some future generation of Christians would endure the coming Great Tribulation and would only afterwards be "translated" (raptured) upon Christ's return to Earth at the very end of this period. For nearly two millennia, the entire Body of Christ held a *Post*-Tribulation Rapture view. After his book was published in 1827, Darby spent the rest of his days working to popularize his theory throughout Great Britain, the United States, and Canada. But it was not until the publication of Hal Lindsey's book in 1970 that the Pre-Tribulation Rapture truly entered the mainstream of Christian belief. In the years that followed, Lindsey's influence on Christian—and even non-Christian—culture was profound. *The Late Great Planet Earth* provided inspiration for a 1972 film by Russell Doughten, about a young girl who faces the Great Tribulation after missing the Rapture, called *A Thief in the Night*—the very film that I watched so many years ago in a barn meeting in the Northern California countryside, and that became the original inspiration for this book series.[177] And two decades later, Lindsay's book provided the doctrinal basis for a wildly popular series of books (an entire media empire, in fact) that thrust the Pre-Tribulation Rapture even into secular mainstream thought: the *Left Behind* series, by Dr. Tim LaHaye and Jerry B. Jenkins.[178]

The Pre-Tribulation Rapture doctrine has not completely permeated Christianity. It may surprise many to learn that today

---

[174] *The Late Great Planet Earth*, Hal Lindsey & Carole C. Carlson (1970; Zondervan)
[175] Discussed in Chapter 5 "The Pre-Tribulation Rapture," in the section "Church Not Mentioned During Depiction of Tribulation in Book of Revelation"
[176] *The Origin of the pre-Tribulation Rapture Teaching*, John L. Bray (1992; John L. Bray Ministry, Inc.)
[177] Depicted in the Introduction
[178] *Left Behind*, Tim LaHaye & Jerry B. Jenkins (1995; Tyndale House Publishers)

CONCLUSION

the majority of Christians worldwide who believe in a literal End Times (a future seven-year Great Tribulation concluded by the Second Coming of Jesus Christ) hold to the much older traditional belief about the order of End Times events: that is, that Christians will remain on Earth throughout the Tribulation period and will be resurrected or raptured only upon Christ's return at the very end (the Post-Tribulation Rapture view).[179] But a majority of *Evangelical* Christians (non-mainline Protestants, of which there are some 360 million adherents worldwide) subscribe to the Pre-Tribulation Rapture model popularized by Hal Lindsey, Tim LaHaye, and other teachers of our generation.[180] Now that we're at the end of the first book of this series—a main focus of which was the timing of the Rapture, as you no doubt noticed—let's ask a question that perhaps you've been asking from the start. Does it really matter what one believes about the timing of the Rapture? Remember my pastor friend who once quipped, "I'm Pan-Trib—whatever happens, it will all pan out in the end"?[181] Even if popular Evangelical belief about the Rapture is wrong—if the Bible, in fact, plainly tells us that the Rapture is not going to happen until Christ's return at the *end* of the Great Tribulation—what harm is there in believing in a Pre-Tribulation Rapture?

One Bible passage that should be familiar to us now—we've looked at it a several times throughout this book—is Paul's description of the Great Tribulation in his second letter to the church at Thessalonica (2 Thessalonians 2:1-4):

1 Now, brethren, concerning the coming of our Lord Jesus Christ and our gathering together to Him, we ask you,
2 not to be soon shaken in mind or troubled, either by spirit or by word or by letter, as if from us, as though the day of Christ had come.

---

[179] Spirit and Power—A 10-Country Survey of Pentecostals (October 2006; Pew Research Center's Religion & Public Life Project); Global Survey of Evangelical Protestant Leaders (June 2011; Pew Research Center's Religion & Public Life Project)
[180] *Ibid.*
[181] Mentioned in Chapter 2 "Finding a Model for the Timing of the Rapture"

3 Let no one deceive you by any means; for that Day will not come unless the falling away comes first, and the man of sin is revealed, the son of perdition,
4 who opposes and exalts himself above all that is called God or that is worshiped, so that he sits as God in the temple of God, showing himself that he is God.

Here—in addition to confirming for us that the Rapture ("our gathering together" to Jesus at His return; verse 1) will certainly not take place before the start of the Great Tribulation (with its central defining event, the Abomination of Desolation; verse 4)—Paul tells us that something will happen in conjunction with the Antichrist's rise to power. He says that there will be a "falling away" of some kind (verse 3). The Greek word that this term is rendered from is *apostasia*, and it is of course from this that we get our English word "apostasy." Merriam-Webster's Collegiate Dictionary defines "apostasy" as "renunciation of a religious faith."[182] Paul is not concerned, of course, with adherents of other religions forfeiting their faith: he is describing a falling away of *Christians*. And, again, he is relating this to the reign of the Antichrist. What could possibly explain this phenomenon, what many teachers of the Gospel refer to as the Great Apostasy or the Great Falling Away? Further in 2 Thessalonians chapter 2, Paul provides us some insight (2 Thessalonians 2:9-12; bracketed comment mine):

9 The coming of the lawless one [the Antichrist] is according to the working of Satan, with all power, signs, and lying wonders,
10 and with all unrighteous deception among those who perish, because they did not receive the love of the truth, that they might be saved.
11 And for this reason God will send them strong delusion, that they should believe the lie,
12 that they all may be condemned who did not believe the truth but had pleasure in unrighteousness.

Paul tells us here that the main trap of the Antichrist—that is, what causes most of the world to follow him, including, apparently, many

---

[182] *Merriam-Webster's Collegiate Dictionary* (2008; Merriam-Webster, Inc.)

Christians—is *deception*. He operates in "lying wonders" (verse 9) and "unrighteous deception," and the ones who fall for his lies are those who do not have a "love of the truth" (verse 10). We should understand "love of the truth" to mean an unswerving commitment to whatever God's Word tells us, regardless of personal desires, hopes, and fears. Paul's words are particularly strong here. Does he indeed mean to include Christians in this? Will there really be Christians who, in our not-too-distant future, will surrender their faith to the wiles of the Antichrist? In His great dissertation on the End Times, Jesus confirms this in very plain terms (Matthew 24:23-24):

> 23 "Then if anyone says to you, 'Look, here is the Christ!' or 'There!' do not believe it.
> 24 "For false christs and false prophets will rise and show great signs and wonders to deceive, if possible, even the elect."

Here, Jesus, speaking to His Disciples—to all of us—warns that in the Last Days "false christs and false prophets" (verse 24) — including, and presumably especially, the ultimate false christ, the Antichrist—would "deceive, if possible, even the elect" (verse 24); that is, even the very Body of Christ. We might be tempted to interpret Jesus' words here—"to deceive, *if possible*, even the elect" (verse 24)—to mean that the Antichrist, though he can't, would deceive Christians if he could. But, of course, He likely wouldn't mention this contingency if it wasn't a real threat. Instead, Jesus is telling us that it *is* possible for the elect—for His followers—to be deceived by the Antichrist.

And the stakes are incredibly high. Earlier in this book, we briefly touched on the question of "once saved, always saved."[183] Many Christians believe that salvation is achieved by a simple prayer whereby Jesus is accepted as one's personal Savior, and this is all that it takes for eternity with Him to be assured. Others insist that there is more to it than this—that salvation is an ongoing process that requires the individual to remain steadfast in his or her faith. Whatever the case—however sure, or however tentative, a person's

---

[183] Discussed in Chapter 8 "The Letters to the Seven Churches," in the section "Revelation 3:1–3:6 ~ The Fifth Letter: The Dead Church"

promise of salvation may be in this dispensation—the Book of Revelation tells us one sure way that someone can forfeit his or her eternal life during the Great Tribulation (Revelation 14:9-11; bracketed comment mine):

> 9 Then a third angel followed them, saying with a loud voice, "If anyone worships the beast [the Antichrist] and his image, and receives his mark on his forehead or on his hand,
> 10 he himself shall also drink of the wine of the wrath of God, which is poured out full strength into the cup of His indignation. He shall be tormented with fire and brimstone in the presence of the holy angels and in the presence of the Lamb.
> 11 And the smoke of their torment ascends forever and ever; and they have no rest day or night, who worship the beast and his image, and whoever receives the mark of his name."

Here, John tells us in no uncertain terms that *anyone* who follows the Antichrist—anyone who "worships [him] and his image" and "receives his mark on his forehead or on his hand" (the meaning of which we'll discuss at length later in this book series; verse 9)—will experience "the wrath of God" and will be "tormented with fire and brimstone...forever and ever" (verses 10-11). All hope of salvation will be gone. And "anyone" means anyone: atheist, agnostic, Buddhist, Hindu, Muslim, Christian, or anything else. Satan isn't selective. When the time comes, he'll drag anyone that he can with him to Hell. For the unbeliever, falling for the deceptions of the Antichrist will mean that any chance of one day being "born again" is lost forever. And for the believer, it will mean that his or her promise of eternal life is irreversibly revoked.

Most Christians have heard about the Antichrist, and most understand that all those who bow down to him will face dire consequences. So, how can we explain even one Christian submitting to the Antichrist's (counterfeit) rule? What is the "Great Deception" that will lead to a multitude of Christians falling prey to the guise of the coming "son of perdition," Satan personified? In C.S. Lewis' *The Screwtape Letters*, a high-ranking demon named Screwtape writes a series of letters to his nephew, Wormwood, wherein he mentors the younger demon in his efforts to secure the damnation of a certain British man. In the preface to the book, Lewis says that one of the greatest "errors into which our race can fall about the devils…is to disbelieve in their existence."[184] Perhaps the Great Deception is the cleverest of twists on this theme. When the seven-year Great Tribulation starts and the Antichrist begins his ascent to power, a vast number of Christians will succumb to the greatest of all possible lies: that this isn't the Antichrist, because, as bad as things are, this can't be the Great Tribulation; because we're not going to be on Earth for the Great Tribulation.

I am aware of how strong a criticism this is. But, to be clear, I believe that the widespread embrace—in our generation—of the Pre-Tribulation Rapture doctrine is destined to be a major factor in the Great Falling Away. Christians as a whole—especially when we are "in our flesh," moved more by our own physical needs and desires and by outward circumstances than by our redeemed spirits—are a flaky bunch. The Bible tells us, in both the Old Testament and the New Testament, that "the just shall live by faith."[185] In fact, this is what makes us "just" (righteous before God)[186]. But how many of us consistently practice this? When crisis comes—when my personal finances take a major hit, when I or a loved one gets a bad report from a doctor, when the economy nosedives into recession, when a natural disaster strikes—do I truly trust God with all of my being? Or do I panic a little (or a lot) and start searching for a natural solution, perhaps with some faith but mainly from a position of worry and concern and even fear? Some Christians can honestly say that, faced with bad circumstances, they manage to stay in faith. Many—most—cannot. Most of us, when confronted by life's trials and tribulations, find it very difficult to "not be afraid; only believe."[187] For some of us, even the smallest of tests—a flat tire, a lost purse or wallet, a rude grocery store clerk, a lousy parking spot—can throw us into a tailspin. So, what's going to happen when unprecedentedly bad times come, times in which—as

---

[184] *The Screwtape Letters: How a Senior Devil Instructs a Junior Devil in the Art of Temptation*, C.S. Lewis (1961; Time, Inc.)
[185] Habakkuk 2:4; Romans 1:17; Galatians 3:11; Hebrews 10:38
[186] Hebrews 11:6; Romans 3:22
[187] As Jesus instructed Jairus when news came that his daughter was dead; Mark 5:21-43

we'll see in Part 2 of this book series—the world that we know is thrust into utter chaos? And when, in the midst of this, a certain man steps onto the world stage and presents himself as a great peacemaker and global problem solver, and he has answers to the nightmare into which the world has been plunged, and a plan to rebuild, and a way for us to feed our families…how many of us will be able to resist him? In different times, his identity—his true nature—might be clear to most Christians. But during times of extreme stress or trauma—and remember that what is coming upon the Earth is "great tribulation, such as has not been since the beginning of the world until this time, no, nor ever shall be"[188]—it is human nature to grasp at any possibility of temporal salvation. And much of the Body of Christ, as things stand now, will be going into this period with the doctrinal license to be in complete denial—to ourselves and to one another—about who the Antichrist really is.

Of course, a correct understanding of the last of the Last Days—including that we're actually going to go through them in their entirety, and all of the other details upon which this book series will attempt to shed light—only gets us so far. God tells us through the Prophet Hosea that "My people are destroyed for lack of knowledge."[189] But knowledge about the Last Days is only the beginning. In the times that are coming, knowledge alone won't save anyone. But if that's true, then what will? What can you take with you into the Great Tribulation that will *absolutely ensure* your survival, most likely your physical survival, and certainly your *spiritual* survival, the salvation of your soul? You are about to read the most important words of your life.

Be Filled with the Holy Spirit!

Why did Jesus come to the Earth? Most Christians, from the newest believer to the most mature, would answer: to die on the Cross so that "whoever believes in Him should not perish but have everlasting life."[190] This is absolutely true, of course. In fact, this is

---

[188] Matthew 24:21
[189] Hosea 4:6
[190] John 3:16

the most important Truth throughout our Universe and across all time. And yet, this is an incomplete answer.

Have you ever wondered what it was like to be one of Jesus' original Disciples, to walk with Him in the flesh, to hear Him teach from His own mouth, to see Him do miracles—feed the multitudes, heal the sick, calm the storm, walk on water? It must have been awe-inspiring for Peter, John, Matthew, and the others: being in the very presence of the Messiah, the Son of God, having the deepest of truths revealed to them, knowing that their every need would be met. And yet Jesus told them something that at the time must have seemed exceedingly paradoxical (John 16-5-7):

> 5 "But now I go away to Him who sent Me, and none of you asks Me, 'Where are You going?'
> 6 But because I have said these things to you, sorrow has filled your heart.
> 7 Nevertheless I tell you the truth. It is to your advantage that I go away; for if I do not go away, the Helper will not come to you; but if I depart, I will send Him to you.

Here, Jesus tells His Disciples that He must leave so that the "Helper" could come to them. But wasn't He Himself the ultimate Helper? Jesus was, of course, referring to that other aspect of God, the so-called Third Person of the Holy Trinity, the Holy Spirit. And He tells His Disciples that it is going to be to their "advantage" (verse 7)—to their benefit—for the Spirit to be intimately with them in His stead. He explains the nature of what was soon coming (John 14:16-17; emphasis mine):

> 16 And I will pray the Father, and He will give you another Helper, that He may abide with you forever—
> 17 the Spirit of truth, whom the world cannot receive, because it neither sees Him nor knows Him; but you know Him, for He dwells with you *and will be in you.*

The Holy Spirit was already *with* the Disciples—just as He is with every true follower of God. But here Jesus is telling them that a very different kind of relationship with the Holy Spirit was soon going to be made available to those who are in Christ. The *Shekhinah*—the manifest, we might even say *physical*, presence of the Holy Spirit—that once dwelled inside the Holy of Holies in the Temple in Jerusalem would now dwell inside those of us who would invite the Holy Spirit in. Just hours after Jesus revealed this promise, He was arrested and crucified. Three days later, He rose from the grave in His glorified body. And forty days after that,[191] He stood atop the Mount of Olives with His Disciples and reminded them what was coming (Acts 1:4-5):

> 4 And being assembled together with them, He commanded them not to depart from Jerusalem, but to wait for the Promise of the Father, "which," He said, "you have heard from Me;
> 5 for John truly baptized with water, but you shall be baptized with the Holy Spirit not many days from now."

Moments after He spoke these words, Jesus ascended into the heavens and out of the Disciples' sight[192]...and eight days later, on the Jewish holiday of *Shavuot*—which takes place fifty days after Passover (the time of Jesus' crucifixion), and which is called in the Greek "Pentecost"—Jesus' promise to His Disciples was fulfilled (Acts 2:1-4; emphasis mine):

> 1 When the Day of Pentecost had fully come, they were all with one accord in one place.
> 2 And suddenly there came a sound from heaven, as of a rushing mighty wind, and it filled the whole house where they were sitting.
> 3 Then there appeared to them divided tongues, as of fire, and one sat upon each of them.
> 4 *And they were all filled with the Holy Spirit* and began to speak with other tongues, as the Spirit gave them utterance.

This—the indwelling of the Holy Spirit—was not merely a parting gift from Jesus; not just a little something to placate us, to hold us over in His absence and while we await His return. The gift of the Holy Spirit is, in fact, a fundamental part of the purpose of Christ.

---

[191] Acts 1:1-3
[192] Acts 1:9-11

CONCLUSION

God sent His Son into the world not merely to save us from the consequences of our sins, but so that the very power that was once attached to the Ark of the Covenant—that parted the waters of the Jordan River so that the Israelites could safely cross into the Promised Land,[193] that toppled the statue of Dagon in the land of Philistia and killed an untold multitude of Philistines with a plague,[194] that for centuries served as a conduit between God and the Jews, that even before the coming of their promised Messiah allowed for the atonement of the entire nation of Israel[195]—would now be *inside of us.*

And yet, how many Christians throughout the centuries and within our own generation view the indwelling of the Holy Spirit (and especially the evidences of this, the ways that the Holy Spirit manifests in the believer) at best as a bonus feature of salvation, an optional add-on for those of us who want a little more punch in our Christianity—a little speaking in tongues, maybe some shouting and dancing in church, perhaps an occasional miracle or two—and, at worst, as demonic in nature? In our previous section, we talked about the Great Deception that is coming against the Body of Christ in these final days, but this deception—the degradation (or outright denial) of the centrality of the indwelling of the Holy Spirit to every born-again believer in Jesus Christ—has been weakening and dulling Christians for centuries. And the end result of it will be to make millions of us dangerously susceptible to the Antichrist when he appears.

Numerous times throughout this book, we've looked at Jesus' great End Times dissertation in Matthew chapter 24. In this, Jesus foretells the tumultuous conditions that will precede the last of the Last Days. He describes the Abomination of Desolation, when the Antichrist usurps the Temple in Jerusalem and declares war on God's people. He warns of false christs and false prophets. Jesus is preparing us for the most perilous period in human history—again, as He puts it in Matthew 24:21, "great tribulation, such as has not been since the beginning of the world until this time, no, nor ever

---

[193] Joshua 3:1-17
[194] 1 Samuel 4:1-11, 5:1-12
[195] Leviticus 16:1-34

shall be." And He concludes His words with several parables meant to equip us, His saints, to survive this time. One of these is the Parable of the Ten Virgins (Matthew 25:1-12):

1 "Then the kingdom of heaven shall be likened to ten virgins who took their lamps and went out to meet the bridegroom.
2 Now five of them were wise, and five were foolish.
3 Those who were foolish took their lamps and took no oil with them,
4 but the wise took oil in their vessels with their lamps.
5 But while the bridegroom was delayed, they all slumbered and slept.
6 "And at midnight a cry was heard: 'Behold, the bridegroom is coming; go out to meet him!'
7 Then all those virgins arose and trimmed their lamps.
8 And the foolish said to the wise, 'Give us some of your oil, for our lamps are going out.'
9 But the wise answered, saying, 'No, lest there should not be enough for us and you; but go rather to those who sell, and buy for yourselves.'
10 And while they went to buy, the bridegroom came, and those who were ready went in with him to the wedding; and the door was shut.
11 "Afterward the other virgins came also, saying, 'Lord, Lord, open to us!'
12 But he answered and said, 'Assuredly, I say to you, I do not know you.'"

Let's look closely at this parable. Presumably, we're all familiar with the Biblical symbolism of the Bridegroom and the Bride. In Revelation 19:6-9a, we read of a great proclamation that is made from Heaven at the end of the Great Tribulation, immediately prior to Jesus' return to Earth:

6 And I heard, as it were, the voice of a great multitude, as the sound of many waters and as the sound of mighty thunderings, saying, "Alleluia! For the Lord God Omnipotent reigns!

> 7 Let us be glad and rejoice and give Him glory, for the marriage of the Lamb has come, and His wife has made herself ready."
> 8 And to her it was granted to be arrayed in fine linen, clean and bright, for the fine linen is the righteous acts of the saints.
> 9 Then he said to me, "Write: 'Blessed are those who are called to the marriage supper of the Lamb!'"

This, of course, is a depiction of the Resurrection/Rapture event, when all of the saints of God—those deceased and those who are still alive on the Earth at the Second Coming—rise in our physical bodies to meet Jesus in the air, to be with Him for eternity. The concept is clear. Jesus is the Bridegroom, and we—the Church, the Body of Christ—are His Bride. In the Parable of the Ten Virgins, however, we are not yet referred to as a bride but as "virgins." In this parable, we are not yet married to Jesus. We have not yet become the Bride of Christ; we are merely awaiting the Bridegroom's arrival (the Second Coming). And make no mistake—Jesus *is* talking about Christians in this parable. First, we see that all ten virgins have lamps, which corresponds to one of the ways that Jesus describes His followers (Matthew 5:14-16):

> 14 "You are the light of the world. A city that is set on a hill cannot be hidden.
> 15 Nor do they light a lamp and put it under a basket, but on a lampstand, and it gives light to all who are in the house.
> 16 Let your light so shine before men, that they may see your good works and glorify your Father in heaven."

Second, all of the lamps have at least some oil in them. Oil is used throughout the Old and New Testaments for the purpose of anointing, and there is always an implication of a connection to the Holy Spirit. One clear example of this is when the Prophet Samuel anointed David to be king over the nation of Israel (1 Samuel 16:13a):

> 13 Then Samuel took the horn of oil and anointed him in the midst of his brothers; and the Spirit of the Lord came upon David from that day forward...

Finally, in our parable all ten virgins are *betrothed* to the Bridegroom. They are slated to become the Bride. All ten have been "saved." They are born-again believers. In the Parable of the Ten Virgins, *we* are the virgins. And some of us—a full half, according to this parable—don't make it. When the Bridegroom comes, five of the ten virgins aren't "ready" (verse 10) and, consequently, they are shut out of the wedding. By the time that Jesus arrives at the end of the Great Tribulation, they have lost their salvation.

Again, it is not among our tasks to thoroughly address the issue of "once saved, always saved," the question of whether or not it is possible for a born-again believer to lose his salvation. However, in our previous section we identified one sure way to do precisely this during the Tribulation period. A person—Christian or otherwise—needs only to "worship the beast and his image, and receive his mark on his forehead or on his hand,"[196] and "he shall be tormented with fire and brimstone…forever and ever."[197] Presumably, this is the fate of our five lost virgins. When the Bridegroom returns, He "does not know them" (verse 12 of our parable; paraphrased). They have nullified their betrothal by giving in to the Great Deception of the Antichrist. They have become part of the Great Falling Away.[198]

An important question—indeed, the most important for this generation—is, what is the difference between the five wise virgins and the five foolish ones? What distinguishes the Christian who will spiritually survive the Great Tribulation—who will keep his salvation to the very end—from the one who will surrender to the seductions of the Antichrist and forfeit his eternal life? In our parable, it is the virgins who have kept their lamps full of oil who are invited into the wedding when the Bridegroom comes. And it is the virgins who have allowed their oil to dwindle who are shut out. When Jesus returns to Earth at the end of the Great Tribulation, it is *only those believers who have remained filled with the Holy*

---

[196] Revelation 14:9 (paraphrased)
[197] Revelation 14:10-11 (paraphrased)
[198] 2 Thessalonians 2:1-4

Spirit who He will find worthy to become the Bride of Christ. Only these will have managed to keep their salvation through the greatest time of testing the world has ever experienced. Only these will have been empowered to recognize and resist the Antichrist, to live by faith, and to be led by the Spirit. Only these will have overcome[199] and endured to the end.[200]

Some of us may breathe a sigh of relief at this point. After all, when one receives Jesus Christ as his personal savior, one automatically receives the gift of the indwelling of the Holy Spirit, right? This seems to be the promise that the Apostle Peter made to the crowd that he preached to on the Day of Pentecost, following his own indwelling (Acts 2:38):

> 38 Then Peter said to them, "Repent, and let every one of you be baptized in the name of Jesus Christ for the remission of sins; and you shall receive the gift of the Holy Spirit."

However, later in the Book of Acts, we read a different sort of account (Acts 8:14-17):

> 14 Now when the apostles who were at Jerusalem heard that Samaria had received the word of God, they sent Peter and John to them,
> 15 who, when they had come down, prayed for them that they might receive the Holy Spirit.
> 16 For as yet He had fallen upon none of them. They had only been baptized in the name of the Lord Jesus.
> 17 Then they laid hands on them, and they received the Holy Spirit.

Here, we find a group of Christians—believers who "had received the word of God" (verse 14) and who had "been baptized in the name of the Lord Jesus" (verse 16). The salvation event had already taken place. However, none of them had been filled with the Holy Spirit: "as yet He had fallen upon none of them" (verse 16). This was why Peter and John came to them—so that they could lay

---

[199] The Seven Letters to the Seven Churches: Revelation chapters 2 and 3
[200] Matthew 24:13

hands on them and pray for them "that they might receive the Holy Spirit" (verse 15). This story, then, strongly implies that the indwelling of the Holy Spirit does not automatically occur when we are born again. If this is the case, it is conceivable that many Christians today—millions, perhaps—are entirely "saved" but are not filled with the Holy Spirit. Like the Disciples before the Day of Pentecost, the Holy Spirit is *with* them, perhaps, but He is not *in* them.[201]

Even if this is not the case—if we're misinterpreting the above passage, and every born-again believer is, in fact, automatically filled with the Holy Spirit when he receives salvation—it is clear from the Parable of the Ten Virgins that none of us automatically *remains* filled. In the parable, all ten virgins *do* appear to have some degree of the indwelling of the Holy Spirit. Each of them is producing light, which we might relate to the "fruit of the Spirit" that Paul describes in Galatians 5:22-23a:

> 22 But the fruit of the Spirit is love, joy, peace, longsuffering, kindness, goodness, faithfulness,
> 23 gentleness, self-control...

However, the ten foolish virgins' lamps are growing dim. They have allowed the Holy Spirit inside of them to dwindle. They're becoming unfruitful. And, by the time Jesus returns to Earth at the Second Coming, these foolish virgins are lost. Does this mean that every Christian in this condition—once filled, perhaps, with the Holy Spirit but now not-so-filled—is lost? Should such a believer die today, will his soul be forbidden entry into Heaven? Certainly not. Being filled with the Holy Spirit is not what saves us: it is faith in Jesus Christ alone that does, as Paul states plainly in Romans 10:8b-9:

> 8 ..."The word is near you, in your mouth and in your heart" (that is, the word of faith which we preach):
> 9 that if you confess with your mouth the Lord Jesus and believe in your heart that God has raised Him from the dead, you will be saved.

---

[201] John 14:17

This, then, is clearly not the meaning of the Parable of the Ten Virgins. Jesus is not saying that being filled with the Holy Spirit is what qualifies us to become the Bride of Christ at His return. Rather, He is warning us that if we do not *remain filled with the Holy Spirit*—if we allow the oil in our lamps to burn down and we do not continuously replenish it—we will be vulnerable to the trap that Satan is setting for the Body of Christ even as you read these words.

In Chapter 8 of this book,[202] we examined the Seven Letters to the Seven Churches in chapters 2 and 3 of Revelation. Recall that (contrary to some teachings) all of these letters pertain to all believers throughout history and can be viewed as a general encouragement/admonishment, in particular to the last-of-the-Last-Days Body of Christ—us. One of these letters is especially pertinent to the topic at hand—the fifth letter, addressed to the church in Sardis, commonly referred to as "The Dead Church" (Revelation 3:1-6):

1 "And to the angel of the church in Sardis write, 'These things says He who has the seven Spirits of God and the seven stars: "I know your works, that you have a name that you are alive, but you are dead.
2 "Be watchful, and strengthen the things which remain, that are ready to die, for I have not found your works perfect before God.
3 "Remember therefore how you have received and heard; hold fast and repent. Therefore if you will not watch, I will come upon you as a thief, and you will not know what hour I will come upon you.
4 "You have a few names even in Sardis who have not defiled their garments; and they shall walk with Me in white, for they are worthy.
5 "He who overcomes shall be clothed in white garments, and I will not blot out his name from the Book of Life; but I will confess his name before My Father and before His angels.

---

[202] Chapter 8 "The Letters to the Seven Churches"

> 6 "He who has an ear, let him hear what the Spirit says to the churches.'"

In this letter, Jesus makes reference to the fact that He when He returns to Earth at the Second Coming He will be coming "as a thief" (verse 3); that is, unexpectedly. However, recall the words of Paul that we examined in Chapter 3 of this book[203] (1 Thessalonians 5:2-6):

> 2 For you yourselves know perfectly that the day of the Lord so comes as a thief in the night.
> 3 For when they say, "Peace and safety!" then sudden destruction comes upon them, as labor pains upon a pregnant woman. And they shall not escape.
> 4 But you, brethren, are not in darkness, so that this Day should overtake you as a thief.
> 5 You are all sons of light and sons of the day. We are not of the night nor of darkness.
> 6 Therefore let us not sleep, as others do, but let us watch and be sober.

We see, then, that for the "watchful" Christian (verse 3 of our letter and verse 6 above), Jesus does *not* come as "a thief in the night" (verse 2). We are not supposed to be caught unawares by the Second Coming event. And notice the penalty for not watching, for being caught by surprise at Jesus' return: in verse 5 of the letter to Sardis, Jesus seems to be saying that these believers will have their "names blotted...from the Book of Life" (paraphrased). They will have lost their salvation by the end of the Great Tribulation. These are the ones most vulnerable to the Great Deception. This is the group of Christians most susceptible the Great Falling Away. And what is their one defining feature? They are "dead" (verse 1 of our letter).

By "dead," Jesus does not mean that they are *physically* dead, of course. These believers are *spiritually* dead. And by spiritually dead, He does not mean that they are not saved—otherwise, He would not be addressing them as part of the Church. He would not tell

---

[203] Chapter 3 "Building Confidence for Our Model"

them to "strengthen the things which remain" (verse 2), to remember what they "have received and heard" (verse 3), and to "hold fast and repent" (verse 3). And they would not be in danger of having their names blotted from the Book of Life—rather, their names would not be there to begin with. So, in what way are they spiritually dead? They are producing works, but their works are not "perfect before God" because it is their own fruit, not the "fruit of the Spirit."[204] They have allowed their oil to dwindle and their lamps are going out.

How Can I Be Filled?

What, then, is our assurance that we will not be counted among these—those Christians who fail during the Great Tribulation, who surrender their eternities to the enemy of our souls? What can we do to guard ourselves against the false promises of the counterfeit messiah, to equip ourselves to hold fast to our faith and not give in to fear, to procure the power to overcome and endure to the end? How can we ensure that we will be found worthy to walk with Jesus in garments of white; that, at His return, we will become what He paid so steep a price for us to become, His Bride? What is our defense against the times that are coming? It is simple. *We must get filled—and we must stay filled—with the Holy Spirit.*

And, good news: By "simple," I really do mean simple. Many Christians who desire the Holy Spirit have the mistaken perception that there is some sort of formula, a special mode of conduct that draws the Holy Spirit to us. They believe that the more righteously we conduct ourselves, the more "anointed"—the more filled with the Spirit—we'll be. But the precise opposite is true: our anointing is not the result of our good works. Rather, our righteousness manifests as a result of the Holy Spirit being inside of us. We don't need to pray more, read our Bibles more, attend church, tithe, do good deeds, or have more faith in order to be filled. Instead, it is when we are filled with the Holy Spirit that all of these things—and so much more—naturally (or, more precisely, supernaturally) flow from deep within us. Jesus once said this of those who are of the Holy Spirit (John 3:8):

---

[204] Galatians 5:22-23

> 8 "The wind blows where it wishes, and you hear the sound of it, but cannot tell where it comes from and where it goes. So is everyone who is born of the Spirit."

The Holy Spirit is like the wind. In fact, the Greek word used throughout the New Testament to refer to the Spirit is *pneuma*, which means "wind." And like the wind, He cannot be defined or corralled or obtained. He is not a thing—a special power or force—to be acquired: He is a Person. Because He is a Person, the only way to be filled with the Holy Spirit is to *be in relationship with Him*. This begins, simply enough, with asking our Father to introduce Him to us. And, according to Jesus, this request will certainly be granted (Luke 11:11-13):

> 11 "If a son asks for bread from any father among you, will he give him a stone? Or if he asks for a fish, will he give him a serpent instead of a fish?
> 12 Or if he asks for an egg, will he offer him a scorpion?
> 13 If you then, being evil, know how to give good gifts to your children, how much more will your heavenly Father give the Holy Spirit to those who ask Him!"

As simple as this sounds, for some Christians all of this may still seem very mysterious. Perhaps up to now you just haven't heard a lot about the indwelling of the Holy Spirit. Perhaps you're a new believer or you belong to a church where the Holy Spirit is discussed very little or not at all. Maybe this all just sounds weird. But considering what's at stake—considering the days that are ahead—I encourage you not to simply dismiss this. *You need to be filled.* If you need a little help, there's more good news: that's what the Body of Christ is for! Consider this account from the Book of Acts (Acts 19:1-6):

> 1 And it happened, while Apollos was at Corinth, that Paul, having passed through the upper regions, came to Ephesus. And finding some disciples
> 2 he said to them, "Did you receive the Holy Spirit when you believed?" So they said to him, "We have not so much as heard whether there is a Holy Spirit."

CONCLUSION

> 3 And he said to them, "Into what then were you baptized?" So they said, "Into John's baptism."
> 4 Then Paul said, "John indeed baptized with a baptism of repentance, saying to the people that they should believe on Him who would come after him, that is, on Christ Jesus."
> 5 When they heard this, they were baptized in the name of the Lord Jesus.
> 6 And when Paul had laid hands on them, the Holy Spirit came upon them, and they spoke with tongues and prophesied.

Find a local church that emphasizes the power of the Holy Spirit. Or find a fellow believer in your own church who happens to be filled. There are Spirit-filled believers in Christian churches throughout the world and in every denomination. They may be a minority in many churches, but they're there. Or tune in to a radio or television ministry that teaches about the Holy Spirit and call in. The point is, there are Christians everywhere who are filled with the Spirit who will pray with you. *And you will be filled!*

But becoming filled with the Holy Spirit is only the beginning of your relationship with Him. Like any relationship, this one must be nurtured in order to endure. It must grow continually. It must mature and increase. This is not a singular event. Being filled with the Spirit is a lifelong adventure that must be actively lived. But this is a journey that only the Holy Spirit can lead you on. Your relationship with Him is private and intimate, between the Spirit and you. The only instruction that I can offer is what the Apostle Paul wrote to the Christians at Ephesus: "Pray always with all prayer and supplication in the Spirit"[205] so "that you may be able to withstand in the evil day."[206] The key to our survival—in this time, and in the times that are ahead of us—is to *pray continuously in the Spirit*, each and every day. Do this, and you will stay filled. *And you will spiritually survive the times that are coming.*

The days are dark, and they're growing darker. Being in denial about the reality of the times that we live in won't spare us from

---

[205] Ephesians 6:18 (paraphrased)
[206] Ephesians 6:13

what is in our very near future. Stockpiling food and water and guns won't save us either. And as important as it is, even holding to precisely the right doctrine—about the timing of the Rapture or about anything else—isn't the key to our ultimate salvation. The Spirit of God—the *Shekhinah*, the power that raised Christ from the dead,[207] the very power that created the Universe—is. And, thanks to Jesus' sacrifice on the Cross, the Holy Spirit can live inside of us, and the Spirit will lead us through the days ahead, every step of the way. This is Jesus' promise to us (John 16:13):

> 13 When He, the Spirit of truth, has come, He will guide you into all truth; for He will not speak on His own authority, but whatever He hears He will speak; and He will tell you things to come.

During the days that are coming, more than at any other time in human history, we're going to need the revelation that comes only from the Holy Spirit. And, as we'll see in Part 2 of this book series, the Great Tribulation is bringing upon this Earth very formidable days indeed.

• • •

Thank you, Father God, for your Son Jesus—the True Christ—, for the gift of the Holy Spirit, and for your soon-coming Kingdom. Amen!

---

[207] Romans 8:11

amazon.com

Thanks for reading! If you enjoyed this book I'd be very grateful if you'd **post a short review on Amazon**. Your support really does make a difference, and I read all of the reviews personally: http://thesefinaldays.org/book1/review (redirects to Amazon)

While I'm asking for favors, might I also request:
- **Recommend this book to your friends**
- Like my Facebook page:
  http://facebook.com/thesefinaldays
- Subscribe to my YouTube channel:
  http://youtube.com/thesefinaldays

Finally, I invite you to **check out all of the books in this series**. You can find them on my Amazon author page: http://amazon.com/author/ryanspeakman

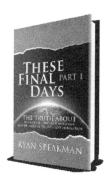  

Thanks for your support!

THESE FINAL DAYS ONLINE

Web: http://thesefinaldays.org
Facebook: http://facebook.com/thesefinaldays
YouTube: http://youtube.com/thesefinaldays
Amazon: http://amazon.com/author/ryanspeakman

Booking Information

Pastor Ryan Speakman is available to speak at your church, club, or event. Contact Ryan for booking information:

These Final Days Ministries
P.O. Box 1331
Lake Havasu City, AZ 86405

Phone: 928-486-7014
E-Mail: ryan@thesefinaldays.org

Ryan is also available for television, radio, and print interviews, and can speak with authority on a wide variety of topics: the End Times, the timing of the Rapture, the Third Temple, the Antichrist, Israel, the Israeli-Palestinian conflict, Islamism and Islamist terrorism, and the Holy Spirit in these final days.

Made in the USA
Coppell, TX
29 January 2020